BuzzFeed
ULTIMATE BOOK OF
QUIZZES

QUESTIONS AND ANSWERS ON LIFE, LOVE, FOOD, FRIENDSHIP, TV, MOVIES, AND MORE

RUNNING PRESS
PHILADELPHIA

Copyright © 2020 by BuzzFeed
Cover copyright © 2020 by Hachette Book Group, Inc.

Running Press
Hachette Book Group
1290 Avenue of the Americas, New York, NY 10104
www.runningpress.com
@Running_Press

Printed in Canada

First Edition: October 2020

Published by Running Press, an imprint of Perseus Books, LLC, a subsidiary of Hachette Book Group, Inc. The Running Press name and logo is a trademark of the Hachette Book Group.

The Hachette Speakers Bureau provides a wide range of authors for speaking events. To find out more, go to www.hachettespeakersbureau.com or call (866) 376-6591.

The publisher is not responsible for websites (or their content) that are not owned by the publisher.

Photographs on pp. 17, 20, 26, 49, 52, 60, 66, 72, 77, 102, 120, 152, 168–169, 179, 180, 186, 202–203, 219, 220, 228, 244, 256, 273, 298, 302, and 303 copyright Getty Images

Print book cover and interior design by Jason Kayser.

Library of Congress Control Number: 2020936113

ISBNs: 978-0-7624-9940-3 (paperback), 978-0-7624-9937-3 (ebook)

FRI

10 9 8 7 6 5 4 3 2 1

Introduction

IS YOUR PHONE DEAD? Are you sitting in the one spot of your house that has terrible Wi-Fi? Did you travel back to 1998 and try to log onto the internet only to find out you couldn't because your older brother was on the phone? Enter *BuzzFeed: Ultimate Book of Quizzes*.

Inside, you'll find a treasure trove of activities that will predict your love life, test your brain, make you hungry, and reveal some deep truths about you. We know you've been lying awake at night wondering which decade you were meant for and the zodiac sign your soul mate is. You've been training your whole life to solve celebrity brainteasers and complete the hardest Disney quiz ever made. The time has come. By the end of this book, you'll know everything from your celebrity dog name to what you should major in, based on your favorite foods.

Ready to spend hours upon hours of boredom-busting offline fun? Grab your best writing utensil and your favorite people because you're about to LOL, OMG, WTF, and WIN your way through this amazingly awesome collection of quizzes and activities—now get to it.

Can We Accurately Guess If You're the First Child, the Baby, or Somewhere in Between?

Okay, so, you're at a party. Fun! What are you most likely doing?

A Huddling in a circle with your closest friends.

B. Roaming around, chatting, meeting new people.

C. Dancing on the table, making out, or both at the same time.

D. Holding your friend's hair back while they puke.

Now you're preparing for a road trip. How do you usually get ready?

A. Roll out of bed the day of and hope everyone else took care of it.

B. Research routes and calculate gas money because you'll obviously be driving the whole way.

C. You do everything yourself; you don't need anyone's help.

D. Buy snacks and make a playlist.

Uh-oh, someone's trying to start a fight with you. What's your game plan?

A. Totally shut down. Confrontation is not your thing.

B. Calm them down and/or try to reason with them. Fighting is never the answer.

C. Fight back. They're clearly in the wrong if they're trying to argue with you.

D. Cry and cry. Why is everyone always picking on you?!

You have a wedding to go to this weekend! What do you wear?

A. Uh, probably just rent an outfit at the last minute.

B. Run over to a store and buy something nice! Why not?

C. Borrow something from a friend or sibling. All your clothes are too casual.

D. That nice outfit you keep in your closet for special occasions.

Aww yeah, now it's dinnertime. What's cookin'?

A. Something delicious-looking you found on Pinterest.

B. Cooking? Please. Seamless is enough effort for you.

C. Whatever everyone else likes.

D. One of your standard go-to meals. You know what you like.

Crap, one of your parents' birthdays just snuck up on you out of nowhere. Now what?

A. They mentioned . . . something . . . they wanted recently. That'll work.

B. Birthdays never sneak up on you. You've had a present stored away for weeks.

C. Confer with your siblings or friends to figure out something nice and meaningful.

D. Someone else got a gift you can go in on . . . you're pretty sure about that, anyway.

You just ran out of toilet paper while going to the bathroom! What do you do?

A. Scream out, asking if anyone is there to help you.

B. Make do with the remaining scraps and then drip dry.

C. Use the extra roll you always keep next to the toilet as backup.

D. Waddle over to the cabinet to get a fresh roll; you always have more there.

And finally: Are you always right?

A. Of course.

B. Yeah, but no one ever listens to me.

C. I guess, but I don't feel like I have to prove that to anyone but myself.

D. Being right doesn't matter as long as we get along.

If You Got Mostly A's:
You're the youngest child! People call you a baby and they're not wrong. But babies are lovable, right?! You like attention and are always down to have a good time, even when people tease you a little.

If You Got Mostly B's:
You're the oldest child! You're pretty mature and you have always set high standards for yourself. You often find yourself taking care of your sibling(s) and friends, but hey, that's love.

If You Got Mostly C's:
You're the only child! No siblings? No problem. Growing up solo has made you pretty independent and very resourceful—and you're definitely not afraid to speak your mind.

If You Got Mostly D's:
You're the middle child! You're no monkey in the middle—you're a pretty chill person! You like to have a good time and you're always there for people, including your many friends when they need you.

What Decade Do You Belong In?

The first slang word you see is the decade you belong in.

1980s
bitchin'
gnarly
brill

1990s
as if
booyah
scrub

2000s
crunk
that's hot
chillax

2010s
extra
thirsty
shade

2020s
drip
tea
mood

B	S	D	N	C	H	I	H	U	A	H	U	A	Y	D
S	H	P	U	G	H	E	A	T	D	A	N	E	X	R
F	A	C	R	U	N	K	H	O	W	B	O	X	E	I
R	D	B	H	R	D	E	R	C	O	O	D	I	E	P
B	E	D	D	L	M	A	T	I	A	O	L	L	H	U
C	O	B	R	I	L	L	P	T	N	Y	C	L	M	E
J	G	E	V	M	A	N	S	H	A	A	H	E	D	A
T	F	O	A	O	E	R	M	A	N	H	I	X	P	Z
L	T	E	A	B	V	M	A	T	T	E	L	T	L	H
M	D	N	X	A	R	O	T	S	M	E	L	R	E	R
B	A	S	I	F	T	H	X	H	N	T	A	A	B	T
J	U	U	X	O	A	I	M	O	O	D	X	Z	Q	S
S	H	I	B	A	S	N	U	T	H	I	S	T	Z	U
F	R	B	I	T	C	H	I	N	L	D	H	G	P	L
G	H	U	S	T	H	I	R	S	T	Y	A	N	N	D
G	Q	Z	P	O	U	E	R	C	N	I	D	A	S	G
I	C	K	T	G	B	E	Y	R	O	U	E	R	D	R
F	P	I	T	B	U	L	L	U	E	A	R	L	E	R
P	O	W	H	I	P	P	E	B	G	Y	L	Y	V	I

Answers on p. 309

ACKNOWLEDGMENTS

Special thanks to Jasmin Sandal, Spencer Althouse, Sarah Aspler, Delia Cai, Rachel Dunkel, Tessa Fahey, Jay Fleckenstein, Shelby Heinrich, Rebecca O'Connell, Jess Probus, Syd Robinson, Michael Spohr, Ivy Tai, Sarah Wainschel, Audrey Engvalson, Andrew Ziegler, and to all the BuzzFeed quiz writers and illustrators past and present who have helped us know ourselves better by telling us which celebrity is our soul mate, when (or if!) we'll get married, whether we're smarter than an eleven-year-old, and where we should vacation next.

Can We Guess Your Zodiac Sign?

PARTY ANIMAL OR WALLFLOWER?

- Party animal
  - Fight for what's right, or go with the flow?
    - Fight
      - Lone wolf or queen bee?
        - Lone Wolf
          - Truth or dare?
            - Truth → **SAGITTARIUS**
            - Dare → **ARIES**
        - Queen bee → **LEO**
    - Flow

- Wallflower
  - Neat freak or a little bit messy?
    - Neat freak
      - Corner office or a seat at the table?
        - Corner office → **CAPRICORN**
        - A seat at the table → **VIRGO**
    - Messy
      - Talk it over or take a walk?
        - Talk → **CANCER**
        - Walk → **AQUARIUS**

- It really depends on the day
  - Commitment-phobe or completely ready to settle down?
    - Commitment-phobe → **GEMINI**
    - Ready to settle down → **LIBRA**
  - Living in the present or living on another planet?
    - Present → **TAURUS**
    - Planet
      - One true love or passion aplenty?
        - Love → **PISCES**
        - Passion → **SCORPIO**

Build a Pizza and We'll Determine Where You'll Be in 5 Years

What kind of crust do you want?

A. Thin

B. Thick

C. Deep

D. Stuffed

Choose a sauce:

A. Tomato

B. White

C. BBQ

D. Pesto

Pick a meat topping:

A. Pepperoni

B. Sausage

C. Chicken

D. No meat

Add in another topping:

A. Jalapeños

B. Mushrooms

C. Pineapple

D. I'm good

Any extra stuff?

A. Crushed red pepper

B. Pepperoncini

C. Ranch dressing

D. Parmesan cheese

How many slices do you want?

A. One

B. Two

C. Three

D. The whole damn pie

If You Got Mostly A's:

Working at a new hotshot job! That's right. In five years' time, you'll be working at a new job, in a new environment, and you'll be making new work friends. You may have even entered a whole new tax bracket! Everyone needs a change every couple of years or so and this one is yours.

If You Got Mostly B's:

Doing something completely different! In five years, you'll look back and you'll ask yourself, "Who was that person?" Everything will change, from where you're living to where you're working. You will have new career goals and overall life goals. It's never too late to change the course of your life.

If You Got Mostly C's:

Living with your significant other! You've had your ups and downs in romance. You've dated around, you've found someone you like, and now, you're gonna move in with them. This is a pretty huge step, so congrats!

If You Got Mostly D's:

Doing exactly what you're doing! Nothing will change in five years. Nothing. You will keep going about your life doing you and it'll probably be the same five years from now, which may not be a bad thing!

What Kind of Ghost Are You?

How did you die?

A. Under mysterious circumstances
B. Of natural causes
C. I don't wanna talk about it

How do you spend your time?

A. Shaking chains
B. Moving random objects around
C. Just floatin'

Do you have any unfinished business?

A. So much
B. Mostly just unreturned library books
C. Hmm . . . ?

Who's your celebrity crush?

A. Casper
B. Nearly Headless Nick
C. I don't much care for fame

boo

Where is your local haunt?

A. Graveyards, abandoned hospitals, dark forests
B. Any old house will do
C. Right behind you

If you could communicate with the other side, what would you say?

A. "Investigate my death!"
B. "Boo!" of course
C. I don't need words to commune with the living

If You Got Mostly A's:
You're a ghost who will show up in photos.

If You Got Mostly B's:
You're felt but not seen.

If You Got Mostly C's:
You're an orb of light.

Check off All the Top Songs from the 2010s You've Heard and We'll Guess Your Age

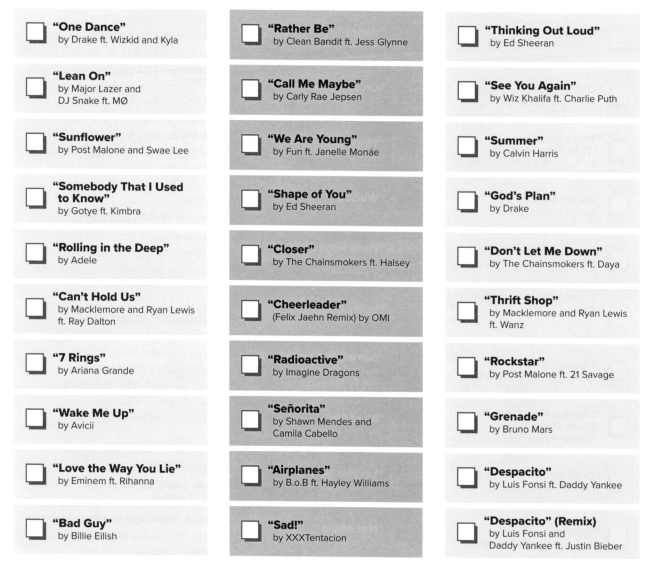

- ☐ **"One Dance"** by Drake ft. Wizkid and Kyla
- ☐ **"Lean On"** by Major Lazer and DJ Snake ft. MØ
- ☐ **"Sunflower"** by Post Malone and Swae Lee
- ☐ **"Somebody That I Used to Know"** by Gotye ft. Kimbra
- ☐ **"Rolling in the Deep"** by Adele
- ☐ **"Can't Hold Us"** by Macklemore and Ryan Lewis ft. Ray Dalton
- ☐ **"7 Rings"** by Ariana Grande
- ☐ **"Wake Me Up"** by Avicii
- ☐ **"Love the Way You Lie"** by Eminem ft. Rihanna
- ☐ **"Bad Guy"** by Billie Eilish

- ☐ **"Rather Be"** by Clean Bandit ft. Jess Glynne
- ☐ **"Call Me Maybe"** by Carly Rae Jepsen
- ☐ **"We Are Young"** by Fun ft. Janelle Monáe
- ☐ **"Shape of You"** by Ed Sheeran
- ☐ **"Closer"** by The Chainsmokers ft. Halsey
- ☐ **"Cheerleader"** (Felix Jaehn Remix) by OMI
- ☐ **"Radioactive"** by Imagine Dragons
- ☐ **"Señorita"** by Shawn Mendes and Camila Cabello
- ☐ **"Airplanes"** by B.o.B ft. Hayley Williams
- ☐ **"Sad!"** by XXXTentacion

- ☐ **"Thinking Out Loud"** by Ed Sheeran
- ☐ **"See You Again"** by Wiz Khalifa ft. Charlie Puth
- ☐ **"Summer"** by Calvin Harris
- ☐ **"God's Plan"** by Drake
- ☐ **"Don't Let Me Down"** by The Chainsmokers ft. Daya
- ☐ **"Thrift Shop"** by Macklemore and Ryan Lewis ft. Wanz
- ☐ **"Rockstar"** by Post Malone ft. 21 Savage
- ☐ **"Grenade"** by Bruno Mars
- ☐ **"Despacito"** by Luis Fonsi ft. Daddy Yankee
- ☐ **"Despacito" (Remix)** by Luis Fonsi and Daddy Yankee ft. Justin Bieber

- [ ] **"Humble"**
  by Kendrick Lamar

- [ ] **"Old Town Road" (Remix)**
  by Lil Nas X ft. Billy Ray Cyrus

- [ ] **"Waka Waka (This Time for Africa)"**
  by Shakira ft. Freshlyground

- [ ] **"Danza Kuduro"**
  by Don Omar ft. Lucenzo

- [ ] **"Dark Horse"**
  by Katy Perry ft. Juicy J

- [ ] **"Cheap Thrills"**
  by Sia

- [ ] **"Uptown Funk"**
  by Mark Ronson ft. Bruno Mars

- [ ] **"I Took a Pill in Ibiza" (Seeb Remix)**
  by Mike Posner

- [ ] **"Only Girl (in the World)"**
  by Rihanna

- [ ] **"Psycho"**
  by Post Malone ft. Ty Dolla $ign

- [ ] **"Happy"**
  by Pharrell Williams

- [ ] **"On the Floor"**
  by Jennifer Lopez ft. Pitbull

- [ ] **"Starships"**
  by Nicki Minaj

- [ ] **"Whistle"**
  by Flo Rida

- [ ] **"Party Rock Anthem"**
  by LMFAO ft. Lauren Bennett and GoonRock

- [ ] **"In My Feelings"**
  by Drake

- [ ] **"Something Just Like This"**
  by The Chainsmokers and Coldplay

- [ ] **"All of Me"**
  by John Legend

- [ ] **"Let Her Go"**
  by Passenger

- [ ] **"Not Afraid"**
  by Eminem

If You Checked 0–10:
You're 35–40 years old. So, this is not the decade where your musical tastes lie, and it shows!

If You Checked 11–20:
You're 11–15 years old. You've heard a few of these songs, but you were too young to fully enjoy the musical talents to come out of the 2010s.

If You Checked 21–30:
You're 17–20 years old. You've sung along to about half of these songs and they've provided you with the soundtrack to some important moments in your life.

If You Checked 31–40:
You're 18–23 years old. Yup, you consider some of these songs required listening and others, not so much. You've given those iconic songs a second listen and skipped on the remainder.

If You Checked 41–50:
You're 24–29 years old. The 2010s are where you've thrived! You listen to a ton of music, whether that's on the radio or through your favorite streaming service, and you know most of these songs' lyrics by heart.

Can You Actually Pass This Fourth-Grade Spelling Test?

Which is the correct spelling?

1. A. Pengin
   B. Penguin
   C. Pinguin
   D. Pengniu

2. A. Neighbor
   B. Neighber
   C. Neibor
   D. Neigbour

3. A. Eclypse
   B. Eclipce
   C. Eclypce
   D. Eclipse

4. A. Tomorrow
   B. Tommorrow
   C. Tommorow
   D. Tomorow

5. A. Decive
   B. Deceive
   C. Deseeve
   D. Deceve

6. A. Temrature
   B. Temporture
   C. Temperature
   D. Temperture

7. A. Villan
   B. Villain
   C. Villian
   D. Villen

8. A. Austrailia
   B. Austraila
   C. Australlia
   D. Australia

9. A. Utensil
   B. Utencil
   C. Utensel
   D. Utinsel

10. A. Exageration
    B. Exagerasion
    C. Exaggerasion
    D. Exaggeration

11. A. Sinonim
    B. Synomim
    C. Synonym
    D. Sinonym

12. A. Metropolitian
    B. Metropolitan
    C. Metrapolitan
    D. Metrapolittian

ANSWER KEY

1. B; 2. A; 3. D; 4. A; 5. B; 6. C; 7. B;
8. D; 9. A; 10. D; 11. C; 12. B

NOW ADD UP YOUR SCORE!

If You Got 0–3 Correct:
You FAILED! GET. IT. TOGETHER.

If You Got 4–8 Correct:
You Got a C+! Okay, but nothing
to hang up on the fridge.

If You Got 9–12 Correct:
You Got an A+! HANG. THIS. TEST.
UP. ON. THE. FRIDGE.

Cake vs. Pie Bracket

Pick your favorite contender from each pairing on the left and right.
An item that's not selected gets eliminated. The winner takes on the winning item from
the next pairing and so on until you have one final winner. You can fill out as you go,
snap a pic and share online, and compare your results with friends.

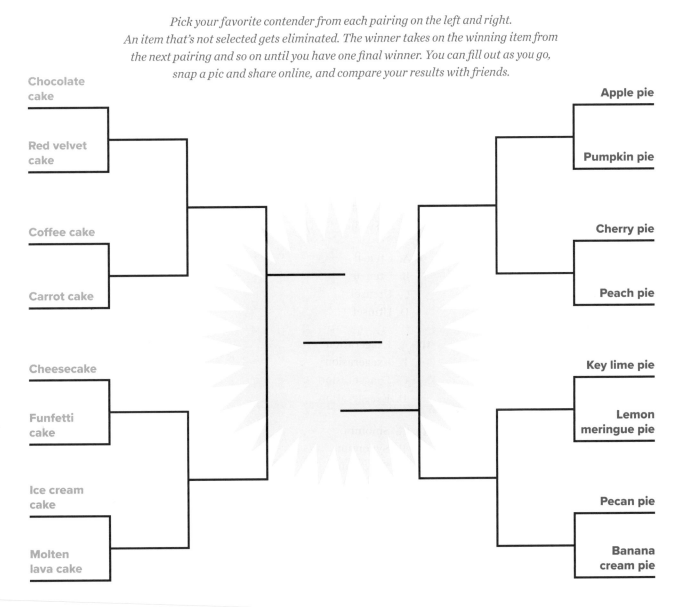

Chocolate cake

Red velvet cake

Coffee cake

Carrot cake

Cheesecake

Funfetti cake

Ice cream cake

Molten lava cake

Apple pie

Pumpkin pie

Cherry pie

Peach pie

Key lime pie

Lemon meringue pie

Pecan pie

Banana cream pie

Biggest Fear Word Search

The first word you see is your biggest fear.

```
G D D U G M U A D O Z R I W E M
W H R X G O A D L V J W Q T O R
S M D P V X B M G H O S T S H D
J L C T R Y D T N L L J S R V Y
B P F Q F N F Z C K C W H K Y Y
J N M G H O D D E A T H Z O G D
P U B L I C S P E A K I N G U S
D F U D Z S G V B H I I I C Q Z
D T Z H E I G H T S G V N K J C
P X R G C L O W N S N H X A U W
K F S N A K E S P I D E R S Z J
B F L O N E L I N E S S E N R Y
I I Q M W E N A H Z N P Z N Y
Y B M Q Y E S R F J Q M J Y B C
F W F C S W O C F I T I C I S M
K E B M A Y Q S K U N B N O J Z
```

Build a Roommate for Under $50

Circle the items you want to purchase. The goal is to try not to go over your budget.

$30	Actually does their own dishes	Is someone you genuinely enjoy hanging out with	Always pays their portion of the rent on time	Never eats your food
$20	Doesn't mind if you have a pet	Runs it by you when they have someone over	Takes out the trash	Doesn't borrow anything of yours without asking
$10	Doesn't leave passive-aggressive notes	Has very quiet sex as a courtesy to you	Cleans out the fridge every once in a while	Doesn't monopolize the TV
$5	Plays music at a very comfortable volume	Is very democratic about household disputes	Leaves some hot water for you after they take a shower	Replaces the toilet paper roll

Are You Actually an Adventurous Eater?

Check off all the foods you've tried.

☐ Escargot	☐ Gravlax	☐ Ackee and saltfish
☐ Falafel	☐ Xiaolongbao	☐ Fried plantains
☐ Ramen	☐ Laksa	☐ Arancini
☐ Tagine	☐ Poutine	☐ Black pudding
☐ Bratwurst	☐ Pierogi	☐ Cochinita pibil
☐ Tortilla Española	☐ Arepas	☐ Jollof rice
☐ Foie gras	☐ Bourekas	☐ Lumpia
☐ Spätzle	☐ Steamed pork buns	☐ Biryani
☐ Moussaka	☐ Banh mi	☐ Baklava
☐ Cacio e pepe	☐ Conch fritters	☐ Époisse de Bourgogne
☐ Saag paneer	☐ Pão de queijo	☐ Brigadeiro
☐ Uni	☐ Croquettes	☐ Mochi
☐ Smørrebrød	☐ Goulash	☐ Pastel de nata
☐ Mole	☐ Pancit	☐ Poffertjes

- [ ] **Sticky rice with mango**
- [ ] **Semifreddo**
- [ ] **Horchata**
- [ ] **Pisco sour**

- [ ] **Soju**
- [ ] **Mango lassi**
- [ ] **Port wine**
- [ ] **Aperol spritz**

If You Checked 0–15:

You have lots of new foods to try.
When it comes to eating, you usually stick to the same foods you know and love. But there's a whole world out there including countries with amazing cuisines and dishes that might open your eyes to new things. Try going out of your comfort zone and tasting some totally new flavors.

If You Checked 16–32:

You've got a pretty global palate.
You've tried a solid number of different dishes from around the world. That's great! Since you've already started exploring new cuisines and expanding your horizons, keep it up! There are so many more delicious foods out there.

If You Checked 33–50:

You're a total world foodie. Wow, look at you! You're a super adventurous eater who loves trying new things. You've already tried a ton of different cuisines and flavors and you're willing to take a bite of just about anything. TBH, the way you eat is probably a metaphor for how you live your whole life—with an open mind and a desire to experiment with new things.

What's Your Racehorse Name?

MONTH YOU WERE BORN

January: Chicago

February: Gatsbury

March: Coleslaw

April: Lightning

May: Our Only

June: Nimble

July: Secret

August: The Humble

September: Doctor

October: Gym Rat

November: Ace

December: International

FAVORITE HORSE SNACK

Sugar cube: Excalibur

Carrot: Perfection

Apple slice: Headlock

Peppermint: Storm

Hay: Father

Salt lick: McGraw

Grapes: Disgrace

Grass: Gerkin

Ice cube: Senator

Watermelon: A-Lister

Friends Trivia Crossword Puzzle

ACROSS

1 Phoebe's alter ego

6 Costume Joey dresses in to teach Ben about Hanukkah

7 Phoebe's twin

9 _____ Club that Ross and Will started in high school

13 Soap opera Joey starred on

15 A state of total awareness, according to Ross

16 Ross's first wife

17 Number of erogenous zones, according to Monica

19 Dessert Rachel tries making for Thanksgiving

21 Vegas game Monica wins

22 Top Brown Bird cookie seller prize

23 Number of seasons aired

24 Song Rachel sings to quiet Emma

25 Chandler's middle name

DOWN

1 Made out with the high school librarian

2 What Ross dresses as to teach Ben about Hanukkah

3 Your one true love, according to Phoebe

4 Pees on Monica after she's stung by a jellyfish

5 Color of door with picture frame on it

8 What Rachel first wore in the pilot

10 _____ point, according to Joey

11 Vegas machine game Phoebe gets lurked at

12 Touch football trophy name

14 Chandler's job, according to Rachel

18 Country Chandler flies to, to avoid Janice

20 Janice's catchphrase

Answers on p. 309

Everyone Has a Dog Breed That Matches Their Personality—Here's Yours

How would your closest friends describe you?

A. Fabulous
B. Loyal
C. Hilarious
D. Tall
E. Goofy
F. Playful
G. Confident
H. Stubborn
I. Adorable

Which dish would you bring to a potluck?

A. Potato salad
B. Mac 'n' cheese
C. Deviled eggs
D. Garlic bread
E. Coleslaw
F. Brownies
G. Green bean casserole
H. Cupcakes
I. Wine

What's your favorite holiday?

A. Christmas or Hanukkah
B. Thanksgiving
C. Halloween
D. Easter
E. Fourth of July
F. Boxing Day
G. St. Patrick's Day
H. Your birthday
I. I hate all holidays

Pick a condiment:

A. Ketchup
B. Mayo
C. Relish
D. Mustard
E. Sriracha
F. Pesto
G. Ranch
H. BBQ sauce
I. Soy sauce

If you won the lottery, what's the first thing you would buy?

A. A big house
B. A fancy car
C. Plane tickets
D. Clothes
E. New phone
F. Shoes!!
G. I would donate it all
H. I would pay off loans or debt
I. I would save it all!

cute

If You Got Mostly A's:

You're a labradoodle! You're known for your intelligence, kindness, and cheerful disposition! You're a self-confident pup who rarely comes across as aggressive. There's nothing you love more than helping people! Actually . . . you might love swimming more. Well, what are you waiting for? Jump in!

If You Got Mostly B's:

You're a golden retriever! You're an adventurous extrovert who loves to make friends! And you've got a big soft spot for the simple things in life. You're not complicated. All you need in your life is the breeze, a bone, and a comfy bed. Oh! And lots of snuggles. *squeals*

If You Got Mostly C's:

You're a mutt! Your personality is a combination of the best of breeds! And you will not be confined to any sort of box. You're the best type of pup to invite over for a dinner party, because you've got the best stories. You love experiencing new things and pushing the boundaries. Plus, you're ridiculously cute!

If You Got Mostly D's:

You're a great dane! You're so humble that you don't even realize how much you stand out! You're truly one of a kind. At first, people might think you're intimidating, but after they get to know you, they absolutely fall in love. Not only are you confident and unique, but you've got an old soul.

If You Got Mostly E's:

You're a pug! Let's be honest: You're a total goofball. You're hilarious and adorable and you love the spotlight! Not only that, but you're empathetic and thoughtful. Just look at those adorable puppy eyes! You tend to be highly emotional, but that's what's so great about you.

If You Got Mostly F's:

You're a shiba inu! You are so barking cute! You're an adventurous introvert who likes to be affectionate and playful, as long as it's on your own terms. Your little fiery personality is contagious and always puts a smile on someone's face.

If You Got Mostly G's:

You're a German shepherd! You're one sleek and powerful pup! You're highly intelligent and genuinely love helping others. And when it comes to challenges, you're relentless. But you also love to relax! You're just as affectionate and loving as you are focused and courageous!

If You Got Mostly H's:

You're a pitbull! You're ridiculously lovable and loyal. Sure, you might feel misunderstood at times, but what's important is that you've got a good heart. Once people get to know you, they instantly love you. Plus, you're the best cuddle buddy around!

If You Got Mostly I's:

You're a corgi! You're so adorable that it's borderline mesmerizing. There's just something about your li'l booty and short legs that make people lose their minds. And who could blame them? You're so charismatic and majestic! You, my friend, are a pup who truly lives up to the hype.

Can We Guess Where in the US You Live in Just 5 Questions?

It's Saturday morning and you're:

A. Hiking
B. Sleeping in
C. Chasing after kids
D. Eating
E. Running errands
F. Tinkering in the garage

Would you rather be:

A. Hot
B. Cold

Which T-shirt pattern are you most drawn to?

A. Tie-dye
B. All-over cat print
C. Fruit
D. Plain white
E. Plain black
F. Plaid

The absolute best fries are from:

A. In-N-Out
B. Steak 'n Shake
C. Whataburger
D. Burger King
E. Shake Shack
F. Wendy's

How do you like to unwind?

A. Weed
B. Reality TV
C. A glass of wine
D. A six-pack of beer
E. Jogging
F. Chocolate

If You Got Mostly A's:
You live on the West Coast! You're all chill and probably like to hike.

If You Got Mostly B's:
You live in the Midwest! You hail from America's heartland.

If You Got Mostly C's:
You live in the Southwest! Not to be confused with the Deep South.

If You Got Mostly D's:
You live in the Southeast! Don't even get you started on humidity.

If You Got Mostly E's:
You live in the Northeast! You're all about that cold winter life.

If You Got Mostly F's:
You live in the Rocky Mountains! You're outdoorsy AF.

Can You Find All 12 Disney Princesses?

Snow White
Cinderella
Aurora
Ariel
Belle
Jasmine
Pocahontas
Mulan
Tiana
Rapunzel
Merida
Moana

```
P O R X N I D D A L A M A D I L E I R A
S O A D I R E M E P O U G O O F Y P N S
D R C I B U Z Z R Y R M I K E N Q R E L
Y O S Y E N S I D E N I A R L A R I E E
B I N N C E U P S S D Z N I L Z E N U E
E T D A O P I O L A F I G C E R T C Q P
L I L O L W O C D T B P R E B A T E S Y
L H U E Y D W A Y U A A U N N T A E N T
M I C K E Y I H J C C U M M N I H R O U
O U Z A C O L O U T R K R B B Y E I W H
W R W N K I E N A T S E A O I A L C G S
G S E A R I E T U M E Y P F R J A F N U
L U N O C D I A S U Y A U A A A X T I M
I L D M U F A S A L D M N L P S W A K I
Z A Y S N K Q S N A U U Z L E M U L A N
T S S E C N I R P E J Z E E T I L H O N
I C X S I M B A C O E A L U S N A U B I
A L L E R E D N I C T Z A R A E D G M E
N T H U M P E R J A S Y Y C E J Y O U N
A H A P P Y O C T I N K E R B E L L D E
```

Answers on p. 309

What's Your Mythical Creature Name?

MONTH YOU WERE BORN

January: The Legendary

February: The Fabulous

March: The Heroic

April: The Fantastic

May: The Supernatural

June: The Mesmerizing

July: The Miraculous

August: The Whimsical

September: The Illustrious

October: The Spellbinding

November: The Notorious

December: The Enchanting

LAST DIGIT OF YOUR PHONE NUMBER

1: Pegasus

2: Dragon

3: Fairy

4: Beast

5: Sphinx

6: Loch Ness Monster

7: Manticore

8: Merperson

9: Cyclops

0: Ogre

This Maze Will Determine Your Future Career

ASTRONAUT

FAMOUS WRITER

INTERIOR DESIGNER

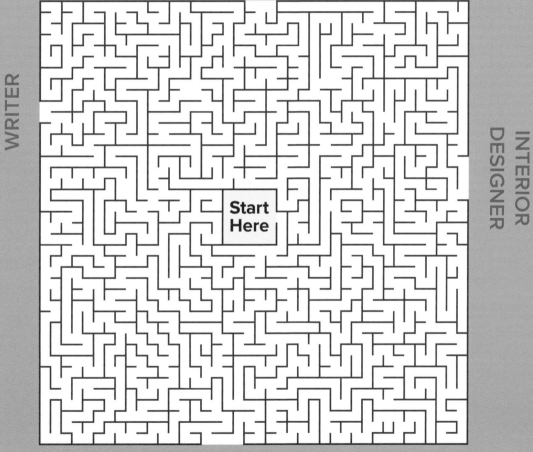

Start Here

MUSIC PRODUCER

Can We Guess Your Personality Type Based on Your Taste in Music?

Which female group "gets" you?

A. The Supremes
B. Bananarama
C. The Bangles
D. TLC
E. The Spice Girls
F. Destiny's Child

What decade had the best music scene?

A. The '60s
B. The '70s
C. The '80s
D. The '90s
E. The '00s
F. This current decade

Which male artist is undeniably amazing?

A. Freddie Mercury
B. Stevie Wonder
C. Frank Sinatra
D. Marvin Gaye
E. Kurt Cobain
F. Prince

You listen to music to . . .

A. Dance
B. Relax
C. Escape
D. Reflect
E. Feel happy
F. Get rowdy

Which music genre is totally underrated?

A. Reggae
B. Bluegrass
C. New wave
D. Bachata
E. Dubstep
F. Jazz

What's the greatest musical act to ever come out of the UK?

A. The Beatles
B. Adele
C. The Who
D. Amy Winehouse
E. The Rolling Stones
F. Stormzy

How do you get your music?

A. Pandora
B. Spotify
C. CDs
D. Tidal
E. iTunes
F. The radio

When you hear the name "John," which musician comes to mind?

A. John Lennon
B. John Legend

If You Got Mostly A's:

You're reflective and deep! You have a vast intellect and an inquisitive mind. You like music that really gets your brain going. You're internally motivated and know that getting lost in thought is the path toward bigger things.

If You Got Mostly B's:

You're eclectic and creative! You have a vivid imagination and curiosity about the world. You like tunes that really get your creative juices flowing. Your personality is as colorful and wonderful as you are.

If You Got Mostly C's:

You're charismatic and social! You are a social butterfly and a people magnet. You like music that's upbeat and can get the party started. You're an absolute joy to be around and are always the life of the party.

If You Got Mostly D's:

You're edgy and innovative! You're hip, cool, and always on top of the latest trends. Your musical tastes are as cutting-edge as you are. You've always thought outside the box, and others look to you for inspiration.

If You Got Mostly E's:

You're assertive and goal-oriented! You're a self-starter and natural-born leader. You're highly ambitious and at the very top of your game. You like music that motivates you and gets you in the mood to take the world on.

If You Got Mostly F's:

You're sassy and classy! You have a quick, razor-sharp wit and the smarts to match. You like music that's empowering, uplifting, and gets you moving. You're a riot and there's never a dull moment when you're around.

Sorry, Only Introverts Are Allowed to Do This Would You Rather

Would you rather
make a phone call to set up an appointment
OR have an overly chatty hairdresser while
getting your hair cut?

Would you rather
sing a karaoke song that you only
~kinda~ know the lyrics to at a crowded bar
OR give a presentation at work?

Would you rather
have a week-long paid vacation where you don't
have to talk to anyone if you don't want to
OR have someone make all your calls for you
for a whole year?

Would you rather
have the entire Disneyland park to yourself every time you go
OR have your own private first-class "pod" every time you fly?

Would you rather

have a chatty driver every time you take a taxi/Uber/Lyft/etc.
OR have someone start a conversation
with you every time you're in line at the grocery store?

Would you rather

always have the perfect excuse to leave a party early
OR always have the middle seat empty next to
you on every flight?

Would you rather

always be able to order food from a touchscreen
and never have to talk to a human
OR never get an unknown or spam call ever again?

Would you rather

have a perfect reading nook in your house
and an endless supply of books
OR your own home theater and an endless supply of snacks?

Would you rather

never have to do a group project ever again
OR never be asked, "Why are you so quiet?" ever again?

Disney MASH

Add together the first and last digit of your phone number to get the magic number! Use that number to go through each category and count through the items; then cross off the item you land on. Start again, skipping over the crossed-off items until there's only one left in each category. Then circle the last item in each category to see your results.

Where will you live?

Arendelle

Neverland

Agrabah

Zootopia

Mount Olympus

Who's your sidekick?

Sebastian

Mushu

Genie

Tinkerbell

Timon

Who's your enemy?

Scar

Maleficent

Hades

Jafar

Ursula

Who will you marry?

Flynn Rider

Elsa

Li Shang

Princess Tiana

Tarzan

Who's your best friend?

Aladdin

Merida

Fairy Godmother

Emperor Kuzco

Megara

What are you searching for?

True love

Your family

Treasure

A way out

Who you really are

Build a Boyfriend for $50

Circle the items you want to purchase. The goal is to try not to go over your budget.

$30	Makes a lot of money	Is open about his emotions	Funny but not embarrassing	Smokin' hot
$20	Loves pets	Doesn't have a crazy ex	Promising career	Isn't scared of commitment
$10	Dresses well	Has more furnishings at his apartment than just a mattress and old liquor	Has great taste in music	Likes watching your shows
$5	Buys you flowers on the regular	Is a good cook	Always texts back	Has a family you like and who likes you

Only People Who Are 100% Weird Have Done 40/40 of These Things

Check off everything that applies to you.

- [ ] Put one hand in the air for no reason while you're in bed.

- [ ] Check other people's windshield wipers while driving to make sure yours aren't going too fast.

- [ ] Pretend to look at something else when someone is blocking the product you want in the grocery store.

- [ ] Hoard photos on your phone because you never know when you're going to need them.

- [ ] Realize you've been singing the wrong lyrics to a song for forever after looking up the actual lyrics.

- [ ] Get immediately repulsed after touching wet food in the sink.

- [ ] Refuse to eat until you find the perfect show on Netflix.

- [ ] Reconsider buying something online after seeing the shipping price.

- [ ] Never pull the right chain to turn on your ceiling fan.

- [ ] Listen to a song, forget you're listening to a song, and are surprised when it's over.

- [ ] Wake up five minutes before your phone alarm goes off and get sad because you could have slept in five more minutes.

- [ ] Become immediately embarrassed when no one laughs at the joke you thought was funny.

- [ ] Smile awkwardly at someone you know but don't know well enough to say hi to.

- [ ] Watch cartoons after a scary movie so you don't have nightmares.

- [ ] Hear a recording of your own voice and immediately hate it.

- [ ] Check behind the shower curtain when you go into a bathroom.

- [ ] Become embarrassed when you think of something awkward you did years ago.

- [ ] Think the '90s were ten years ago.

- [ ] Reread an email immediately after you've sent it.

- [ ] Park in a faraway spot, rather than parallel parking in a close spot.

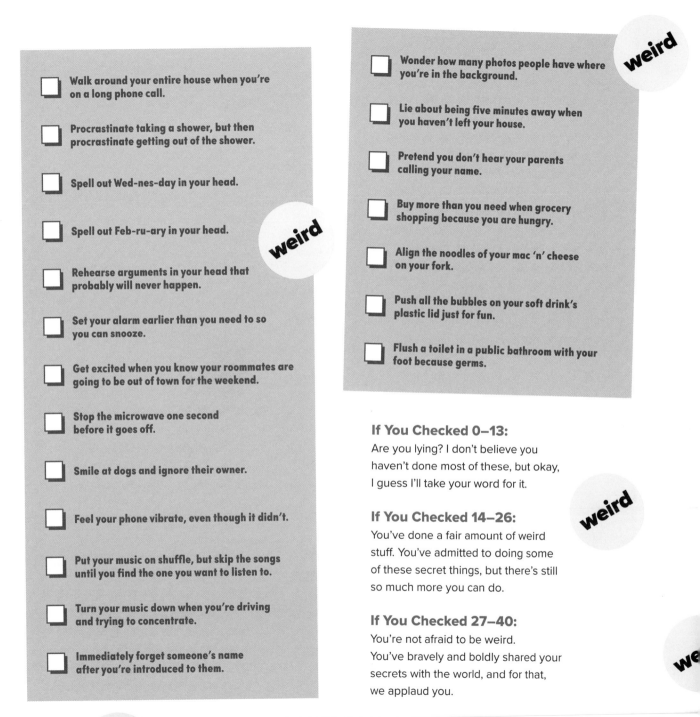

- [ ] Walk around your entire house when you're on a long phone call.

- [ ] Procrastinate taking a shower, but then procrastinate getting out of the shower.

- [ ] Spell out Wed-nes-day in your head.

- [ ] Spell out Feb-ru-ary in your head.

- [ ] Rehearse arguments in your head that probably will never happen.

- [ ] Set your alarm earlier than you need to so you can snooze.

- [ ] Get excited when you know your roommates are going to be out of town for the weekend.

- [ ] Stop the microwave one second before it goes off.

- [ ] Smile at dogs and ignore their owner.

- [ ] Feel your phone vibrate, even though it didn't.

- [ ] Put your music on shuffle, but skip the songs until you find the one you want to listen to.

- [ ] Turn your music down when you're driving and trying to concentrate.

- [ ] Immediately forget someone's name after you're introduced to them.

weird

- [ ] Wonder how many photos people have where you're in the background.

- [ ] Lie about being five minutes away when you haven't left your house.

- [ ] Pretend you don't hear your parents calling your name.

- [ ] Buy more than you need when grocery shopping because you are hungry.

- [ ] Align the noodles of your mac 'n' cheese on your fork.

- [ ] Push all the bubbles on your soft drink's plastic lid just for fun.

- [ ] Flush a toilet in a public bathroom with your foot because germs.

weird

If You Checked 0–13:
Are you lying? I don't believe you haven't done most of these, but okay, I guess I'll take your word for it.

If You Checked 14–26:
You've done a fair amount of weird stuff. You've admitted to doing some of these secret things, but there's still so much more you can do.

weird

If You Checked 27–40:
You're not afraid to be weird. You've bravely and boldly shared your secrets with the world, and for that, we applaud you.

we

weird

What's Your Cat Name and Personality?

COLOR OF THE SHIRT YOU'RE WEARING

Red: Jingle Jangles

Yellow: Cheddar

Blue: Count Fluffington

Purple: Latte

Orange: Kitty Dupree

Green: Fritter

Black: Papaya

Pink: Pearl

Gray: Saint Whiskers

Multicolored: Sir Floof

FAVORITE FOOD

Pizza: Knocks over a glass just to get attention

Sushi: Will try to kill anyone who goes near your tummy and/or toe beans

French fries: Determined to catch the laser pointer

Pasta: Sits on the couch *juuuust* far enough away so people must reach to pet you

Burgers: Will headbutt until you receive the cuddles you desire

Nachos: Brings home leaves and dead birds as a gift

Fried chicken: Wakes everyone up at 4:30 every morning because you're hungry

Ice cream: Hides in every open cabinet and drawer

Mozzarella sticks: Only eats canned food and drinks from the kitchen faucet

Tacos: Hisses at you and then immediately licks your hand

This or That: Teens/Twentysomethings Edition

Teens and twentysomethings will choose completely different answers.

This or that?

A. Cats
B. Dogs

This or that?

A. Vanilla
B. Chocolate

This or that?

A. Bath
B. Shower

This or that?

A. Savory
B. Sweet

This or that?

A. Day
B. Night

This or that?

A. Fruit
B. Vegetables

This or that?

A. Winter
B. Summer

This or that?

A. Spring
B. Fall

This or that?

A. Pancakes
B. Waffles

This or that?

A. Rain
B. Snow

This or that?

A. Coffee
B. Tea

This or that?

A. Silver
B. Gold

This or that?

A. East Coast
B. West Coast

This or that?

A. Peanut butter
B. Jelly

This or that?

A. Breakfast
B. Dinner

If You Got Mostly A's:
You're a twentysomething! You're somewhere within the twenty to twenty-nine age range. If you haven't graduated from college yet, you will soon. You might also be getting your first taste of financial independence and loving every second of it.

If You Got Mostly B's:
You're a teen! Yup, you're definitely between the ages of thirteen and nineteen. You're still a student, and unless you live in a dorm, you're probably still living at home with your parents.

How Well Do You Remember the First *Twilight* Movie?

1. **What is the first line of the movie?**

   A. "I don't regret my decisions."
   B. "Leaving home is a lot like dying."
   C. "I'd never given much thought to how I would die."

2. **Where did Bella live with her mother?**

   A. Santa Fe, New Mexico
   B. Phoenix, Arizona
   C. Carson City, Nevada

3. **What is the name of the town Bella moves to?**

   A. Kent
   B. Edmonds
   C. Forks

4. **What reason does Edward give Bella after he's been absent from school?**

   A. He was out of town
   B. He was sick
   C. He had a family emergency

5. **What is the name of Jacob's tribe?**

   A. Yakama
   B. Quileute
   C. Makah

6. **What kind of car does Edward drive?**

   A. BMW
   B. Mercedes
   C. Volvo

7. **Where is the first time Edward and Bella talk about Edward being a vampire?**

   A. In the woods
   B. Under the bleachers
   C. On the beach

8. **Bella states that she was "_____ and _____ in love" with Edward.**

   A. "Totally and completely"
   B. "Unconditionally and irrevocably"
   C. "Undoubtedly and permanently"

9. **What is Edward dying of when Dr. Cullen turns him into a vampire?**

   A. Spanish influenza
   B. Scarlet fever
   C. Cholera

10. **What is Edward listening to when Bella visits his room?**

   A. Miles Davis
   B. The White Stripes
   C. Debussy

11. **Where does James tell Bella to meet him?**

   A. Her old high school auditorium
   B. The public library
   C. Her old ballet school

12. **How does James trick Bella into believing he has taken her mother hostage?**

   A. He is able to manipulate his own voice to sound like Bella's mom
   B. He is playing the sound from an old home movie in which Bella's mom is calling her
   C. He's playing a recording of Bella's mom's voice he made before he released her

13. **What is the theme of Edward and Bella's prom?**

   A. Casino Night
   B. Under the Sea
   C. Midnight Fantasy

NOW ADD UP YOUR SCORE!

If You Got 0–5 Correct:
Nice try! It's not like you've been going to school as long as Edward, so how can you be expected to know everything?

If You Got 6–10 Correct:
You knocked it out of the park! Your vampire memory is pretty sharp.

If You Got 11–13 Correct:
You are a *Twilight* master! Edward would save your life any day.

ACROSS

2 "Rolling in the Deep"
3 "Hotline Bling"
6 "DJ Got Us Fallin' in Love"
8 "Truth Hurts"
10 "Kiss from a Rose"
15 "Believe"
16 "Thrift Shop"
17 "Loser"
18 "Raise Your Glass"
21 "Lose Yourself"
22 "Your Love Is My Drug"
23 "Jailhouse Rock"
24 "Chandelier"
25 "Don't Stop the Party"

DOWN

1 "Who Will Save Your Soul"
3 "White Flag"
4 "Wake Me Up"
5 "Only Time"
7 "Umbrella"
9 "Royals"
11 "Army of Me"
12 "Hips Don't Lie"
13 "Little Red Corvette"
14 "Single Ladies"
16 "Vogue"
19 "Fields of Gold"
20 "Glamorous"

Artist by Song Title Crossword Puzzle

Answers on p. 309

The First Name You See Is the Name of the Person You'll Marry

```
S A R A H A N N A H S J L G U S
Y B A T Y L E R M E G A N I Z S
L W C H R I S O E R P C M A C Y
V S H A N N O N L J A K E M K D
I B E L I Z A K I Z C H A D Y N
A R L J E N N Y A R I A N I X E
A A Q P E T E R A I N L Y A M Y
N D K M A A V A N D R E W N A T
N A T A L I E N O A H Y X A L I
A P R I L O L S P E N C E R I N
L R M K Y L E I A B I E M M A O
X I A D A M A R U I N J L U C Y
P L M A T T H V L I A M Y S A M
```

If You Score 6/10 on This Logic Quiz, You're Smarter Than the Average Person

Beneath each question, fill out your response in the space provided, check your answers, and then add up your score. Go!

1. You just bought a rooster. You expect to get three fresh eggs every morning. After two weeks and three days with the bird, how many eggs do you have?

2. What word in the dictionary is always spelled incorrectly?

3. You're running a marathon and you just passed the person who was in second place. What place are you in now?

4. In what month do people get the least sleep?

5. How much dirt is there in a hole that is three feet wide, four feet long, and five feet deep?

6. A doctor gives you three pills and tells you to take one every half hour. How long do the pills last?

7. You walk into a pitch-black room, and you only have ONE match. You have some newspaper, a candle, and some firewood in front of you. Which should you light first?

8. What has a head and tails but no body?

9. Jane and Bob have four daughters. Each of their daughters has one brother. How many children do Jane and Bob have in total?

10. How many times can you subtract five from twenty-five?

NOW ADD UP YOUR SCORE!

If You Got 0–5 Correct:
Hmm. Not this time. Sure, you got stumped a few times, but hey—some of these were pretty hard!

If You Got 6–10 Correct:
You're smarter than the average person! When it comes to trick questions, there's no tricking you!

win

CONGRATS!

Can You Unscramble the Names of the 50 Most Mentioned Characters in the *Harry Potter* Books?

RAHYR ETPROT_____

ONR ALEYSEW_____

NORMIHEE REGANRG_____

LASUB ODERMUDBEL_____

SUBERU IADRGH_____

RUSSEVE PANES_____

DREMOTLV_____

URISIS LCAKB_____

CARDO FLOMAY_____

DFER ASEWLYE_____

SEMUR ILPNU_____

ROGGEE SAWELYE_____

LENIVLE BGOOTLNMTO_____

RATURH SLAWYEE_____

NYGNI LESYAEW_____

VNEIAMR NAACLGGOLM_____

LOMYL EELWSYA_____

REDLOOS GEDIMRUB_____

STARLOA DAM-YEE DOMOY_____

NENVOR SEDYLUR_____

LENUCIROS GDUFE_____

REEPT ERGTWPIET_____

BOYDB_____

ULDYDE URDLESY_____

OCARHE GHNLSUOR_____

EPYRC EEAWLSY_____

AULN VEOOLOGD_____

ERCDIC GYDORGI_____

IEUATPN SLREYUD_____

EHARRKEC_____

LBLI YWLEASE_____

ATRBY HCORCU RS_____

RUAGS CLFIH_____

ORTVKI RMUK_____

OELIYRDG RAKHOTLC_____

LSLIBY TEYRANEWL_____

URFLE LERACDUO_____

CLIUUS AOYLMF_____

DULO GNBAMA_____

AHRDNMYPOA SONTK_____

OGRYEGR ELYGO_____

NVCIENT RBBAEC_____

TAXELRIBL ESLNGEART_____

OCH GNACH_____

ANED HTMOSA_____

IVEORL ODOW_____

WDEGIH_____

SJMEA TRPTOE_____

RIAT KREESET_____

MSAESU INGFINAN_____

●●●

How Many Classic and Not-So-Classic Disney Movies Have You Actually Seen?

Check all the movies you've seen all the way through.

- [ ] Snow White and the Seven Dwarfs
- [ ] Pinocchio
- [ ] Fantasia
- [ ] Dumbo
- [ ] Bambi
- [ ] Saludos Amigos
- [ ] The Three Caballeros
- [ ] Make Mine Music
- [ ] Melody Time
- [ ] The Adventures of Ichabod and Mr. Toad
- [ ] Cinderella

- [ ] Alice in Wonderland
- [ ] Peter Pan
- [ ] Lady and the Tramp
- [ ] Sleeping Beauty
- [ ] 101 Dalmatians
- [ ] The Sword in the Stone
- [ ] The Jungle Book
- [ ] The Aristocats
- [ ] Robin Hood
- [ ] The Many Adventures of Winnie the Pooh
- [ ] The Rescuers

- [ ] The Fox and the Hound
- [ ] The Black Cauldron
- [ ] The Great Mouse Detective
- [ ] Oliver & Company
- [ ] The Little Mermaid
- [ ] The Rescuers Down Under
- [ ] Beauty and the Beast
- [ ] Aladdin
- [ ] The Lion King
- [ ] Pocahontas
- [ ] Toy Story
- [ ] The Hunchback of Notre Dame
- [ ] Hercules
- [ ] Mulan

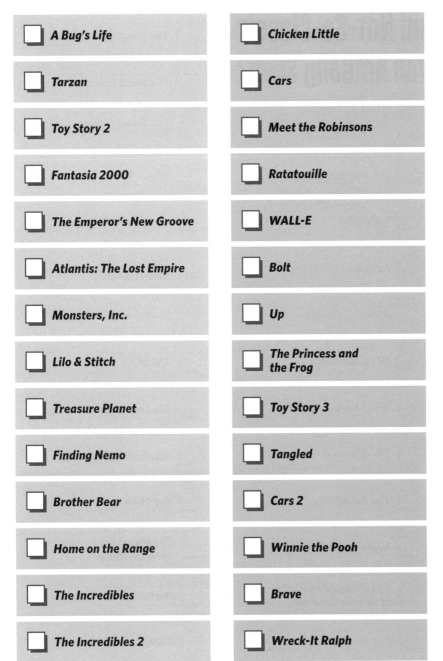

- ☐ A Bug's Life
- ☐ Tarzan
- ☐ Toy Story 2
- ☐ Fantasia 2000
- ☐ The Emperor's New Groove
- ☐ Atlantis: The Lost Empire
- ☐ Monsters, Inc.
- ☐ Lilo & Stitch
- ☐ Treasure Planet
- ☐ Finding Nemo
- ☐ Brother Bear
- ☐ Home on the Range
- ☐ The Incredibles
- ☐ The Incredibles 2

- ☐ Chicken Little
- ☐ Cars
- ☐ Meet the Robinsons
- ☐ Ratatouille
- ☐ WALL-E
- ☐ Bolt
- ☐ Up
- ☐ The Princess and the Frog
- ☐ Toy Story 3
- ☐ Tangled
- ☐ Cars 2
- ☐ Winnie the Pooh
- ☐ Brave
- ☐ Wreck-It Ralph

- ☐ Monsters University
- ☐ Frozen
- ☐ Big Hero 6
- ☐ Inside Out
- ☐ Coco
- ☐ Frozen 2

If You Checked 0–23:
You've seen most of the major ones, but you've missed more than a few. But this isn't all bad, 'cause the Magic Kingdom awaits!!!

If You Checked 24–60:
You've seen a lot, but you've got more to go. Good news is, you're in for a treat! These are the perfect films to watch on a rainy day or when you're just in the mood.

If You Checked 61–70:
You're a Disney scholar!!! You must have majored in Disney or something in college, because you've spent a lot of time studying both the new hits and the classics!

Are You More Like Tina Fey or Amy Poehler?

Donuts or waffles?

A. Donuts
B. Waffles

Top hat or monocle?

A. Top hat
B. Monocle

Cats or dogs?

A. Cats
B. Dogs

Boston or Chicago?

A. Boston
B. Chicago

Sketch comedy or Improv?

A. Sketch comedy
B. Improv

Broad City or _The Mindy Project_?

A. _Broad City_
B. _The Mindy Project_

Cheese or chocolate?

A. Cheese
B. Chocolate

Soccer or Tennis?

A. Soccer
B. Tennis

Thelma or Louise?

A. Thelma
B. Louise

Tea or Coffee?

A. Tea
B. Coffee

Polka dots or stripes?

A. Polka dots
B. Stripes

Beyoncé or Nicki Minaj?

A. Beyoncé
B. Nicki Minaj

Jerry or Kenneth?

A. Jerry
B. Kenneth

If You Got Mostly A's:

You're Tina Fey! You're a born leader and a multitalented creative force, always trying new things and excelling in pretty much all of them. The best thing about you? You're never afraid to poke fun at yourself and just have a good time with your friends.

If You Got Mostly B's:

You're Amy Poehler! You are a force of true good in this world, with optimism that inspires everyone around you. You seem to have boundless energy and tackle every goal with a level of grace that makes everyone wish they were more like you.

The Very Difficult, Practically Impossible Sandwich Bracket

Pick your favorite contender from each pairing on the left and right.
An item that's not selected gets eliminated. The winner takes on the winning item from
the next pairing and so on until you have one final winner. You can fill out as you go,
snap a pic and share online, and compare your results with friends.

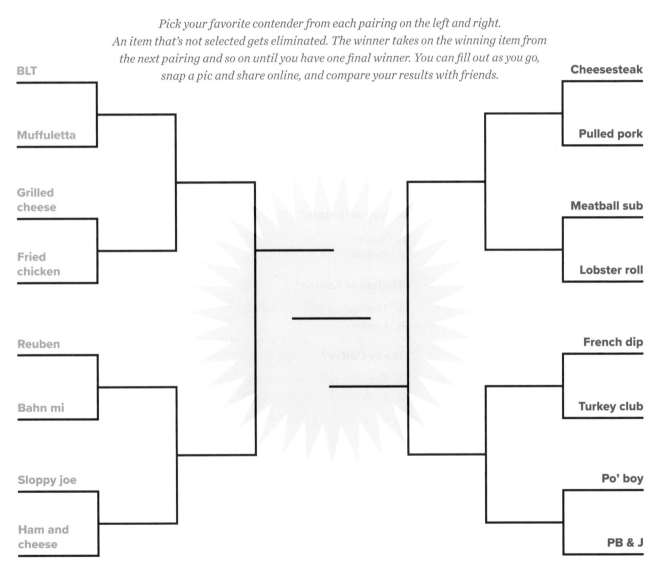

BLT

Muffuletta

Grilled cheese

Fried chicken

Reuben

Bahn mi

Sloppy joe

Ham and cheese

Cheesesteak

Pulled pork

Meatball sub

Lobster roll

French dip

Turkey club

Po' boy

PB & J

1. **What's the name of the student newspaper at Riverdale High?**

   A. *The Blue & Gold*
   B. *The Riverdale Times*
   C. *The Riverdale Gazette*
   D. *The Riverdale Press*

2. **What's the name of the Lodges' former butler?**

   A. Smith
   B. Smithy
   C. Smithers
   D. Smitty

3. **Where does Mary Andrews live?**

   A. Philadelphia
   B. Chicago
   C. Boston
   D. Denver

4. **What sweet treat does Veronica bring Betty in "Chapter Two: A Touch of Evil"?**

   A. Cupcakes
   B. Cake pops
   C. Cheesecake
   D. Brownies

5. **What color is Miss Grundy's car?**

   A. White
   B. Red
   C. Blue
   D. Black

Only True *Riverdale* Fans Can Score at Least 11/14 on This Quiz

6. **Which holiday did Jason Blossom die on?**

   A. Labor Day
   B. Memorial Day
   C. Fourth of July
   D. Halloween

7. **Which city did Veronica Lodge live in before moving to Riverdale?**

   A. San Francisco
   B. New York
   C. Los Angeles
   D. Seattle

8. **Where do Archie and Veronica first kiss?**

   A. At Pop's Chock'lit Shoppe
   B. In a closet
   C. At school
   D. In front of the Pembrooke

9. **What's the Blossom family business?**

   A. Restaurant
   B. Construction
   C. Drive-in movie theater
   D. Maple syrup

10. **Which of these TV shows is also based on *Archie* comics?**

    A. *Sabrina the Teenage Witch*
    B. *Scooby-Doo, Where Are You!*
    C. *Supernatural*
    D. *Pretty Little Liars*

11. **Who discovers Jason Blossom's body at Sweetwater River?**

    A. The Southside Serpents
    B. The Blossoms
    C. Kevin Keller and Moose Mason
    D. Archie Andrews and Jughead Jones

12. **Who is the Snake Charmer on the Southside Serpents?**

    A. Toni Topaz
    B. Penny Peabody
    C. Sweet Pea
    D. Jughead Jones

13. **True or false: Betty Cooper is older than her brother Chic Smith.**

    A. True
    B. False

14. **What was the last movie to play at the drive-in theater before it closed?**

    A. *Rebel without a Cause*
    B. *Invasion of the Body Snatchers*
    C. *Some Like It Hot*
    D. *The War of the Worlds*

NOW ADD UP YOUR SCORE!

If You Got 0–4 Correct:
You're new to *Riverdale*. Welcome to the *Riverdale* fandom! Get caught up by binge-watching the series over your favorite milkshake. It'll be like you're hanging with the gang at Pop's Chock'lit Shoppe.

If You Got 5–10 Correct:
You're a *Riverdale* fan. You've seen most, if not all, of the series and know exactly which character is your favorite. The real question: Are you team Bughead or team Varchie?

If You Got 11–14 Correct:
You're completely obsessed with *Riverdale*. It's clear you've been a *Riverdale* die-hard since the beginning and you can quote the series like there's no tomorrow. You wouldn't dare miss an episode and you always have your own theories about what's going to happen next. If only you could visit Pop's Chock'lit Shoppe IRL—then your *Riverdale* dreams would be complete.

How Dateable Are You Actually?

On average, how many dates a month do you go on?

A. Zero
B. One to two dates
C. Three
D. Four
E. Five
F. More than six dates a month

Your typical Friday night looks like . . .

A. Pizza + Netflix
B. The clerb
C. Dranks with friends
D. A quiet dinner
E. Sleep
F. Hanging with my SO

What's your weakness?

A. I'm perpetually late
B. I'm too confrontational
C. Too detail-oriented
D. My expectations are usually too high
E. I'm impatient
F. I don't have any weaknesses

When asked to cook, what do you do?

A. LOL, cooking what's that?
B. I'll order in
C. Roll up my sleeves and get cookin'
D. Cooking is my passion
E. Politely suggest that they cook
F. Call my mom and get her best recipe

What are your thoughts on marriage?

A. I want to get married ASAP
B. Marriage is in the cards for me, but not right now
C. Haha, no
D. Can I find a date first, geez
E. If it happens, it happens
F. The title of "marriage" isn't important to me, but a commitment is

Your ex hits you up after you change your Facebook status to "in a relationship." What do you do?

A. They were the love of my life, so I'd go back
B. Tell them to never contact me again
C. I wouldn't respond at all
D. I'd talk to them, but have no intentions of getting back together
E. I'd alert my current partner to the fuckery and get their advice
F. Haha, no

Pick a celeb to marry:

A. Rihanna
B. Kristen Stewart
C. J. LO
D. Chris Pratt
E. Mahershala Ali
F. The Rock

If You Got Mostly A's:
You're 50% dateable! The glass is half full. Or is the glass half empty? Either way, being 50 percent dateable ain't half bad!

If You Got Mostly B's:
You're 82% dateable! Nobody's perfect, but you're damn close. You've got all the right things to make a perfect date. If you're in a relationship, good for you! And if you're not in a relationship, just carry on doing you and you'll have what you want in no time.

If You Got Mostly C's:
You're 65% dateable! You've got a little bit of this and a little bit of that, but guess what? You're still a catch. If dating is something you want, just do it!

If You Got Mostly D's:
You're 10% dateable! Here's the thing: Being 10 percent dateable isn't the end of the world. It just means that there are a few easy and simple things you can do to up your game. That means be confident, believe in yourself, maybe even get a new hobby. This is by no means permanent and remember: It's just a quiz.

If You Got Mostly E's:
You're 30% dateable! You enjoy the company of others, but you're more than happy staying in or treating yourself to a nice dinner for one. You're known for being the Choosy Friend, and hey, that's great! No need to settle for anything less than perfect.

If You Got Mostly F's:
You're 99% dateable! You're a friggin' catch! If you're currently with someone they need to thank their lucky stars. If you're not dating but want to be, all you have to do is put yourself out there. Your charm, wit, and effortless style could win anyone over.

LOL

CONGRATS!

Can You Recognize These Foods in Different Languages?

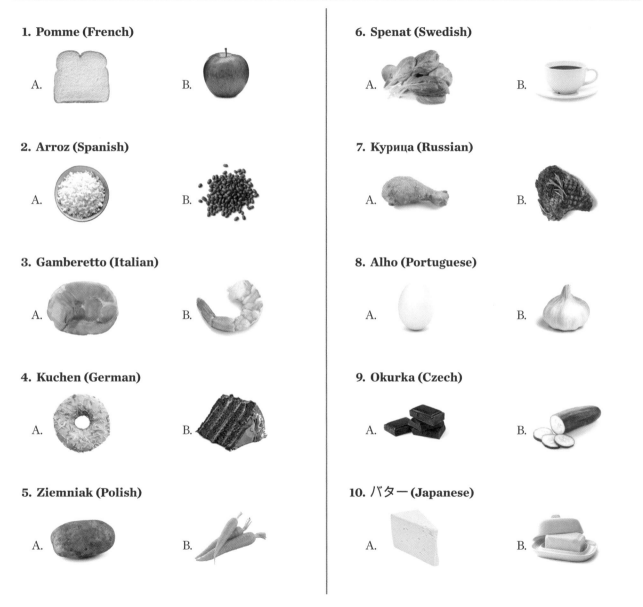

1. Pomme (French)

A.   B.

2. Arroz (Spanish)

A.   B.

3. Gamberetto (Italian)

A.   B.

4. Kuchen (German)

A.   B.

5. Ziemniak (Polish)

A.   B.

6. Spenat (Swedish)

A.   B.

7. Курица (Russian)

A.   B.

8. Alho (Portuguese)

A.   B.

9. Okurka (Czech)

A.   B.

10. バター (Japanese)

A.   B.

10. B. It's butter! *Cheese* in Japanese is "チーズ."
9. B. It's cucumber! *Chocolate* in Czech is "Čokoláda."
8. B. It's garlic! *Egg* in Portuguese is "ovo."
7. A. It's chicken! *Beef* in Russian is "говядина."
6. A. It's spinach! *Coffee* in Swedish is "kaffe."
5. A. It's potato! *Carrot* in Polish is "marchewka."
4. B. It's cake! *Donut* in German is "krapfen."
3. B. It's shrimp! *Ham* in Italian is "prosciutto."
2. A. It's rice! *Beans* in Spanish is "frijoles."
1. B. It's apple! *Bread* in French is "le pain."

NOW ADD UP YOUR SCORE!

If You Got 0–3 Correct:

Yikes! You failed. Don't feel too bad about it. You'll just have to travel the world, eating whatever you come across to perfect your language skills.

If You Got 4–6 Correct:

You did just okay! You're not a language expert, but you're not an amateur either.

If You Got 7–10 Correct:

Wow! You're a master of food *and* language. Congratulations! Go reward yourself with something delicious.

№1

OMG

What Should Your College Major Be?

What's your favorite way to spend a weekend?

A. Sketching in a park
B. Reading a new book
C. Playing with your pets
D. Hanging out with your friends
E. Babysitting
F. Baking cupcakes
G. Having a movie marathon

What's your dream city to live in?

A. New York City
B. Seattle
C. Miami
D. Chicago
E. Dallas
F. Phoenix
G. Los Angeles

Where would you want to study abroad?

A. Rome, Italy
B. London, England
C. The Maldives
D. Dublin, Ireland
E. Barcelona, Spain
F. Paris, France
G. Sydney, Australia

How would your friends describe you?

A. Creative
B. Captivating
C. Passionate
D. Empathetic
E. Determined
F. Detail-oriented
G. Expressive

When are you happiest?

A. When I create something new
B. When I feel heard
C. When I volunteer
D. When I can relate to others
E. When I make a difference in someone's life
F. When I get to perform

Which is the most infuriating?

A. When people are close-minded
B. Incorrect grammar
C. When people don't ask to say hi to your dog
D. When people don't communicate with you
E. Not being able to solve a puzzle
F. Burning your dinner
G. Being overlooked

What's your favorite pastime?

A. Doodling on your notes
B. Scrolling through social media
C. Looking at travel Instagrams
D. Watching documentaries
E. Finding some new craft to try
F. Looking at food Instagrams
G. Binge-watching your favorite TV show

Mostly A's: Art
You should major in art! Wherever you are, you're always creating something whether it's doodles on your notes or fully detailed portraits on a canvas. You're an artist through and through.

Mostly B's: English
You should major in English!
You've been captivating others with your storytelling forever and now's the time to try writing those stories down. You'd get to write poetry, fiction, and nonfiction and you'd also get to read. Like, A LOT!

Mostly C's: Marine Biology
You should major in marine biology!
You've always loved animals, so this is the perfect way to help them *and* the environment. Plus, having the ocean as your classroom wouldn't suck . . .

Mostly D's: Psychology
You should major in psychology!
You've always thought talking about emotions was interesting and deeply complex. You might even get to help some people along the way!

Mostly E's: Education
You should major in education!
You've always loved kids, and they need teachers who are compassionate and determined, so you sound like the perfect match.

Mostly F's: Culinary Arts
You should major in culinary arts!
Your friends and family all know you're an incredible chef—now it's time to take your recipes to the next level!

Mostly G's: Theater
You should major in theater!
You've always loved the spotlight and have felt most at home on a stage, so why not pursue a degree in theater? It's your time to shine!

Are You a Thinker, a Solver, or a Doer?

Check off everything that applies to you.
Whichever list you check the most is your result!

THINKER

- [ ] Very quiet
- [ ] Hates attention
- [ ] Gets stressed out easily
- [ ] Terrible at confrontation
- [ ] Always has a new idea
- [ ] More of a visual learner than a verbal learner
- [ ] Enjoys talking things out
- [ ] Daydreams a lot
- [ ] Cat person
- [ ] Likes ordering takeout

You got ____ / ____

SOLVER

- [ ] Likes to doodle
- [ ] Has a vivid imagination
- [ ] Throws great parties
- [ ] Sends memes
- [ ] Doesn't like constructive criticism
- [ ] Very good at video games
- [ ] Strong, silent type
- [ ] Apathetic
- [ ] Is always about two trends behind
- [ ] Says, "Are you ready to rock and roll" when you leave the house

You got ____ / ____

DOER

- [ ] Never sits still
- [ ] Always makes to-do lists
- [ ] Hikes on the weekends
- [ ] Always has the most to say
- [ ] More of a verbal learner than a visual learner
- [ ] You don't look before you leap
- [ ] Constantly motivated
- [ ] Impatient
- [ ] Hates when you don't understand a joke
- [ ] If you're sitting at a table with a pen, you'll drum on that table

You got ____ / ____

Complain about Your Ex and We'll Guess Your Favorite Carb

My ex was too:

A. Needy
B. Selfish
C. Rude
D. Boring
E. Immature
F. Nice

Our relationship could have used more:

A. Communication
B. "Me time"
C. Date nights
D. Affection
E. Balance
F. Sex

When I think about my ex, I:

A. Want to cry
B. Want to scream
C. Want to text them
D. Want to text their hot friend
E. Want to throw a tomato at them
F. I don't think about my ex

My ex was annoyingly:

A. Jealous
B. Clingy
C. Smelly
D. Loud
E. Shady
F. Inadequate . . . in bed

I'm totally over my ex but I kind of miss their:

A. Lips
B. Cuddles
C. Jokes
D. Pet
E. Sex
F. Literally nothing

Honestly, I hope they:

A. Are doing well
B. Have found someone nice
C. Are as lonely as me
D. Text me back
E. Return my books
F. Burn in hell

If You Got Mostly A's:
Pizza is your favorite carb. Bread, sauce, cheese—what more do you need?

If You Got Mostly B's:
Bagels are your favorite carb. They say there's the equivalent of four pieces of bread in an average bagel . . . mmmmmm bread.

If You Got Mostly C's:
Donuts are your favorite carb. Like a bagel, but better . . . because it's sweet.

If You Got Mostly D's:
Pasta is your favorite carb. Red sauce, white sauce, penne, ziti, ravioli, tortellini—any kind of ini, I don't care, just give it to me.

If You Got Mostly E's:
Garlic bread is your favorite carb. Some would say the purest form of carbs.

If You Got Mostly F's:
Potatoes are your favorite carb. Fried, baked, mashed, whatever—the potato is the most perfect carb and I'll fight anyone who disagrees.

Can You Correctly Spell Commonly Misspelled Words?

Pick the correct spellings for each pair.

1. A. secretary
   B secretery

2. A. liason
   B. liaison

3. A. heirarchy
   B. hierarchy

4. A. address
   B. adress

5. A. allegiance
   B. allegaince

6. A. pronounciation
   B. pronunciation

7. A. tomorrow
   B. tommorow

8. A. visious
   B. vicious

9. A. seize
   B. sieze

10. A. ordeurves
    B. hors d'oeuvres

ANSWER KEY

1. A; 2. B; 3. B; 4. A; 5. A; 6. B;
7. A; 8. B; 9. A; 10. B

If You Got 9–10 Correct:
You can spell better than 91 percent of Americans!

If You Got 5–8 Correct:
You spell about average!

If You Got 0–4 Correct:
You need to brush up on your spelling!

Celebrity Name Scramble

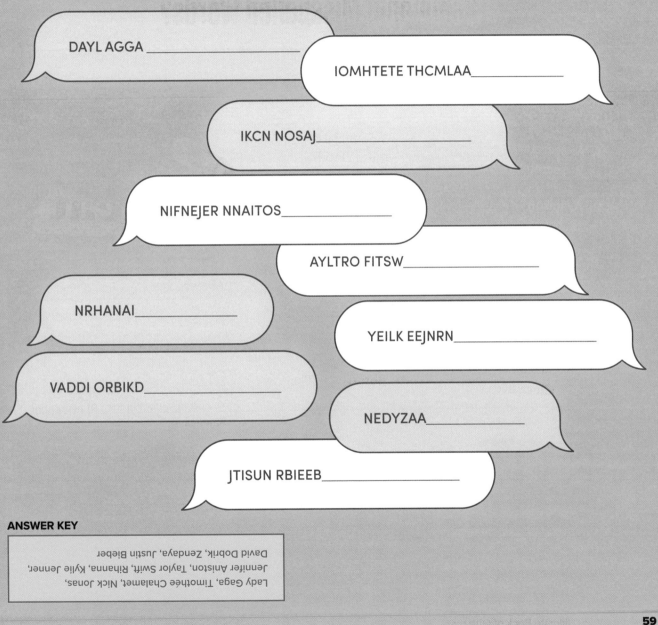

DAYL AGGA _____

IOMHTETE THCMLAA_____

IKCN NOSAJ_____

NIFNEJER NNAITOS_____

AYLTRO FITSW_____

NRHANAI_____

YEILK EEJNRN_____

VADDI ORBIKD_____

NEDYZAA_____

JTISUN RBIEEB_____

ANSWER KEY

Lady Gaga, Timothée Chalamet, Nick Jonas,
Jennifer Aniston, Taylor Swift, Rihanna, Kylie Jenner,
David Dobrik, Zendaya, Justin Bieber

Pick Some Booze and We'll Guess What Type of Guys You're Into

You're at brunch. What are you drinking?

A. Mimosa in a little flute glass
B. MANmosa in a pint glass
C. Bloody Mary
D. Coffee with some booze that I brought in a flask because I'm a garbage human
E. I don't even drink, why am I taking this quiz?

It's, like, 4 p.m. It's hot and you want a drink. What are you having?

A. A nice, frosty cold beer
B. Margs
C. Whiskey on the rocks
D. Frosé
E. I don't even drink, I'm just taking this quiz to see what kind of guys I'm into

You're out to dinner at a regular-ass, kinda-nice place. What's your first drink?

A. Brewski
B. Red, red wine
C. White wine
D. A cosmo or some other sweet cocktail
E. I don't even drink and/or I'd like to drink something not listed at this hypothetical dinner

You're pre-gaming with friends before a night out. What are you guys drinking?

A. Wine
B. Tequila
C. Cheap beer
D. Whatever is the cheapest at my deli, TBH
E. I told you, I don't drink, and/or your choices are dumb!

It's getting late and you're one drink away from being, like, perfectly blitzed. What do you order?

A. A beer, I'm gonna ease into this
B. One or several shots
C. A brown liquor cocktail
D. A clear liquor cocktail
E. You know I don't drink. Please just give me a man.

If You Got Mostly A's:

You're into sweet nerds. You never thought you'd be into guys who like comic books and sci-fi, but it turns out it's great to watch *Game of Thrones* with someone who actually knows WTF is going on.

If You Got Mostly B's:

You're into silver daddies. You like them a little older, a little grayer, a whole lot *mmmph*-ier? You don't know how to describe it, but you know you like it. You like it a lot.

If You Got Mostly C's:

You're into skaters. Despite every logical bone in your body, you can't help but be attracted to skaters. They're dirty and smelly. They're always asking to borrow your car and if their friend Adrian can crash on your couch, but you can't help it. When you hear those wheels rollin', your heart starts pounding.

If You Got Mostly D's:

You're into frat bros. You know you shouldn't like them but . . . the abs. The chiseled jawlines. The good haircuts. The nice cars. The boat shoes and the pastel shorts. The polo shirts, and the fact they might actually *play* polo. If you're being honest, you'd trade your moral integrity to live off that Wall Street paycheck, no questions asked.

If You Got Mostly E's:

You're into refined and well-dressed. He comes from a good family, went to a good school, and knows how to dress himself. His manners are impeccable, and when you go to the museum he doesn't even have to pretend to know what the art is about. He actually knows!

Can You Guess the Movie from a Continuous Line Drawing?

1.

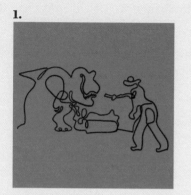

A. *Jurassic World*
B. *The Lost World: Jurassic Park*
C. *Jurassic Park III*
D. *Jurassic Park*

3.

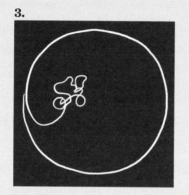

A. *Moon*
B. *Transformers: Dark of the Moon*
C. *E.T.*
D. *Apollo 13*

5.

A. *The Dark Knight*
B. *It*
C. *The Purge*
D. *Problem Child*

2.

A. *Sling Blade*
B. *Forrest Gump*
C. *Good Will Hunting*
D. *500 Days of Summer*

4.

A. *Smokey and the Bandit*
B. *Back to the Future*
C. *Radio Flyer*
D. *Days of Thunder*

6.

A. *An American in Paris*
B. *Cabaret*
C. *Oklahoma!*
D. *West Side Story*

7.

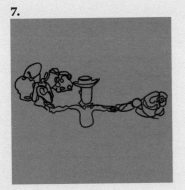

A. *The Magnificent Seven*
B. *Avengers: Age of Ultron*
C. *Toy Story 3*
D. *Dances with Wolves*

8.

A. *My Fair Lady*
B. *Beauty and the Beast*
C. *Mean Girls*
D. *The Sound of Music*

9.

A. *The Hobbit: An Unexpected Journey*
B. *Raiders of the Lost Ark*
C. *The Goonies*
D. *The Mummy*

10.

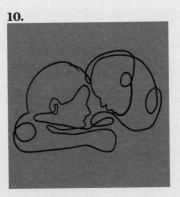

A. *Cinderella*
B. *Out of Africa*
C. *Romeo and Juliet*
D. *Titanic*

NOW ADD UP YOUR SCORE!

If You Got 0–3 Correct:

You're a visual enthusiast! So you missed a couple (or more) of these. NBD! You still love going to the movies and enjoying the ride along the way!

If You Got 4–6 Correct:

You're a visual aficionado! You've seen your fair share of movies and obviously the best scenes have really stuck with you. You know a winning combination of story and visual beauty when you see it!

If You Got 7–10 Correct:

You're a visual genius! You know your stuff! Not only are you a movie buff, but you've also got a really great eye. You can recognize greatness from a mile away.

What's Your Fantasy Book Name?

FIRST LETTER OF YOUR FIRST NAME

A: A Song

B: A Land

C: A Castle

D: A Spell

E: A Knight

F: A Kingdom

G: A Journey

H: A Sword

I: A Tree

J: A Bird

K: A River

L: A Queen

M: A Mountain

N: A Marriage

O: A King

P: A Game

Q: A War

R: A Dagger

S: A Jewel

T: A Quest

U: A Whisper

V: A Ring

W: A Touch

X: A Flame

Y: A Forge

Z: A Lake

FIRST LETTER OF YOUR LAST NAME

A: of Fairies

B: of Air

C: of Silver

D: of Friendship

E: of Scarlet

F: of Fire

G: of Greed

H: of Magic

I: of Beauty

J: of Steeds

K: of Eternity

L: of Blood

M: of Iron

N: of Dragons

O: of Winter

P: of Worlds

Q: of Power

R: of Demons

S: of Gold

T: of Glass

U: of Ships

V: of Elves

W: of Towers

X: of Music

Y: of Ice

Z: of Armor

Take This Weird Food Test and We'll Tell You Your Age and Location

Pick a weird American food.

Olive Loaf *You're 84 and live in Florida!*	**Jell-O Salad** *You're 45 and live in Texas!*	**Ambrosia Salad** *You're 50 and live in New Jersey!*
Green Bean Casserole *You're 69 and live in Ohio!*	**The Donut Burger** *You're 18 and live in New York!*	**The KFC Double Down Sandwich** *You're 26 and live in North Carolina!*
Chicken Gizzards *You're 16 and live in Georgia!*	**Meatloaf** *You're 21 and live in California!*	**Pickled Pigs' Feet** *You're 33 and live in Pennsylvania!*

ew

This Short *Harry Potter* Test
Will Reveal a Hard Truth about You

Which character do you identify with the most?

A. Harry

B. Ron

C. Hermione

D. Luna

E. Neville

F. Hagrid

Which defining moment in the series made you feel the happiest?

A. When Harry, Ron, and Hermione bring their children to Platform 9 ¾

B. When Harry soars atop Buckbeak

C. When Harry receives his letter(s) of admittance to Hogwarts

D. The formation of Dumbledore's Army

E. When Luna wore the lion-topped hat in support of the Gryffindor Quidditch team

F. Ron's Felix Felicis–assisted Quidditch win

Which character do you miss the most?

A. Remus

B. Fred

C. Dobby

D. Sirius

E. Dumbledore

F. Hedwig

If You Got Mostly A's:

You're often embarrassed about things you did in the past. You'll just be sitting there minding your own business and enjoying yourself, when—BAM—you remember something you did a decade ago that was super embarrassing. Then you have to stop what you're doing to cringe about the past for a bit. Luckily, the more you think about a particular thing, the less power it has over you.

If You Got Mostly B's:

You feel like other people are more successful than you. Whenever you hear how your friends are doing or look on Facebook, it always seems as though everyone is miles ahead of you in terms of, you know, life. At times, you have to just remind yourself that people just project that stuff out and really nobody has anything figured out.

If You Got Mostly C's:

You have a hard time admitting it when you're wrong. You have a lot of strength of conviction, but that can turn on you when it turns out that your convictions weren't correct. You'll do pretty much anything to avoid admitting that you were wrong, including tweaking the truth a bit.

If You Got Mostly D's:

You find it hard to make new friends. You're not the type of person to organize big group outings or walk up to a stranger and become friends with them. But when you do make a friend, you tend to be a close, loyal, and generous friend to that person. It's really more about quality than quantity anyway, right?

If You Got Mostly E's:

You sometimes fantasize about being a hero. Your life is fine, but it's a little uneventful. You dream of being in a world like Harry Potter's, where you think you could make a big difference. Or, heck, you'd love to just make a big difference in this world. If only you had magic . . .

If You Got Mostly F's:

You tend to overthink things a lot. Should you send that text? Did you accidentally offend someone in the way you phrased that comment? These are the kinds of questions you find yourself asking a lot, agonizing over every detail of the decisions you make. It means you're very careful in what you do, but you can also get stressed out if you let your everyday decisions overwhelm you.

Which Disney Couple Are You and Your Significant Other?

How do you settle disputes with your SO?

A. By hugging it out
B. Through arguing
C. By giving them the silent treatment
D. By reaching a compromise
E. By apologizing
F. With makeup sex

What's your ideal date?

A. Dinner and movie
B. A day at the beach
C. Strolling in a park
D. Cocktails
E. A night in watching Netflix
F. Camping

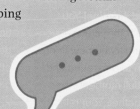

Pick a Disney character who's perfectly fine being single:

A. Maleficent
B. Captain Hook
C. Cruella de Vil
D. Genie
E. Elsa
F. Kuzco

What's a great couples food to share?

A. Popcorn
B. Pizza
C. Chili cheese fries
D. Milkshake
E. Spaghetti
F. Ice cream

What's a cute pet name for that special someone?

A. Snookums
B. Cuddle Butt
C. Sugar Bear
D. Mi Amor
E. Sweet Cheeks
F. Honey Pot

What's the grossest thing you can do around your partner?

A. Burp
B. Pick your nose
C. Pee
D. Fart
E. Scratch yourself
F. Not brush your teeth

What's the most important component in a relationship?

A. Loyalty
B. Openness
C. Shared values
D. Honesty
E. Respect
F. Physical chemistry

If You Got Mostly A's:

You're Aladdin and Jasmine! You and your significant other crave adventure, excitement, and trying new things. Both of you are fun to be around and there is seldom a dull moment when both of you are together. Your relationship is a nonstop joyride and you wouldn't have it any other way.

If You Got Mostly B's:

You're Anna and Kristoff! You're in the type of relationship where you can truly be yourself. Both of you are trustworthy, yet funny and adorably awkward. No matter what, you always keep each other happy and laughing.

If You Got Mostly C's:

You're Simba and Nala! You have a special bond that has really stood through trials and tribulations. You might have had challenges like distance and time to deal with, but you always make it work. Your bond is strong, and when it comes to your partner, nothing can keep you apart.

If You Got Mostly D's:

You're Belle and Adam! Your relationship is deep and took a while to develop. You really didn't know each other very well at first, but you still gave it a chance.

If You Got Mostly E's:

You're Mulan and Li Shang! You have the type of relationship where one person is always trying to make the other better. You're both competitive and strive for greatness, and that's a good thing. You're a powerful couple and the sky's the limit in terms of what you both can do.

If You Got Mostly F's:

You're Ariel and Eric! You have a special something with someone who's different than you and you make it work. Both of you don't mind the differences and complement each other's personalities well. Opposites attract and your bond is living proof of that.

You're Moving to the First State You See . . .

```
N E W M E X I C O O E H E F R G M Z P B
I N D I A N A J F H I O W A N N I M B F
T E N N E S S E E I E T X V K L S I R O
E Z C O L O R A D O H H F E J I S N V K
P Y E J Y H N O R T H C A R O L I N A L
R H O D E I S L A N D S G M L L S E N A
M A R Y L A N D D N R O E O U I S S E H
Q L V F T U R A E O W U O N P N I O W O
S H T L E W P H L R E T R T E O P T H M
S J V O X R E S A T S H G I N I P A A A
N E B R A S K A W H T C I V N S I Y M N
E A U I S M U S A D V A A I S C C G P E
W Q V D U D Q H R A I R Z R Y N F A S V
J A L A B A M A E K R O Q G L E I R H A
E O W Y O M I N G O G L I I V W K K I D
R A M U T A H X F T I I D N A Y A A R A
S Y A M I C H I G A N N A I N O N N E K
E N I M I S S O U R I A H A I R S S U H
Y Y N F S O U T H D A K O T A K A A P H
O R E G O N W I S C O N S I N H S S R I
```

Tell Us What Kind of Hero You Are and We'll Reveal Your Arch Nemesis

What's your superpower?

A. I can fly

B. I'm super strong

C. I can read minds

What's your tragic backstory?

A. I don't want to talk about it

B. I was exposed to toxic waste

C. I was unfairly fired from my corporate job

What does your costume look like?

A. Big cape and boots

B. A leotard, of course

C. Just my regular clothes and a tiny mask

Who is your sidekick?

A. A small child

B. A talking animal

C. I work alone

What's your heroic catchphrase?

A. "Me no likey crime."

B. "Stop, drop, and roll into jail."

C. "I only love justice and my mama, I'm sorry."

If You Got Mostly A's:

Your nemesis is Professor Goop. Armed with a PhD, a tenure position at an Ivy League school, and a deep well of evil in his heart, Professor Goop seems—at times—unstoppable. In your darkest moments, you think him and his sidekick The TA will bring about the end of the world with their deathly slime ray and seemingly unlimited private funding. But you've stopped death rays of all kinds before. You'll get them one day. Time to accept your honorary degree from Justice University.

If You Got Mostly B's:

Your nemesis is The Paradox. Often using crime as a method of justice, you infuriatingly don't know if you should even attempt to stop their misdeeds. Whenever you come close to catching them, they yell something like "THIS SENTENCE IS A LIE!"—such a head scratcher that when you stop for a moment to think, they slip away. "If that's true, that's . . . not true!" you yell after them for the fifth time this month.

If You Got Mostly C's:

Your nemesis is Bradley Cooper. After you both fell for the same woman back in 2009 and she chose him, you simply didn't like the guy. You're a bona fide hero! And what's he ever done? Write, direct, and star in one of the greatest modern movie musicals? Have striking blue eyes and a perfect personality? You don't buy it for a second. Sure, there's real crime to stop, but your beef with Bradley is your top priority right now.

Everyone Is a Combination of One Savory and One Sweet Food—What's Yours?

How would you describe yourself in one word?

A. Brave
B. Practical
C. Witty
D. Free-spirited
E. Lovable
F. Giving

Pick a type of cheese:

A. Brie
B. Swiss
C. Manchego
D. Burrata
E. Gorgonzola
F. Cheddar

Pick a candy:

A. Twix
B. Sour Patch Kids
C. Reese's Peanut Butter Cups
D. M&M's
E. Gummy Bears
F. Starburst

Pick a snack food:

A. Potato chips
B. Apple and PB
C. Yogurt-covered pretzels
D. Trail mix
E. Popcorn
F. Carrots and hummus

Choose a food TV show:

A. *Chopped*
B. *Chef's Table*
C. *Iron Chef*
D. *Ugly Delicious*
E. *Diners, Drive-Ins, and Dives*
F. *The Great British Bake Off*

Pick a fast-food chain:

A. McDonald's
B. Taco Bell
C. Chick-fil-A
D. KFC
E. In-N-Out Burger
F. Wendy's

Pick a food city to visit:

A. Mexico City
B. San Francisco
C. Bangkok
D. Tokyo
E. Florence
F. Copenhagen

If You Got Mostly A's:

You're nachos and ice cream! You have layers of personality and you're constantly down to try new things. People love you because you're both spontaneous and reliable.

If You Got Mostly B's:

You're cheese and chocolate! You're smart and practical, which are two qualities that help you get far in life. You're constantly succeeding and gaining the admiration of others. Of course, you still know how to indulge and treat yourself every once in a while.

If You Got Mostly C's:

You're pizza and donuts! You're outgoing, witty, and even a bit of a goofball. You don't take yourself too seriously and you always know how to have a good time. You're also one of the most caring and loyal people who is always there for a friend in need.

If You Got Mostly D's:

You're mozzarella sticks and s'mores! You are full of life and one of the most vibrant people around. Your passion and energy follow you wherever you go. You're the kind of person who always looks on the bright side and your positivity is contagious.

If You Got Mostly E's:

You're French fries and chocolate chip cookies! Just as French fries and chocolate chip cookies are timeless classics, you are always in style. You're also kind and comforting, which is more reason people are always drawn to you.

If You Got Mostly F's:

You're mac 'n' cheese and apple pie! You're laid back, relaxed, and always happy to go with the flow. You're a great judge of character and you always look for the good in people. Sometimes you come off as childish, but really, you just love to make the most of every opportunity to have a good time.

How Good Are You at Taking Care of Yourself?

Check off all the things you've done for yourself in the past month.

- [ ] Stayed hydrated.

- [ ] Stretched.

- [ ] Took the time to properly moisturize.

- [ ] Gave yourself a small massage, dry brushed, scratched yourself with a head or back scratcher, or something similarly sensory.

- [ ] Kept your (however brilliant) shower thoughts at bay and focused on how good the water felt.

- [ ] Did your laundry.

- [ ] Changed your sheets.

- [ ] Made yourself a meal you love.

- [ ] Enjoyed that meal without any distractions.

- [ ] Made some low-stakes art or craft.

- [ ] Read a fun, lighthearted book.

- [ ] Spent time outdoors.

- [ ] Jammed to a song or playlist that made you happy.

- [ ] Took a little time each day to keep your living space clutter-free.

- [ ] Made a concerted effort to turn off your phone, computer, or TV.

- [ ] Took yourself to the movies, went solo to a museum, etc.

- [ ] Chilled with some animals, if you're into that.

- [ ] Napped when you needed one.

- [ ] Masturbated.

- [ ] Planned something for yourself to look forward to.

- [ ] Took time to appreciate something nice that happened.

- [ ] Wrote that thing down in a gratitude list.

- [ ] **Considered progress you've made in some part of your life.**

- [ ] **Recorded that in a pick-me-up journal.**

- [ ] **Talked honestly and openly to a loved one.**

- [ ] **Talked honestly and openly to multiple loved ones.**

- [ ] **Tried earnestly and without expectations to understand someone better.**

- [ ] **Said "no" to something that felt overwhelming.**

- [ ] **Wrote down your negative thoughts, if just to get them out of you.**

- [ ] **Planned ahead of time so you weren't stressed later.**

- [ ] **Downloaded a de-stressing or meditation app.**

- [ ] **Let yourself cry.**

- [ ] **Considered talking to a mental health professional.**

NOW ADD UP YOUR SCORE!

If You Checked 0–10:

Self-care? What self-care? It can be tempting in your busy life to never pause for a breath, but it's not always sustainable. Could you block out five to thirty minutes during your day to try some of the items above?

If You Checked 11–22:

You're halfway there, practicing self-care! It's clear you're trying to look out for your mental health. No pressure, but could you say no to *one* more commitment this month and have some "you" time instead?

If You Checked 23–33:

You're a self-care connoisseur! Way to go! As with airplane oxygen masks, you're best at caring for others when you've first cared for yourself.

1. **Where are the McCallisters going for Christmas?**

   A. London
   B. Paris
   C. NYC
   D. Miami

2. **Why doesn't Kevin want to share a bed with Fuller?**

   A. Kevin wants to sleep in his own bed
   B. If Fuller drinks Pepsi, he jumps on the bed
   C. Kevin is afraid of sleeping in the attic
   D. If Fuller has something to drink, he wets the bed

3. **How much did pizza for the whole family cost?**

   A. $100
   B. $125.50
   C. $122.50
   D. $128.75

4. **What's the name of the neighbor kid who gets miscounted for Kevin?**

   A. Peter
   B. Mitch
   C. Harry
   D. Jeff

5. **Kevin accidentally steals THIS from the pharmacy.**

   A. A comb
   B. Spray-on deodorant
   C. Aftershave
   D. A toothbrush

6. **Who are the gangsters in *Angels with Filthy Souls*?**

   A. Johnny and Snakes
   B. Snakes and A.C.
   C. A.C. and Johnny
   D. A.C. and Harry

7. **Gus Polinski is best known as the . . .**

   A. Polka King of Chicago
   B. The King of Polka, Polka, Polka
   C. Polka King of the Midwest
   D. Polka King of Sheboygan

8. **What does "Santa" give Kevin?**

   A. A candy cane
   B. Tic Tacs
   C. Tootsie Rolls
   D. A parking ticket

9. **Which burglar gets injured FIRST?**

   A. Harry
   B. Marv

10. **True or false: Marv gets an "M" burned into his hand.**

    A. True
    B. False

11. **What do Harry and Marv say they're going to do to Kevin after they catch him?**

    A. Burn his head with a blowtorch
    B. Smash his face with an iron
    C. Shove a nail through his foot
    D. LITERALLY ALL OF THESE

12. **And finally, who has the last line in the movie?**

    A. Kevin
    B. Buzz
    C. Kevin's dad
    D. Old Man Marley

ANSWER KEY

NOW ADD UP YOUR SCORE!

If You Got 0–3 Correct:
You're a *Home Alone* newbie! Okay, you've MAYBE seen *Home Alone* once or twice, but TBH, you wouldn't consider it your favorite or anything. Maybe it's time to give it another watch?

If You Got 4–6 Correct:
You're a *Home Alone* fan! You've definitely seen the movie more than once and you thought it was great, but it's not like you're obsessed with it or anything. Still, though, you're looking forward to catching it on TV this holiday season!

If You Got 7–9 Correct:
You're a *Home Alone* expert! You've seen this movie A LOT, like more than most people. Sure, you haven't memorized every detail and scene, but who cares! You still think it's a great movie and always look forward to watching it.

If You Got 10–12 Correct:
You're a *Home Alone* aficionado! You've seen *Home Alone* more times than you can count. In fact, for your money, *Home Alone* is the greatest holiday film ever made and nothing can ever top it! You probably own a copy of it and love watching it even when it's NOT the holidays!

Extrovert Bingo

Check off or mark the squares that apply to you (things you own, have done, or things that have happened to you). The more you fill out, the more you're an extrovert! See if you can get five across, down, or diagonally. Then snap a picture and upload online to share your results!

Loves attending sporting events	Camera roll is 60% selfies, 40% your dog	"LOOK! A DOG!"	24,861 unopened email notifications	Loves singing karaoke regardless of singing ability
Updating accomplishments section of résumé as a fun pastime	Dating for sport	Iced coffee!!!!!!!!	"I'm an ENFP"	EXCLAMATION POINTS!!!!!!!!!!!!!
Friendly Competition <3	Flawless winged eyeliner	**Free Space** (Go Pet a Stranger's Dog)	*more iced coffee*	$45 kickboxing class
Craves That Buzz™	Top of your Instagram stories that look like "------------------"	Downloaded a meditation app and has used it maybe once	Drama Club	Held position of power in said Drama Club
texts therapist	Best friend is a tier, not a person	Nothing better than the sound of your own voice	Volunteering to go first	On first-name basis with local bartenders

Introvert Bingo

Check off or mark the squares that apply to you (things you own, have done, or things that have happened to you). The more you fill out, the more you're an introvert! See if you can get five across, down, or diagonally. Then snap a picture and upload online to share your results!

Lady in the streets, crumbs in the sheets	Finding the dog at the party	"If not, no worries!" at the end of emails	*Despises* small talk	Oversharing on social media
Rehearsing your order one hundred times in your head	Going to the movie theater solo	Intense daydreams	Thinking before you speak	Screening all your phone calls
Scheduling time to "do nothing"	Hates when people "order a few dishes to share"	**Free Space** (Go Take a Nap)	Buying more throw pillows as self-care	Great listener
Binge-watching as a hobby	More internet friends than IRL friends	Avoiding people you know in public	Owns more blankets than bras	Skipping the party to sleep and watch *The Office*
Not speaking in Ubers	Reading as an escape	Looking up the menu before going to a restaurant	Dating is torture, flirting is hell	Makes bed, then immediately gets into it

Tell Us How Many of These Dishes You Can Cook and We'll Guess Your Age

Check off everything that you've successfully made from scratch.

- [ ] Spaghetti Bolognese
- [ ] Lasagna
- [ ] Eggplant parm
- [ ] Gnocchi
- [ ] Soup
- [ ] Chili
- [ ] Fried eggs
- [ ] Pancakes
- [ ] Mashed potatoes
- [ ] Schnitzel
- [ ] Pizza

- [ ] Goulash
- [ ] Dumplings
- [ ] Pesto
- [ ] Curry with rice
- [ ] Hollandaise sauce
- [ ] Meatballs
- [ ] Roast chicken
- [ ] Steak
- [ ] Salmon
- [ ] Risotto
- [ ] Spinach and artichoke dip
- [ ] Vegetable stir-fry

- [ ] Crème brûlée
- [ ] French toast
- [ ] Croque monsieur
- [ ] Banana bread
- [ ] Hummus
- [ ] Mac 'n' cheese
- [ ] Sweet potato fries
- [ ] Chicken potpie
- [ ] Guacamole
- [ ] Enchiladas
- [ ] Ramen

If You Checked 0–4:

You're 16–20 years old! You're not used to cooking for yourself just yet, but hopefully in a couple of years you'll take some interest in the ~culinary arts~.

If You Checked 5–8:

You're 21–25 years old! You're a cooking novice. Slowly but surely you're trying to learn, and that's what matters.

If You Checked 9–13:

You're 26–30 years old! You know how to make a decent amount of dishes, which shows that you're not a total cooking newbie.

If You Checked 14–17:

You're 31–35 years old! You've made around half of the meals mentioned. You like to dabble here and there, but cooking isn't your favorite pasttime.

If You Checked 18–23:

You're 36–40 years old! You know your way around a kitchen and love any occasion that allows you to flex your chefing skills.

If You Checked 24–34:

You're 37–45 years old! Okay, are you a chef?! Because you've been around the *chopping* block and it shows!

Disney Movies Bracket

Pick your favorite contender from each pairing on the left and right. An item that's not selected gets eliminated. The winner takes on the winning item from the next pairing and so on until you have one final winner. You can fill out as you go, snap a pic and share online, and compare your results with friends.

Beauty and the Beast

Mulan

The Little Mermaid

Pocahontas

Cinderella

Sleeping Beauty

Peter Pan

Alice in Wonderland

Snow White

Fantasia

Tarzan

Dumbo

Hercules

The Emperor's New Groove

Meet the Robinsons

Atlantis: The Lost Empire

Tangled

Frozen

Moana

Lilo & Stitch

Wreck-It Ralph

Bolt

The Hunchback of Notre Dame

The Nightmare before Christmas

Zootopia

The Princess and the Frog

The Lion King

Aladdin

Pinocchio

The Jungle Book

101 Dalmatians

Lady and the Tramp

Which Celebrity Should Be Your Roommate?

What's your favorite snack?

A. Cookies

B. Smoothie

C. Pizza

D. Fruits and veggies

E. Chips and salsa

F. Parfait

What's your favorite decor style?

A. Sleek and minimal

B. Plants everywhere!

C. Shabby chic

D. Marble countertops

E. Vintage finds

F. Rustic and moody

Which song do you dance around your room to?

A. "Sing" by Ed Sheeran

B. "Anaconda" by Nicki Minaj

C. "Go Your Own Way" by Fleetwood Mac

D. "Black Skinhead" by Kanye West

E. "Holy Grail" by Jay Z

F. "Let's Get It On" by Marvin Gaye

What show do you binge-watch?

A. *Friends*

B. *Law & Order*

C. *The Office*

D. *The Real Housewives*

E. *Orange Is the New Black*

F. *Keeping Up with the Kardashians*

What city do you want to live in?

A. New York City

B. Miami

C. London

D. Los Angeles

E. Memphis

F. Toronto

How clean are you?

A. I'll pick stuff up when I get around to it

B. A little mess never hurt nobody

C. I like it to be clean, but I'm not a neat freak

D. Anything below sparkling clean is unacceptable

E. Um, that's what a maid is for

F. I clean something as it starts to get messy

If You Got Mostly A's:

Taylor Swift would be your roommate! You guys will make perfect roommates! You'll be there for one another during breakups and binge sessions. Think: empty bottles of wine, family dinners, and lots of journaling together.

If You Got Mostly B's:

Drake would be your roommate! You'll stay up late and have long philosophical conversations with Drake. He'll pick you up in times of sorrow and you'll definitely throw amazing parties together.

If You Got Mostly C's:

Harry Styles would be your roommate! You'll learn a lot from living with Harry. He'll help you understand British slang, totally reinvent your style, and you may even end up with matching tattoos!

If You Got Mostly D's:

Kim Kardashian would be your roommate! Get ready for your apartment to be spotless and your Instagram to be *fire*. You'll truly find *your light* with Kim as your roommate and finally be able to work on building your own personal brand.

If You Got Mostly E's:

Beyoncé would be your roommate! Wow. How did you get so lucky?! Beyoncé will introduce you to a lot of important people and you'll cook incredible meals together, while receiving free singing lessons. Score!

If You Got Mostly F's:

Justin Timberlake would be your roommate! No need for an alarm in the morning—Justin will wake you up to the sounds of his sweet voice and the smells of his Southern cooking. You'll crack each other up while writing comedy sketches and busting moves at the club.

Your Cheese Preferences Will Determine the Number of Kids You'll Have

Which cheesy food do you prefer?

A. Gooey grilled cheese
B. Cheese pizza
C. Macaroni and cheese
D. Cheese nachos

Which flavor of cheese is your favorite?

A. Pepper Jack
B. Cheddar
C. Colby Jack
D. Mozzarella

Which of these cheeses is best as a snack?

A. String cheese
B. Cream cheese
C. A slice of cheese
D. Cottage cheese

Which sophisticated cheese are you?

A. Gouda
B. Brie
C. Bleu
D. Feta

Which cheese appetizer tantalizes your taste buds?

A. Mozzarella sticks
B. Cheesy garlic bread
C. Cheese fries
D. Cheese dip

If You Got Mostly A's:
You will have three kids. Your cheese habits tell us you will be the parent of three cheese-adoring cherubs.

If You Got Mostly B's:
You will have two children. You will have two kids whose cheese habits will highly resemble your own. Now that's a future to look forward to.

If You Got Mostly C's:
You will have one child. You and your kid will be the dynamic cheese duo.

If You Got Mostly D's:
You will have fur babies, not human babies. You won't have any kids, but that's okay because your life will be complete with your cheese and your pets.

Instagramable Cities Scramble

OOTYK_____

NOOLDN_____

NWE OKRY_____

GOHN OKGN_____

OSL SEALGEN_____

YESYDN_____

ABDIU_____

ACROI_____

ANSWER KEY

Tokyo, London, New York, Hong Kong, Los Angeles, Sydney, Dubai, Cairo

Friends Fans Beware:
This Would You Rather Test Is Pretty Brutal

Would you rather
have a meal cooked by Monica
OR get a massage from Phoebe?

Would you rather
eat Rachel's trifle OR eat Thanksgiving in a box?

Who would you rather
spend a day alone with Eddie OR spend a day alone with Janice?

Would you rather
listen to Ross give a lecture OR listen to Ross play the bagpipes?

Would you rather
carry and give birth to your brother's triplets
OR help Ross move a couch?

Would you rather
have a pet monkey OR have a chick and a duck?

Would you rather
have a one-night stand with Joey OR marry Chandler?

Would you rather

date someone who lives in a filthy apartment
OR date a clean freak, like Monica?

Would you rather

be forced to eat an entire Thanksgiving turkey
OR get your head stuck inside a raw turkey?

Would you rather

take sailing lessons from Rachel
OR take guitar lessons from Phoebe?

Would you rather

be haunted by the ghost of Mr. Heckles
OR be haunted by Estelle's ghost?

Would you rather

watch Ross and Rachel's sex tape, Monica and Richard's sex tape,
OR Monica and Chandler's sex tape?

Who would you rather

be roommates with Rachel, Joey, Ross, Monica,
Chandler, OR Phoebe?

If You Had 15 of These 37 Things Growing Up, Then You Were Definitely Rich

Check off everything you had growing up.

- ☐ A big-ass projection TV that weighed eight hundred pounds
- ☐ An exotic reptile as a pet
- ☐ A TiVo
- ☐ A trampoline
- ☐ A collection of Super Soakers
- ☐ Playmobil toys and play sets
- ☐ A big-ass dollhouse thing
- ☐ A life-size Barbie
- ☐ A treadmill in your furnished basement
- ☐ A working air hockey table

- ☐ Some kind of pinball machine in your furnished basement
- ☐ A CD burner
- ☐ Snapple in glass containers
- ☐ A home theater
- ☐ Cable
- ☐ A piano room
- ☐ A pile of Uggs at the front door
- ☐ An old-timey popcorn machine
- ☐ A large deck with cushioned chairs and couches
- ☐ A hot tub

- [ ] A bathroom attached to your room

- [ ] Matching holiday pajamas

- [ ] A professionally shot and framed picture of your dog who was still alive

- [ ] A refrigerator that looks like a cabinet

- [ ] A trash can in your kitchen that was impossible to find because it also looked like a cabinet

- [ ] An SUV with leather seats

- [ ] A DVD player in your car

- [ ] Surround sound in your house

- [ ] An entire set of encyclopedias

- [ ] A garden fountain

- [ ] Extensive collections of Game Boy accessories

- [ ] A robotic toy animal

- [ ] A subscription to *Nickelodeon* magazine

- [ ] A huge VHS collection

- [ ] A collection of American Girl dolls

- [ ] A Fisher-Price car

- [ ] Lunchables

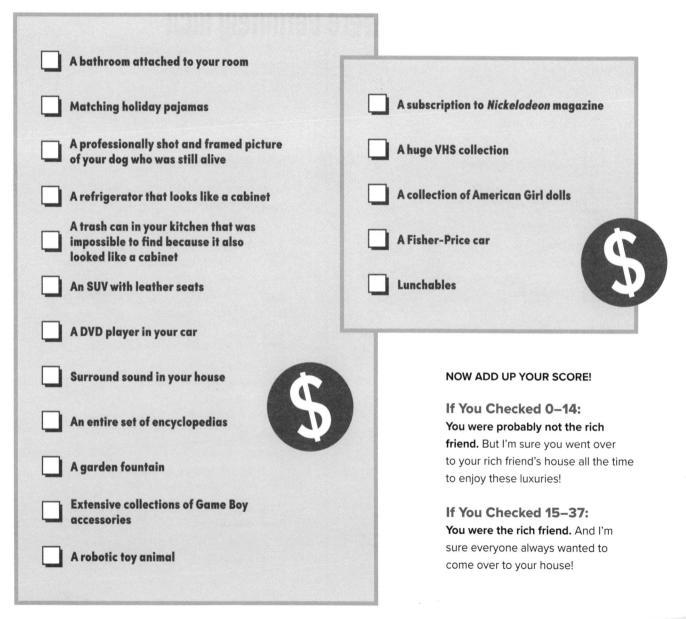

NOW ADD UP YOUR SCORE!

If You Checked 0–14:
You were probably not the rich friend. But I'm sure you went over to your rich friend's house all the time to enjoy these luxuries!

If You Checked 15–37:
You were the rich friend. And I'm sure everyone always wanted to come over to your house!

Where Will You Meet Your Next Significant Other?

Pick a rainy Sunday afternoon activity:

A. Watching Netflix
B. Cuddling
C. Brunch
D. Going somewhere new
E. Sleeping in
F. Reading

What's the best kind of kiss?

A. The one you don't expect at all
B. Drunken makeout, TBH
C. Gentle and romantic
D. The kiss you've waited for for a while
E. Mellow and going on for some time
F. Passionate and even a li'l rough ;)

What's your dating style?

A. A few people at once
B. Just very chill, IDK
C. Hook up first, ask questions later
D. Taking it real slow
E. All depends on your current schedule
F. It varies from person to person

If you were a *Friends* character, you'd be:

A. Monica
B. Phoebe
C. Ross
D. Chandler
E. Rachel
F. Joey

Your idea of a perfect weekend trip:

A. Your local museum
B. A train ride to a nearby city
C. Anywhere with a beach
D. A road trip with your friends
E. Staying in a cozy cabin
F. A last-minute flight to somewhere new

What about a first date makes you the most nervous?

A. The person being a total weirdo
B. Not having anything in common
C. Accidentally saying something *really* dumb
D. Things moving too quickly
E. Just being bored and stuck for a few hours
F. Nothing, it's just a first date!

What's your dating pet peeve?

A. Taking forever to text back
B. Moodiness
C. Feeling pressure to only hang with them
D. Your SO being awkward with your BF
E. Sloppiness
F. A lack of ambition

In your friend group you're the:

A. Mom
B. Party animal
C. Introvert
D. Dependable one
E. Workaholic
F. Chill one

If You Got Mostly A's:
You'll meet them on a dating app. You are as busy as they get and only think to look for dating prospects during your downtime. You might play around with Tinder while Netflixing your favorite sitcom when you actually start to talk to someone pretty damn cool!

If You Got Mostly B's:
You'll meet them at a bar. You are confident as hell (especially with a bit of liquid courage) and you have no issue with approaching a stranger and striking up a conversation. Little do you know that this stranger will end up becoming so much more.

If You Got Mostly C's:
You'll meet them through a mutual friend. Hey, your friends know you best, so who better to pair you up than a solid BFF? You'll all hang out and then you'll slowly realize that the hottie your friend brought along might just be keeper material.

If You Got Mostly D's:
You'll meet them at a cafe/chill setting. They say it happens when you least expect it/aren't trying, and maybe that's true! Right when you're chilling out and reading a book or just having some "you" time, you catch the eye of a stranger and somehow manage to exchange numbers, eventually paving the way to something big.

If You Got Mostly E's:
You'll meet them at work. Ah, the classic "Don't poop where you eat" scenario. Yes, sometimes that's true, but, then again, if you love your job and are somewhat consumed by it, it kinda makes sense to meet someone through work, no? (Not to mention you probably share a lot of the same interests already.) LIFE IS SHORT, TAKE A CHANCE (but only, you know, if there aren't any serious consequences. Check your company policy first!).

If You Got Mostly F's:
You'll meet them in class. Either you're in school, or in the future, despite having graduated, you'll maybe want to take a class in something you're passionate about. And, lo and behold, you'll meet someone in the exact same boat, which will eventually become a ~loooove~ boat.

How Well Do You Remember *The Princess Diaries*?

1. What is Mia's complete name?

A. Amelia Mathilde Thermopolis Renaldi
B. Alexandra Mignonette Thermopolis Renaldi
C. Amelia Mignonette Thermopolis Renaldi
D. Amelia Margaret Thermopolis Renaldi

2. What was her best friend's name?

A. Mandy
B. Alice
C. Sally
D. Lilly

3. Who is responsible for Mia's stunning makeover?

A. Paolo
B. Giuseppe
C. Angelo
D. Giovanni

4. Who played Lana, the bad girl from Mia's school?

A. Jessica Simpson
B. Mandy Moore
C. Amanda Bynes
D. Lindsay Lohan

5. What nation is Mia the princess of?

A. Monaco
B. Belarus
C. Genovia
D. Fontvielle

6. What was that country's national fruit?

A. Bananas
B. Strawberries
C. Pears
D. Apples

7. What is the cat's name?

A. Dumb Milo
B. Little Sebastian
C. Fat Louie

8. Why did Mia have to get married in *The Princess Diaries 2*?

A. In order to be queen
B. To be able to remain living in Genovia
C. To be with her true love

9. Who played Nicholas Devereaux?

A. Freddie Prinze Jr.
B. Chris Pine
C. Shane West
D. Chad Michael Murray

10. Who did Mia's grandmother, Queen Clarisse Renaldi, fall in love with?

A. Her assistant, Michael
B. Her personal chef, John
C. Her head of security, Joe

NOW ADD UP YOUR SCORE!

If You Got 0–3 Correct:

Genovia? Pears? Fat Louie? None of that made *any* sense to you. You should probably watch the movies again and then give this quiz another go.

If You Got 4–6 Correct:

You were almost there. Looks like it's time to re-watch the movies and pay a little more attention this time.

If You Got 7–10 Correct:

Amazing! You might even be the true heir to the Genovian crown. Looks like you know the movies really well!

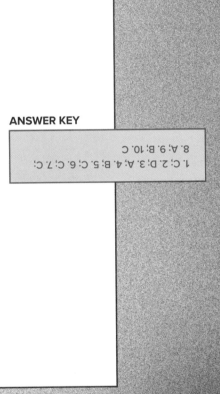

ANSWER KEY

1. C; 2. D; 3. A; 4. B; 5. C; 6. C; 7. C; 8. A; 9. B; 10. C

Order a Few Takeout Meals and We'll Tell You What City You Belong In

You're too lazy to get out of bed. Order breakfast from the local diner:

A. Omelet

B. Pancakes

C. Bagel

D. Bacon and eggs

E. Oatmeal

F. French toast

Your favorite deli now delivers! Pick a sandwich:

A. Grilled cheese

B. Roasted vegetable

C. Italian combo

D. Tuna fish

E. Reuben

F. Chicken Caesar wrap

You're craving Japanese food. What do you order?

A. Sushi

B. Ramen

C. Chicken teriyaki

D. Bento box

E. Yakitori

F. Vegetable tempura

It's Italian food night. Order up!

A. Chicken Parmesan

B. Pizza

C. Lasagna

D. Caprese salad

E. Spaghetti and meatballs

F. Tortellini soup

You want Chinese tonight. Pick something:

A. Dumplings

B. Lo mein

C. Peking duck

D. Orange chicken

E. Beef and broccoli

F. Fried rice

You're craving some comfort food. Whatcha getting?

A. Burger

B. Mac 'n' cheese

C. Chicken noodle soup

D. Fried chicken

E. Potpie

F. Quesadilla

How about something Mediterranean?

A. Hummus plate

B. Falafel

C. Gyro

D. Meat and veggie skewers

E. Tagine

F. Baba ghanoush

Ohh it's Taco Tuesday! Order some Mexican food:

A. Shrimp tacos

B. Chips and guac

C. Fajitas

D. Nachos

E. Burrito

F. Carnitas tacos

You don't have to leave the house for dessert. Order it:

A. Cookies

B. Crêpe

C. Pie

D. Brownie

E. Frozen yogurt

F. I'm not a dessert person

If You Got Mostly A's:

You belong in the laid-back beach city of **San Diego** where the weather is perfect and the surf's always up. From beautiful sites at La Jolla Cove—home to sprawled out sea lions—to heavenly Mexican food that can be found all over town, you'll feel right at home in America's Finest City.

If You Got Mostly B's:

You belong in **Seattle** among the great outdoors and incredible food, where—despite the rain—the people are smiling, the craft beer is always flowing, and the coffee tastes better. It's a perfect city for adventurous eaters, where you'll find everything from oyster bars and omakase counters to Korean steakhouses and vegan eateries.

If You Got Mostly C's:

Just across the bridge from Manhattan, **Brooklyn** is calling your name. From the waterfront streets of Williamsburg to the tree-lined blocks of Park Slope, this borough is teeming with art, culture, style, and, of course, awesome eateries. Think: farm-to-table restaurants with sprawling outdoor gardens, eclectic food markets that span city blocks, and some of the best pizza outside of Italy.

If You Got Mostly D's:

You'll feel right at home in **Nashville**, a place for eating, drinking, singing, dancing, and living. In Music City, honky-tonk meets Southern comfort, and the only thing better than the music is the culinary scene. And it's more than just hot fried chicken and barbecue. You'll find everything from upscale Southern cooking to trendy taco trucks.

If You Got Mostly E's:

You should totally live in **Chicago**. This lake city boasts a huge music and sports scene, but nothing compares to the food. No-fuss classics like deep-dish pizza and hot dogs (*never* served with ketchup) mixed with a creative fine-dining scene make Chicago the perfect Midwest foodie destination. And since you won't be spending your entire paycheck on rent, you'll have some extra cash to spend at top restaurants like Alinea and EL ideas.

If You Got Mostly F's:

With its New England charm, rich history, and diverse neighborhoods lined with awesome restaurants, there aren't many cities quite like **Boston**. Between the North End, Chinatown, Back Bay, and Downtown, you'll find amazing eateries serving oysters, authentic Italian, Asian fusion, and everything in between.

If You've Seen 31/45 of These Movies, You're Probably a Massive Hipster

How many of these movies have you seen? Check off all that apply.

- [ ] Garden State
- [ ] Eternal Sunshine of the Spotless Mind
- [ ] Juno
- [ ] Donnie Darko
- [ ] The Royal Tenenbaums
- [ ] Napoleon Dynamite
- [ ] The Big Lebowski
- [ ] Clerks
- [ ] Trainspotting

- [ ] A Clockwork Orange
- [ ] Little Miss Sunshine
- [ ] 500 Days of Summer
- [ ] American Beauty
- [ ] Moonrise Kingdom
- [ ] Lost in Translation
- [ ] Fight Club
- [ ] Pulp Fiction
- [ ] Scott Pilgrim vs. the World

- [ ] Zombieland
- [ ] The Rocky Horror Picture Show
- [ ] Fantastic Mr. Fox
- [ ] The Perks of Being a Wallflower
- [ ] Fargo
- [ ] Amélie
- [ ] Requiem for a Dream
- [ ] Léon: The Professional
- [ ] American History X

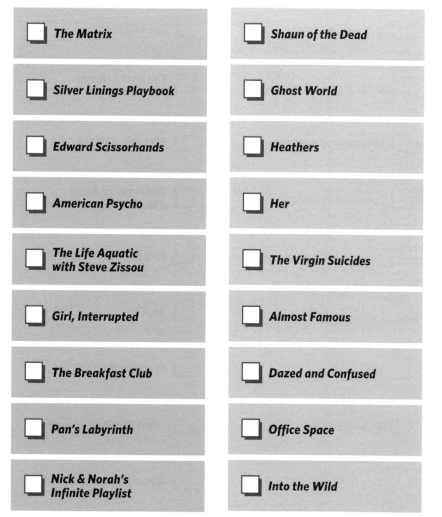

□ **The Matrix**

□ **Silver Linings Playbook**

□ **Edward Scissorhands**

□ **American Psycho**

□ **The Life Aquatic with Steve Zissou**

□ **Girl, Interrupted**

□ **The Breakfast Club**

□ **Pan's Labyrinth**

□ **Nick & Norah's Infinite Playlist**

□ **Shaun of the Dead**

□ **Ghost World**

□ **Heathers**

□ **Her**

□ **The Virgin Suicides**

□ **Almost Famous**

□ **Dazed and Confused**

□ **Office Space**

□ **Into the Wild**

NOW ADD UP YOUR SCORE!

If You Checked 0–15:

You're not hipster. You haven't seen most of these movies, and honestly you haven't even heard of a lot of them. Mainstream movies like the MCU (and maybe even a good rom-com once in a while) are definitely more your speed.

If You Checked 16–30:

You're kinda hipster. You watched a decent chunk of these movies and you're curious to see more. Now go head to your local coffee shop and start reading *The Catcher in the Rye*, you little hipster in training!

If You Checked 31–45:

You're very hipster. Holy smokes, you are very hipster! I'll bet most of us haven't even heard of the rest of the movies you've seen. Congrats on your extensive knowledge of indie films. I tip my fedora to you!

Here's Your Celebrity Soul Mate Based on Your Star Sign: Girls Edition

Pick your sign.

ARIES

ZOE SALDANA (GEMINI)

You are creative, insightful, and highly adaptable. You can be strong-willed and incredibly spontaneous. You may be impatient, and sometimes short-tempered, but it's only because you're so passionate. You would like a woman who can complement your excitement and charisma, but also deal with your assertive temperament. This makes Zoe Saldana, a Gemini, the ideal spark and loyal companion to match your personality.

TAURUS

NINA DOBREV (CAPRICORN)

You're a tenacious, strong, and energetic type. You can be a bit stubborn, but you are also incredibly supportive and patient. You're a hopeless romantic and very generous with your time—especially in the bedroom. These are some of the same qualities you look for in a female, which makes Nina Dobrev, a Capricorn, the perfect partner who appreciates a deep and physical connection.

GEMINI

JENNIFER LOPEZ (LEO)

You are quick-witted, affectionate, and imaginative. You're prone to emotional mood swings and it can be hard to predict how you're going to react to something, but your charisma is infectious, and your accomplishments inspire those around you—especially your romantic partner who happens to be a Leo, like Jennifer Lopez. Her supportive and exuberant nature will help you in your lows and always keep things exciting.

CANCER

BEYONCÉ (VIRGO)

While you tend to be traditional, tender, and loyal, you are also a tough nut to crack. One day you're caring and compassionate, and the next you're on the defensive. This makes Beyoncé, a Virgo, the reliable and structured partner who can perfectly balance you out. Ensuring you stick to your word, your Virgo mate will keep you on track and be the perfect partner to travel and see the world with, as preparation and planning are her strong suits.

LEO

TAYLOR SWIFT (SAGITTARIUS)

You have a strong influence on those around you with your brave and powerful presence. Your playfulness and wittiness can liven up any dull event, and people often look to you to provide comic relief in those moments—which makes Taylor Swift, a dynamic, charming, and up-for-anything Sagittarius, the best companion for you. Her philosophical side will have you captivated, and you'll be able to learn a great deal about each other very quickly.

VIRGO

KATY PERRY (SCORPIO)

Naturally intuitive, you work well with others and are great at giving advice within your friend group. You're inquisitive and remember *all* the tiny details. These aren't necessarily the things you look for in a woman, however. You favor passion and spontaneity from someone like Katy Perry, a Scorpio. Subtle and subdued, your Scorpio match will know exactly how to woo you in the most captivating and charming manner.

LIBRA

KYLIE JENNER (LEO)

With your charm and style, you're all about maintaining a balance in your life. You have an emotional side and tend to favor surrounding yourself with beautiful things, which can sometimes be misconstrued as being vain. Your ideal woman needs to fit these criteria, so a confident Leo like Kylie Jenner would be your ideal match. Her driven and self-assured disposition will inspire you and you will no doubt feel supported by her throughout your relationship.

CAPRICORN

ZENDAYA (VIRGO)

Practical, organized, and patient are your personality staples. You're highly reliable and a great judge of character. When it comes to your goals, you have no problem persevering until they are accomplished. This makes a Virgo like Zendaya, an equally selective and practical person, easy to get along with. You'll be at peace knowing you can rely on one another when planning excursions and adventures together.

SCORPIO

RIHANNA (PISCES)

You're intense yet elusive and you aren't shy about showing your emotional side. You can often be misunderstood, but you enjoy challenging others to figure you out, which plays into your flirtatious side. You need a nurturing partner who will take the time to understand your haphazard ways, someone like Rihanna, a Pisces. True to her sign, she is searching for something special—something out of the ordinary—and you may very well fit the bill.

AQUARIUS

EMMA WATSON (ARIES)

You're easygoing, independent, and artistic. You love to learn and are an excellent communicator, always seeking out new ways to improve yourself. That's why a decisive Aries like Emma Watson would be your perfect match. Together, you'll complement each other's love of being in charge and will likely take turns to lead. Just be honest with your partner, as that is something they value the most, and you'll get the best out of them and your relationship.

SAGITTARIUS

JENNIFER ANISTON (AQUARIUS)

Your adventurous and optimistic sides will allow you to cross paths with a lot of interesting people. However, this also means you don't like to be tied down by people or things; for your attention to be grabbed and sustained, your partner needs to keep up with your spontaneity and enthusiasm. This makes an Aquarius like Jennifer Aniston a perfect partner in life. Her colorful personality will keep you on your toes and she'll be more than happy to plan dates that involve music or dancing.

PISCES

TINA FEY (TAURUS)

Your soulful nature allows you to reflect on your past mistakes and helps you learn from them. You're honest, selfless, and trustworthy. Your ideal match would be someone who honors those characteristics and harmonizes with your best qualities, much like Tina Fey, a Taurus. Her thoughtful and caring tendencies will match yours and you'll be able to enjoy adventurous dates and long and meaningful discussions.

Tell Us Your Favorite Candy and We'll Reveal Your Love Language

Pick some movie theater candy:

A. Junior Mints

B. Milk Duds

C. Peanut M&M's

D. Raisinets

E. Reese's Pieces

Choose a chocolate bar:

A. Snickers

B. 3 Musketeers

C. Hershey's Milk Chocolate

D. Kit Kat

E. Milky Way

What's the best kind of chocolate?

A. Milk

B. Dark

C. White

D. Semi-sweet

E. I don't really like plain chocolate

Pick the worst Halloween candy:

A. Tootsie Roll

B. Candy corn

C. Dots

D. Good & Plenty

E. Smarties

Red or black licorice?

A. Red

B. Black

C. Both

D. Neither

E. Yuck. Who likes licorice?!

Pick an "old person" candy:

A. Werther's Original

B. Hard candy

C. Jujubes

D. Breath mints

E. Peppermint candy

If You Got Mostly A's:

You're into physical touch. It's not just sex that makes you feel loved; hugging, cuddling, holding hands, and other physical expressions of affection are what make you feel loved by your partner.

If You Got Mostly B's:

You're into words of affirmation. Your favorite way to confirm how someone feels about you is to hear them actually *say* it. Whether it's a simple "I love you" or a more detailed account of what they appreciate about you, that's how you feel truly cherished.

If You Got Mostly C's:

You're into quality time. Presents and words can be nice, but what makes you feel really appreciated by your partner is simply spending time with them, like both of you paying attention to each other, whether it's through learning a new hobby or simply talking about each other's days.

If You Got Mostly D's:

You're into receiving gifts. You're not materialistic; your partner could spend nothing at all making you a small token of their appreciation and you'd love it. It's the gesture that they were thinking of you and wanted you to have something they knew you'd love. It's the thought that counts, after all.

If You Got Mostly E's:

You're into acts of service. Small gestures that show you that your partner wants to better your life make you feel all warm and cuddly inside. Whether it's taking out the garbage, bringing you soup when you're sick, or fixing things around the house, you know that it's the simple things that show true love.

What Would Your Rodeo Clown Name Be?

FIRST LETTER OF THE STREET YOU GREW UP ON

A: Bippy

B: Squiggly

C: Stinky

D: Horsey

E: Monsieur

F: Tiny

G: Calamity

H: Yoyo

I: Bozo

J: Zippy

K: Bogo

L: Barely There

M: Shining

N: Buttercup

O: Cookie

P: Alfie

Q: Disco

R: Hayford

S: Bing Bong

T: Stirrup

U: Krusty

V: Giggly

LAST DIGIT OF YOUR PHONE NUMBER

1: Barrels

2: Daddy

3: Lasso

4: Whistles

5: Lederhosen

6: Britches

7: Beans

8: Scoops

9: Pumpkin

0: Juggle

The First Animal You See Is Your Patronus

```
V M U H R W F B F S B L A C K S T A L L I O N C
U A Q E O D I B G A A X H E F D O D A I W C E G L
L N T I G E R S R L T N I U B O R Z O I O X P K
T N B A D G E R I M Q G P K K K K D B Q O C Y D
U Y C W P D D U Z O F O P R G I M G D H D H T L
R L D S P P W D Z N B L O O D H O U N D M E H E
E X N W B E E T L E L D G K U E L S X N O E O L
K B U F F A L O Y O S F R I S Y E O D P U T N E
G C S Q U C L J B S P I I B M W E S R B S A L P
P O I T Y O I E E C A S F M A I A H A R E H Q H
O A C A I C N A A A R H F L S L S E G T B O S A
L S H I R K G R R L R J A Y T D N Z O R B Y W N
A E L O I R S T F I O P U N I C O R N V F M A T
R A C T S A A H L C W B B X F A W T F Q O O N R
B T N T H T L W R O Z R H I F T Y J L G X N P T
E U M E W O A O N C D O E C N J O R Y T T K G A
A R C R O W M R G A F W B G I C W Y G R E E S A
R T R L L H A M L T Z N C U M M L I N W R Y X R
H L Z Z F A N W I L D B O A R L V Z H E R O N D
U E L B H W D I O L Q E D O L P H I N A I E O V
S M U S O K E W N O E A G L E P U R C S E B E A
K I W T U H R S Q U I R R E L P V N Q E R O V R
E W J P N Q V P W J W O L F G I I G Z L X S R K
Y Z C Z D D B G E W B L A C K B E A R Q D U I A
```

If You Can Complete 10/12 of These Famous Quotes, You're a *Friends* Expert

Fill in the blanks, then check if you're correct!

1. "JOEY DOESN'T _____ _____." —Joey

2. "Meet Princess Consuela _____ _____." —Phoebe

3. "Could I BE wearing _____ _____ _____?" —Joey

4. "Just so you know, it's not that common, it doesn't happen to every guy, _____ _____ _____ _____ _____ _____." —Rachel

5. "That's right, Mom and Dad. Your little _____ _____ _____." —Monica

6. "If he doesn't like you, this is all just a _____ point." —Joey

7. "I went to that tanning place your wife suggested." —Ross
   "_____ _____ _____ _____ _____?" —Chandler

8. "They don't know that we know _____ _____ _____ _____." —Phoebe

9. "I'm not great at the advice. Can I interest you _____ _____ _____ _____?" —Chandler

10. "I grew up with Monica. If you didn't eat fast, _____ _____ _____." —Ross

11. "Are you going to set Ross up with someone? Does she already _____ _____ _____ _____?" —Rachel

12. "Jam good, _____ _____, _____ _____." —Joey

NOW ADD UP YOUR SCORE!

If You Got 0–4 Correct:
You're a *Friends* newb. Have you ever seen *Friends*? If you haven't, then congrats on taking a couple of good guesses. If you have, then, well, Monica would be disappointed.

If You Got 5–9 Correct:
You're a *Friends* enthusiast. Could you *be* any closer to being an expert? But you're not there yet. Time to brush up on some episodes. For now, though, you're killing it.

If You Got 10–12 Correct:
You're a *Friends* expert! CONGRATS. YOU GOT AN A+. A 100 percent. The whole shabang. You know your *Friends* quotes in and out and you should be very proud of yourself. Watching reruns every night has really paid off!

ANSWER KEY

1. "share food"
2. "banana hammock"
3. "any more clothes"
4. "and it is a big deal"
5. "Harmonica is hammered"
6. "Moo"
7. "was that place the sun"
8. "they know we know"
9. "in a sarcastic comment"
10. "you didn't eat"
11. "have a wedding dress"
12. "custard good, meat good"

LOL

CONGRATS!

Steal Some Food off Your SO's Plate and We'll Reveal If Your Love Will Survive

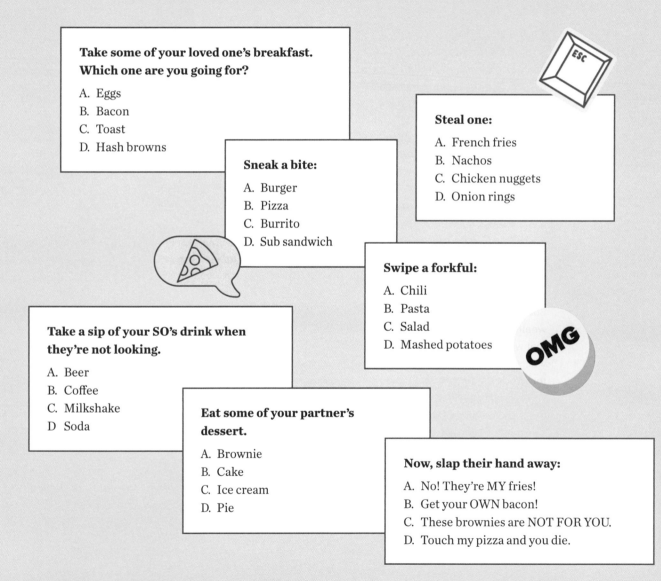

Take some of your loved one's breakfast. Which one are you going for?

A. Eggs
B. Bacon
C. Toast
D. Hash browns

Steal one:

A. French fries
B. Nachos
C. Chicken nuggets
D. Onion rings

Sneak a bite:

A. Burger
B. Pizza
C. Burrito
D. Sub sandwich

Swipe a forkful:

A. Chili
B. Pasta
C. Salad
D. Mashed potatoes

Take a sip of your SO's drink when they're not looking.

A. Beer
B. Coffee
C. Milkshake
D Soda

Eat some of your partner's dessert.

A. Brownie
B. Cake
C. Ice cream
D. Pie

Now, slap their hand away:

A. No! They're MY fries!
B. Get your OWN bacon!
C. These brownies are NOT FOR YOU.
D. Touch my pizza and you die.

If You Got Mostly A's:
You'll decide you're better off as friends. You and your partner will realize that while you love each other, you're not *in* love with each other. You know what you both *do* love, though? Hanging out together and eating some delicious food. You'll end the romantic part of your relationship, but you'll embark on a new adventure as food friends.

If You Got Mostly B's:
You'll break it off after the summer. You two are going to hang in there until the summer ends, but when the weather cools, you'll realize that all that was keeping you together was, well, food. And that was fun, but is that really the basis for a long-term relationship? You'll be sad for a while, but then you'll order some pizza and feel better.

If You Got Mostly C's:
You guys are doomed. Sorry, but all this food stealing isn't going to work out well for you guys. Resentment will grow, more and more food will be stolen from each other, and soon you'll both be screaming, "IF YOU WANTED FRIES THEN WHY DIDN'T YOU ORDER FRIES?!?!" at each other in the middle of a restaurant. It'll be a bit of a messy breakup, but in the end you'll both have your own French fries. Trust me, it's for the best.

If You Got Mostly D's:
You two are totally gonna make it. You both know that love is about compromise and sharing, and that includes food once in a while. After all, you're just sharing the things you love TOGETHER, right? Food just tastes better off your partner's plate and you'll be eating plenty of it for the foreseeable future.

College MASH

The first city you find is the city you'll go to school in, the first name you find is the person you'll end up marrying, and the first major you find is what you'll get a degree in!

```
D W V L W B U S I N E S S I
M X A H H C H I C A G O G W
K R R O B E R T V P W H E D
P A R I S A R T Q K D N I L
H I S T O R Y Z M O R G A N
A R R Y G T O M M Y E V K J
F W N O X H O N U L U L U X
M J O R D A N Y I T J D E S
T E D L O N D O N A G E V L
V U W E C O N O M I C S T T
B L O S A N G E L E S F D H
O R N Y Z B I O L O G Y U W
K A S H L E Y C T L Y C P A
W D B E D N W A L L A C E S
```

Lazy Girl Bingo

Check off or mark the squares that apply to you (things you own, have done, or things that have happened to you). The more you fill out, the more you're a lazy girl! Snap a picture and upload online to share your results!

Sleep with your makeup on	Use dry shampoo instead of showering	Pile up clothes on a chair
Order food when your fridge is full	Paint over already chipped nails	Smell clothes before you wear them
Rest your laptop on your boobs	Kick off your underwear	Take off your bra *before* taking off your shirt first

1. **What's a synonym for *nonchalant*?**

   A. Conditional
   B. Casual
   C. Concerned
   D. Catastrophic

2. **What does *ephemeral* mean?**

   A. Of falsified or erroneously attributed origin
   B. Marked by impulsive vehemence or passion
   C. Lasting a very short time

3. **What's a synonym for *vindicate*?**

   A. Consign
   B. Discredit
   C. Absolve
   D. Convict

4. **What does *hedonist* mean?**

   A. A person who is devoted to the pursuit of pleasure
   B. One who behaves criminally or viciously
   C. One who is despised or rejected

5. **What's a synonym for *surreptitious*?**

   A. Flamboyant
   B. Stealthy
   C. Disloyal
   D. Fortunate

6. **What does *adulation* mean?**

   A. Excessive or slavish admiration or flattery
   B. A rising and falling in waves
   C. To grow toward or arrive at full stature or physical or mental maturity

7. **What's a synonym for *prosaic*?**

   A. Poetic
   B. Talkative
   C. Persistent
   D. Commonplace

8. **What does *panacea* mean?**

   A. Someone or something intensely disliked or loathed
   B. The quality or state of being happy
   C. A remedy for all ills or difficulties

9. **What's a synonym for *querulous*?**

   A. Serene
   B. Adventurous
   C. Gaudy
   D. Fussy

10. What does *veracity* mean?

A. Devotion to the truth
B. Intrepid boldness
C. The highest point of development or achievement

11. What's a synonym for *dearth*?

A. Abundance
B. Lack
C. Eulogy
D. Elegy

12. What does *evanescent* mean?

A. Tending to vanish like vapor
B. Having a noticeable and pleasant smell
C. Free from obscurity or ambiguity

13. What's a synonym for *impute*?

A. Insinuate
B. Entwine
C. Attribute
D. Rationalize

14. What does *maudlin* mean?

A. Overly elaborate or conspicuous
B. Tedious sameness
C. Weakly and effusively sentimental

15. What's a synonym for *quixotic*?

A. Enigmatic
B. Sharp-witted
C. Hideous
D. Idealistic

16. Finally, what does *cogent* mean?

A. Appealing forcibly to the mind or reason
B. Capable of being apprehended
C. Lacking sharpness or quickness of sensibility or intellect

NOW ADD UP YOUR SCORE!

If You Got 0–13 Correct:
You didn't do so hot! Why say "loquacious" when you can just say "talkative," right? Think your friends could do better than you? Challenge them and find out!

If You Got 14–16 Correct:
Your IQ is off the charts! You're basically a walking, talking dictionary. You probably just love throwing around big words every now and then to show off. But like Beyoncé said, If You Got it, flaunt it!

This Is What Your Friends Will Be Like in the Future

First, pick a number: 1, 2, 3, 4, 5. Got your number?
Good, you're going to use it in every prediction! It's time to look into the future.

Prediction: Your *1 = oldest friend, 2 = newest friend, 3 = frenemy, 4 = clingiest friend, 5 = best friend* will marry someone you absolutely hate, and you'll have to see them when their partner isn't around.

Prediction: Your *1 = newest friend, 2 = frenemy, 3 = clingiest friend, 4 = best friend, 5 = oldest friend* will become a C-list celebrity after becoming the villain on a reality TV show.

Prediction: Your *1 = frenemy, 2 = clingiest friend, 3 = best friend, 4 = oldest friend, 5 = newest friend* will move across the country and you'll mainly keep in touch via text and social media.

Prediction: Your *1 = clingiest friend, 2 = best friend, 3 = oldest friend, 4 = newest friend, 5 = frenemy* will have five kids and exclusively talk about raising kids unless you get them drunk.

Prediction: Your *1 = best friend, 2 = oldest friend, 3 = newest friend, 4 = frenemy, 5 = clingiest friend* will become a rich online influencer with over a million followers and always pick up the bill at lunch.

This Relationship Checklist Knows How Long You've Been Dating Your SO

Check off everything you and your significant other have done.

- ☐ You've stayed in on a Friday night just to spend time together.

- ☐ You've canceled existing plans with other people to stay in on a Friday night just to spend time together.

- ☐ You've accidentally worn very similar outfits at the same time.

- ☐ You've snuggled for less than five minutes and rolled to opposite sides of the bed so you could get a real night of sleep.

- ☐ You've survived a vacation together.

- ☐ You've survived an Ikea trip together.

- ☐ Your anniversary is like a bonus holiday and you actively look forward to it.

- ☐ You've burped in front of each other.

- ☐ You've farted in front of each other.

- ☐ You've peed in front of each other.

- ☐ You've shit in front of each other.

- ☐ You've done all these things without even pausing for a second to consider if it's weird.

- ☐ You've helped each other inspect strange bumps in hard-to-reach places.

- ☐ You've endured the "When are you two getting married?" question.

- ☐ You have the story of how you met rehearsed and ready to go in your head.

- ☐ You've had to schedule time apart because apparently it's frowned upon to spend all your time with one person.

- ☐ You've had to defend monogamy in a drunken debate.

- ☐ None of your friends take your dating advice seriously because the last time you were single things were ~different~.

- ☐ You're never totally sure what to do on Valentine's Day.

Continues on next page

- [ ] You know secret ways to cheer them up that wouldn't work on anyone else, like your Danny DeVito impression.

- [ ] There are dating apps that you've barely heard of.

- [ ] And the "How long have you guys been dating?" question.

- [ ] You can tell how the other is feeling just by looking at them.

- [ ] You can communicate by barely speaking.

- [ ] You can communicate without speaking at all.

- [ ] You share grooming products.

- [ ] Your inside jokes are horrible, but there's nothing funnier in the universe to you.

- [ ] It's physically impossible to embarrass yourself in front of them.

- [ ] You are comfortable talking to their parents on the phone.

- [ ] You regularly text members of their family.

- [ ] You have them listed as an emergency contact somewhere.

- [ ] And the "Where's your other half?" question.

- [ ] Money moves between you so frequently you have no idea whose is what.

- [ ] They know your deepest, darkest secret.

- [ ] You know theirs.

- [ ] You barely notice their morning breath anymore.

- [ ] You can talk about which strangers you find attractive without them getting jealous.

- [ ] You've had full conversations about your bodily functions.

- [ ] When you're together, pants are optional.

- [ ] You can successfully order a meal for them.

- [ ] They're the only ones who can talk about your insecurities without you drowning in a pool of self-loathing.

- [ ] You've fallen asleep during sex.

- [ ] You've purposely had sex in under five minutes.

- ☐ You've had "I just need to cum" sex.

- ☐ You can hold a conversation about their hobby because you've absorbed so much information about it.

- ☐ You've actually tried their hobby.

- ☐ You have weird names for each other that you never use in public.

- ☐ You've had to get them a towel because they forgot to bring one into the bathroom.

- ☐ Ditto: toilet paper.

- ☐ You think they look amazing first thing in the morning.

- ☐ You've murdered a hell bug together.

- ☐ You've binged an entire Netflix series together.

- ☐ You've said, "You're just hungry."

- ☐ You know their favorite color, food, and lucky number.

- ☐ You can't imagine being with anyone else.

NOW ADD UP YOUR SCORE!

If You Checked 0–13:

Are you single? You haven't done many of these things at all! And that's okay, it's just funny that you chose to take this quiz.

If You Checked 14–27:

Together for at least one year. Hey, you just need more time before you start poking at cysts in their armpit, but you'll be there soon!

If You Checked 28–41:

Together for at least three years. You're in it for the long haul. You're probably farting in front of your partner as we speak.

If You Checked 42–55:

Together for at least five years. Yeah, you've done it all. You're firmly dating, no ifs, ands, or buts. So pull on a pair of old sweatpants, pop your stinky feet on your partner's lap, and enjoy this thing you've built together.

What Hybrid *Harry Potter* and Disney Character Are You?

Pick a hybrid *Harry Potter* house:

A. Ravendor
B. Slytherpuff
C. Gryfferin
D. Hufferin
E. Ravenpuff
F. Slytherdor
G. Gryffinclaw
H. Huffledor
I. Raverin

How would your friends describe you?

A. Smart
B. Kind
C. Fun
D. Brave
E. Serious
F. Supportive
G. Creative
H. Silly
I. Ambitious

Choose a Disney castle:

A. Castle DunBroch
B. Prince Eric's Castle
C. King Stefan's Castle
D. The Queen of Hearts' Castle
E. The Sultan's Palace
F. The Beast's Castle
G. The Evil Queen's Castle
H. Elsa's Ice Palace
I. King's Castle

What *kind* of smart are you?

A. Music smart
B. Math smart
C. Life smart
D. Visual smart
E. People smart
F. Nature smart
G. Emotional smart
H. Sports smart
I. Word smart

Which Disney villain is the worst?

A. Maleficent
B. Dr. Facilier
C. Hans
D. Mother Gothel
E. The Evil Queen
F. Gaston
G. Ursula
H. Scar
I. Cruella de Vil

Pick a Harry Potter film to watch:

A. *Harry Potter and the Sorcerer's Stone*
B. *Harry Potter and the Chamber of Secrets*
C. *Harry Potter and the Prisoner of Azkaban*
D. *Harry Potter and the Goblet of Fire*
E. *Harry Potter and the Order of the Phoenix*
F. *Harry Potter and the Half-Blood Prince*
G. *Harry Potter and the Deathly Hallows Part 1*
H. *Harry Potter and the Deathly Hallows Part 2*
I. *Fantastic Beasts and Where to Find Them*

If You Got Mostly A's:
You're Hermione and Belle! You're very independent and prefer to spend your time reading books or watching movies. Because of this, you've actually developed an incredible imagination and people really admire that about you! You have a few REALLY CLOSE friends, or maybe even just one best friend, and you know they'd have your back in any situation.

If You Got Mostly B's:
You're Harry and Woody! You're the kind of person a group will often look to for leadership and you're totally comfortable with that. You're actually very humble, so sometimes it's a surprise, but at the end of the day you always know right from wrong and make the best choice for everyone.

If You Got Mostly C's:
You're Ron and Miguel! You're not one to quickly make friends, but that's because people often don't "get" you at first. However, those who *do* make the effort to get to know you better are quick to realize how special you are.

If You Got Mostly D's:
You're Fred and Buzz Lightyear! You're the fun one! Your friends and family can always rely on you to make them laugh and often look to you when they're feeling a bit down.

If You Got Mostly E's:
You're Neville and Thumper! You may not be the first person everyone notices, but if they make the effort to get to know you better, they quickly learn how special you are. Your closest friends rely on you to make them feel better and that's a very important job.

If You Got Mostly F's:
You're Luna and Moana! You're a total risk-taker, but in a good way. You'd never put anyone in danger, but you're always looking for fun new things to do because isn't life just more exciting that way? People may think you're a bit *odd*, but that's only because you don't care WHAT they think!

If You Got Mostly G's:
You're McGonagall and Ariel! You're the kind of person people often refer to as the "mom" of the group. You're great at taking care of others, and whether you know it or not, everyone around you really respects you.

If You Got Mostly H's:
You're Dumbledore and Aladdin! You're the strong, silent type. People are naturally drawn to you because you have a very calming presence about you. You're great in tough situations and always know the right thing to say when someone is feeling bad.

If You Got Mostly I's:
You're Snape and Jasmine! You're opinionated and strong-willed, and that's okay! People might not always agree with your methods and can sometimes be intimidated by your ambition, but in the end it usually works out and everyone is the better for it.

Pick Seven Junk Foods and We'll Tell You What Percent Trash You Are

Pick some chips:

A. Classic
B. Salt and vinegar
C. Tortilla chips
D. Nacho cheese
E. Baked
F. Sour cream and onion

Pick some candy:

A. Reese's Peanut Butter Cups
B. Skittles
C. M&M's
D. Kit Kat
E. Sour Patch Kids
F. Starburst

Pick something hot:

A. Bacon cheeseburger
B. Pizza
C. Fried chicken
D. Hot wings
E. Nachos
F. Tacos

Pick a soda:

A. Coca-Cola
B. Pepsi
C. Ginger Ale
D. Dr Pepper
E. Sprite
F. Mountain Dew

Pick a sweet treat:

A. Ice cream
B. Cake
C. Cupcake
D. Sorbet
E. Brownie
F. Pie

Pick some cookies:

A. Oreos
B. Any type of Girl Scout cookies
C. Keebler Soft 'N Chewy
D. Milano Pepperidge Farm
E. Fig Newtons
F. Nilla Wafers

Now just pick one more thing:

A. Cheetos
B. Oatmeal creme pies
C. Andy Capp's Hot Fries
D. Ho Hos
E. Fritos
F. Cheez-It crackers

OMG

If You Got Mostly A's:
You're 51.5% trash! Slightly more than half trash. You're a trash half full type of person and you ought to be proud of that.

If You Got Mostly B's:
You're 29% trash! Not very trash. Make no mistake, you're garbage. You're just not very garbage percentage-wise.

If You Got Mostly C's:
You're 100% trash! You are full-blown garbage. You're a dumpster filled to the brim—you couldn't really fit any more trash in there.

If You Got Mostly D's:
You're 75% trash! Three-quarters trash! You're very garbage, but not extremely garbage—a very important distinction.

If You Got Mostly E's:
You're 12% trash! Mostly not trash! Your garbage percentage is so low, it's almost nonexistent.

If You Got Mostly F's:
You're 1% trash, 99% recyclable! You're mostly salvageable trash, which is about as good as trash gets. Congratulations on that.

Dog Parent Bingo

Check off or mark the squares that apply to you (things you own, have done, or things that have happened to you). The more you fill out, the more you're a dog parent! See if you can get five across, down, or diagonally. Then snap a picture and upload online to share your results!

Your camera roll is 90 percent your dog	You've given your dog 10+ different nicknames and counting	You made your dog an Instagram	You have something with your dog's face on it (shirt, mug, blanket, etc.)	Your dog has more sweaters than you do
Your lock screen is a photo of your dog	You had a professional photo shoot with your dog	You've thrown your dog a birthday/ adoptiversary party	You've pushed your dog around in a stroller	You've talked to your dog about your problems
You have a *special voice* just for them	You've video chatted with your dog	**Free Space** (Go Video Chat with Your Dog!!!)	You've canceled plans to stay home with your dog	You've made up a song about your dog
You've taken your dog on a trip	You let your dog sleep in your bed every night	You've brought your dog to school/work	You've done a couples Halloween costume with your dog	You've sent out a holiday card with your dog on it
You've held a wedding for your dog and their ~special someone~	You've made art of your dog and displayed it proudly!!!	You and your dog have a matching set of clothes	You've refused to move because your dog fell asleep on you	You've spent more money on your dog's food than on your own

This Is the Hardest Disney Quiz You'll Ever Take

1. What were Mickey and Minnie's original names?

A. Mortimer and Minneola
B. Mickelous and Minerva
C. Mortimer and Minerva
D. Mickelous and Minneola

2. What was the working title for *Fantasia*?

A. *Fantasmic*
B. *The Concert Feature*
C. *Disney's Concert Magic*
D. *The Sorcerer's Apprentice*

3. What did Aladdin steal from the marketplace?

A. A loaf of bread
B. A rug
C. A tiny hat
D. An apple

4. In *Pinocchio*, who called Jiminy Cricket a grasshopper?

A. Lampwick
B. The Blue Fairy
C. Pinocchio
D. Stromboli

5. What was Wall-E's favorite musical?

A. *Showboat*
B. *Meet Me in St. Louis*
C. *Bye Bye Birdie*
D. *Hello Dolly*

6. What is Boo's real name in *Monsters, Inc.*?

A. Mary
B. Suzy
C. Sally
D. Cindy

7. The song "Where Do I Go from Here" is featured in which animated sequel?

A. *Pocahontas II*
B. *Little Mermaid II*
C. *Aladdin and the King of Thieves*
D. *The Lion King II*

8. How many bows are on the skirt of Cinderella's pink dress?

A. Two
B. Three
C. Four
D. Five

9. What was Walt Disney's first live-action film?

A. *The Story of Robin Hood and His Merrie Men*
B. *Treasure Island*
C. *The Shaggy Dog*
D. *The Sword and the Rose*

10. How old was Ariel in *The Little Mermaid*?

A. Nineteen
B. Seventeen
C. Fifteen
D. Sixteen

11. Which one of Donald Duck's nephews wears green?

A. Huey
B. Dewey
C. Louie
D. Hugo

Continues on next page

12. Which dwarf did not sing "Heigh Ho"?

A. Dopey
B. Sleepy
C. Grumpy
D. Bashful

13. In *Alice in Wonderland*, what is the time on the White Rabbit's pocket watch?

A. 12:25
B. 12:30
C. 12:15
D. 12:45

14. Which Disney animated feature has the most songs?

A. *Frozen*
B. *The Jungle Book*
C. *Sleeping Beauty*
D. *Alice in Wonderland*

15. Which movie was NOT based on a Brothers Grimm story?

A. *Tangled*
B. *Snow White*
C. *The Princess and the Frog*
D. *The Little Mermaid*

16. Which of these is NOT an actual Disney short film?

A. *Destino*, a surrealist animated film collaboration between Disney and Salvador Dali
B. *The Story of Menstruation*, an animated anatomical lesson on the reproductive cycle
C. *Mickey Mouse and the Medicine Man*, a short animated comic where Mickey and Donald get high and move to Africa to become drug dealers
D. *Der Fuehrer's Face*, a WWII-era film in which Donald experiences the Nazi regime

17. What is the name of the mortal couple who adopts Hercules?

A. Clio and Calliope
B. Amphitryon and Alcemene
C. Philocetes and Philodendra
D. Alcestis and Admetus

18. What is Jane's last name in *Tarzan*?

A. Seymore
B. Porter
C. Williams
D. Clayton

19. In *The Rescuers*, where is the Rescue Aid Society headquarters located?

A. The United Nations Building
B. The Empire State Building
C. The Tower of Big Ben
D. The Sydney Opera House

20. In _The Jungle Book_, what did King Louis ask Mowgli to teach him?

A. How to dance
B. How to make fire
C. How to be human
D. How to hunt

21. Captain Hook has a hook on which hand?

A. Left
B Right

22. How many eggs does Gaston eat for breakfast in _Beauty and the Beast_?

A. A dozen
B. Two dozen
C. Five dozen
D. Ten dozen

23. In which animated feature would you find a villain named Sykes?

A. _Oliver and Company_
B. _The Aristocats_
C. _The Great Mouse Detective_
D. _The Black Cauldron_

24. A young Jonathan Taylor Thomas provided the voice for which character?

A. Simba in _The Lion King_
B. Chip in _Beauty and the Beast_
C. Tod the Fox in _The Fox and the Hound_
D. Christopher Robin in _Winnie the Pooh_

25. Which Disney princess has the fewest number of lines?

A. Cinderella
B. Snow White
C. Jasmine
D. Aurora

ANSWER KEY

NOW ADD UP YOUR SCORE!

If You Got 0–6 Correct:
Nice try! You're not a full-fledged Disney expert yet, but you'll get there.

If You Got 7–12 Correct:
Not too shabby! You're well on your way to becoming a real Disney expert.

If You Got 13–18 Correct:
You sure know a lot about Disney! But not quite everything. Keep going down the rabbit hole and soon you'll know all there is to know.

If You Got 19–25 Correct:
All hail the champion of Disney facts! You know all the Disney there is to know. You've seen every movie and actually paid attention to all the nitty-gritty details. You're basically a Disney character yourself.

Build a Pizza and We'll Tell You Which Celebrity You'll Marry and Then Divorce

Pick a size:

A. Personal
B. Medium
C. Large
D. Extra large

Choose a crust:

A. Thin
B. Stuffed
C. Deep dish
D. Gluten-free
E. Whole wheat
F. Flatbread

Choose a sauce:

A. Tomato basil
B. Pesto
C. Alfredo
D. Marinara
E. BBQ
F. No sauce

How much cheese?

A. Light
B. Normal
C. Heavy
D. ALL THE FREAKIN' CHEESE, PLEASE!
E. Little more than a sprinkle
F. None

Choose topping #1:

A. Pepperoni
B. Pineapple
C. Mushrooms
D. Onions
E. Sausage
F. Green peppers

Now for topping #2:

A. Chicken
B. Bacon
C. Ham
D. Black olives
E. Jalapeños
F. None

How 'bout topping #3:

A. Spinach
B. Arugula
C. Anchovies
D. Banana peppers
E. Broccoli
F. More cheese

Are you ready to eat your pizza?

A. Yes
B. No
C. IDK why I'm taking this quiz

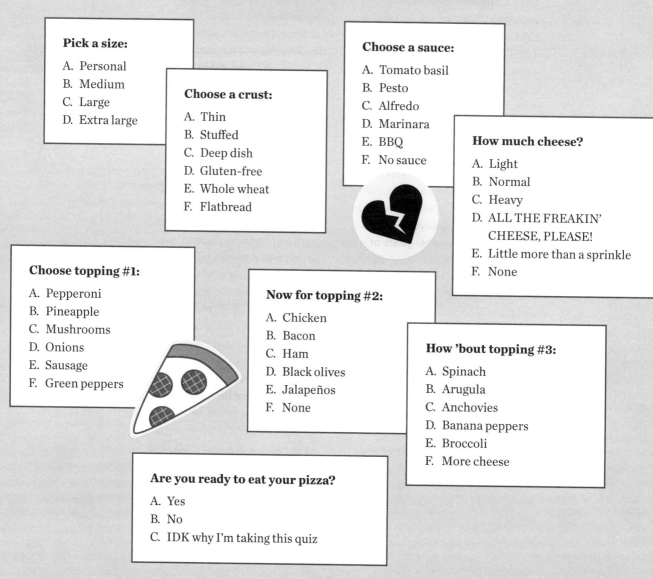

If You Got Mostly A's:

You'll marry and then divorce Leonardo DiCaprio! You and Leo will meet at a charity event and totally hit it off. But after years of traveling the world together, losing all your money, and finding yourselves having to sleep in the carcass of a horse, you'll call it quits, citing irreconcilable differences.

If You Got Mostly B's:

You'll marry and then divorce Zac Efron! You and Zac will be the couple everyone is envious of—fun, easy-going, and always down for an adventure. But after years of Zac singing tunes from *High School Musical* every morning at 7 a.m., you'll decide that enough is enough and the marriage is over.

If You Got Mostly C's:

You'll marry and then divorce Liam Hemsworth! Liam will ask for your number at a Starbucks one summer. Fast-forward three years and three dogs later, you're married! But after realizing that you have completely different parenting styles when trying to train your pups, you'll agree that things would never work if you had actual kids and call it quits.

If You Got Mostly D's:

You'll marry and then divorce Jake Gyllenhaal! You'll meet Jake on the set of one of his movies while interning in Los Angeles one summer, and the rest is history! But after dating for two years and being married for another three, you'll realize the ten-year age difference is just too much and decide you both want different things.

If You Got Mostly E's:

You'll marry and then divorce Zayn Malik! While at one of his shows, Zayn will call you up on stage and you'll end up falling madly in love, getting married, and having some kids. But his insane tour schedule means he's never home, and you start to grow apart. After a year of counseling, you'll decide to divorce but remain close friends for the sake of the children.

If You Got Mostly F's:

You'll marry and then divorce Drake! You and Drake will be married for four years, but two albums, two world tours, and a whole lotta late nights with your hair tied, sweatpants, chillin' with no makeup on later, you'll decide you're both bored AF and were better off as friends.

Seven Styles of Bangs and What They Say about You

Pick the style that's so you.

'70s BANGS

- Crystal mom
- No makeup makeup
- "Should I keep my bangs or grow them out?"
- Applies chapstick every three minutes
- Goes to pet stores just to look at cute animals

BREAKUP BANGS

- "I just need a girls' night!!!!!!!" text
- *Grudgingly downloads Tinder*
- *Deletes Tinder*
- $3 shots
- *Re-downloads Tinder again*

BLUNT BANGS

on sale!

- Type A
- "Always the bridesmaid never the bride"
- Ravenclaw
- Reminds you of you fourth-grade teacher
- Has a mildly successful Etsy business

FRINGE BANGS

- Always cold
- "Follow my dog on Instagram"
- Grocery shops exclusively at farmers' markets
- Owns seven different balsam fir-scented candles
- ~Coffee mornings, wine nights~

MICRO BANGS

- "I'm a Pisces"
- TEVAS
- Needs to pee RN
- Has a stick and poke tattoo from freshman year
- Is vegan but eats pepperoni pizza when hammered

SIDE BANGS

- Always tired
- Dry hands
- Really into baking recently???
- 180+ unchecked Tinder matches
- Definitely used to own several "I<3 Boobies" bracelets

V BANGS

- Cat-eye glasses and red lipstick
- Horny at inconvenient times
- Did theater in high school
- OBSESSED with sphynx cats
- "So I've been thinking about getting my nipples pierced"

Harry Potter MASH

Add together the first and last digit of your phone number to get the magic number!
Use that number to go through each category and count through the items; then cross
off the item you land on. Start again, skipping over the crossed-off items until there's
only one left in each category. Then circle the last item in each
category to see your results.

House

Ravenclaw

Gryffindor

Hufflepuff

Slytherin

Nemesis

Snape

Ron

Dumbledore

Draco

Wand's Core

Unicorn hair

Dragon

Heartstrings

Phoenix Feather

Thestral Hair

BFF

Hagrid

Harry

Hermione

Cho

Favorite Class

Potions

Herbology

Defense Against the
Dark Arts

Transfiguration

Pet

Rat

Owl

Cat

Toad

This Quiz Will Help You Decide on Some Things Right Now!

Your home address = the number of people who look up to you

The last text you sent = the slogan of your next business

The color shirt you're wearing = the color you should dye your hair

The last person you talked to = the person who will secretly betray you

The color of your eyes = the color of your next car

The last four digits of your phone number = your bank balance on December 31

The temperature outside = the month and day that you'll get married (76° = 7/6)

These Questions Will Reveal What Type of Mom You'll Be

It's the annual bake sale at your kid's school. What do you bring?

A. Honestly, I'll probably forget to bring something.

B. Store-bought cookies that I'll try to pass off as my own.

C. Something super simple with five ingredients or less.

D. My favorite recipe that I make every year and the kids (and parents) go crazy for!

You're headed to the pool with your kid and their friend today. What do you bring with you?

A. Nothing. I probably have whatever I need in my car.

B. A bottle of sunscreen, towels, and my phone.

C. Some cash. I can buy whatever I need at the pool.

D. The question is what do I NOT bring with me? I've got sunscreen, floaties, goggles, snacks, extra towels, binoculars, a change of clothes, sunglasses, reading material, baby wipes, pool toys . . .

It's summertime. What will your kid be doing?

A. Summer camp!

B. Swimming lessons for sure.

C. I haven't thought that far ahead, but I do know my kid will be saying "I'm bored" every thirty minutes.

D. Several different activities so they can try new things!

How old will your kid be when you let them have a cell phone?

A. Second or third grade.

B. Middle school.

C. Senior in high school.

D. They can have a cell phone when they're old enough to pay for one.

Your kid refuses to eat dinner at a friend's house. What do you do?

A. Take them to a different room and say you're going to take something away if they don't eat.

B. Ask politely if you can make them something else to eat.

C. Give them a *look* and pray they at least eat some of the food.

D. Apologize for your kid's behavior and tell your kid if they don't eat they aren't getting anything else.

It's Saturday night. What are you doing?

A. That's mom's night out and what we do is none of your business.
B. Probably playing a game or watching a movie with my kid.
C. Drinking wine with a friend or two at one of our houses.
D. Eating and/or sleeping.

It's your kid's birthday. How do you celebrate?

A. I ran to the store last minute, texted some people, and was able to throw together a pretty decent party.
B. With a small birthday dinner at my house with immediate family.
C. We invited the whole class, friends, and family to my place. I love hosting huge parties!
D. We've been celebrating my kid's birthday all week, but the BIG party will be at the hottest spot in town!

Your babysitter canceled last minute and you have an important event to attend. What do you do?

A. Cancel your plans and stay in.
B. Frantically search for a backup babysitter, no matter how much it costs.
C. Call your parents and beg them to watch your kid.
D. Still go to your event but bring your kid with you.

If You Got Mostly A's:

You'll be the hot mess mom. There's no better way to describe you than a complete hot mess! But that's okay—we can't all have our shit together all the time! Plus, you'll love your kiddos more than life itself and that's all that matters. You keep doing you!

If You Got Mostly B's:

You'll be the helicopter mom. You'll love your kids so much and just want the very best for them. Sometimes people will think you overreact, but that is just your way of making sure your kids are safe, happy, and healthy. Keep up the great work, Mom!

If You Got Mostly C's:

You'll be the cool mom. Put those shades on and own it, Momma! You will be ~the coolest~. Every kid will wish they had you as a mom. You'll throw cool parties, you'll have the best snacks, and you'll always be up for something fun!

If You Got Mostly D's:

You'll be the Pinterest mom. You *go*, Mom! Most moms will be envious of how easy you'll make things look. You'll be super talented and creative when it comes to motherhood. You will always have the cutest decorations, parties, and snacks! Everyone will want to be *you*!

Chocolate vs. Cheese Bracket

Pick your favorite contender from each pairing on the left and right.
An item that's not selected gets eliminated. The winner takes on the winning item from
the next pairing and so on until you have one final winner. You can fill out as you go,
snap a pic and share online, and compare your results with friends.

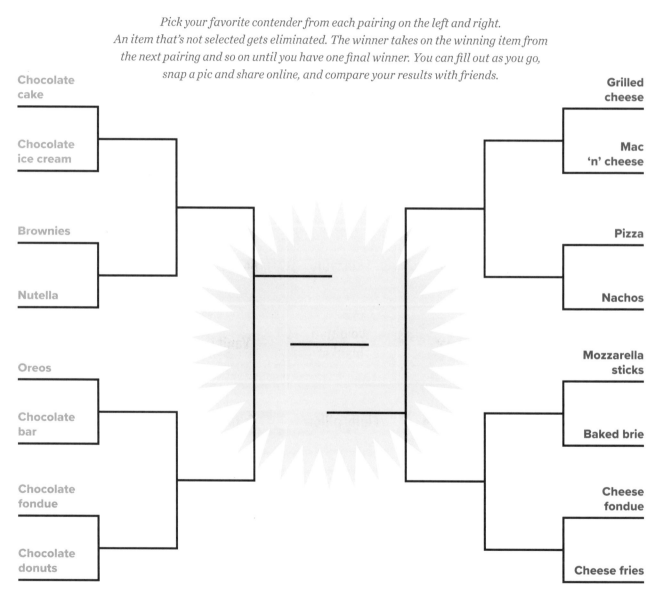

Chocolate cake

Chocolate ice cream

Brownies

Nutella

Oreos

Chocolate bar

Chocolate fondue

Chocolate donuts

Grilled cheese

Mac 'n' cheese

Pizza

Nachos

Mozzarella sticks

Baked brie

Cheese fondue

Cheese fries

Decorate Your Room for $200

Circle the items you want to purchase. The goal is to try not to go over your budget.

$100	Bed Frame	Headboard	Dresser	Accent chair
$80	Clothing rack	Side table	Bookcase	Projector
$60	Duvet	Weighted blanket	Vanity	Wallpaper
$40	Neon sign	Fluffy pillow	Curtains	Makeup mirror
$20	Succulent	Fuzzy slippers	Giant stuffed animal	Fairy Lights

Which language is the best to curse in?

A. Spanish
B. German
C. Chinese
D. Italian
E. Arabic
F. French

Which word makes you cringe the most?

A. Expulsion
B. Chunk
C. Pus
D. Discharge
E. Moist
F. Panties

Which '90s phrase needs to make a comeback?

A. Don't even go there
B. You go girl!
C. You're the bomb diggity
D. Kewl beans
E. As if!
F. Then why don't you marry it?

Can We Guess Your Age Based on the Words You Use?

What's your favorite swear word?

A. Fuck
B. Shit
C. Goddamnit
D. Bloody hell
E. Wanker
F. Bollocks

Pick a word that sounds nasty but actually isn't:

A. Sexagesm
B. Tit-tyrant
C. Clatterfart
D. Fartlek
E. Shittah
F. Jaculate

What's your biggest pet peeve when it comes to grammar?

A. Double negatives
B. "Literally" used figuratively
C. Your/you're
D. The misuse of there, their, and they're
E. Comma splices
F. Incorrect use of apostrophes

What would be harder to give up—cursing or cookies?

A. Cursing
B. Cookies

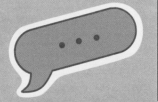

If You Got Mostly A's:

You're 19! You're a teen dream and totally hip. You're up-to-date on all the current slang, hashtags, and abbreviations no matter what.

If You Got Mostly B's:

You're 39! You're at the point in your life where your slang and word usage is a little dated but that doesn't bother you one bit. You're established and educated but still relish the good old days. Over time, you are becoming a total language master.

If You Got Mostly C's:

You're 31! You are full of life and are pretty much an expert on adulthood. You pick up slang here and there, but mostly stick to what works. Your linguistic skills are growing right along with your maturity.

If You Got Mostly D's:

You're 45! You are mature and the words you use reflect that. You are sophisticated and don't curse as much as you used to. You are self-assured and know what you like. You're set in your speech and wouldn't have it any other way.

If You Got Mostly E's:

You're 25! You're young, focused, and on the way to hitting your peak. You keep up with what's cool, but still use a lot of slang from your youth. You're at the right place where you have a good vocab, but you stay on top of what's in.

If You Got Mostly F's:

You're 61! You're wise and intelligent and have truly seen it all. You know language like the back of your hand and balk at the weirdness of new stuff. You know that words can change, but your awesome self never will.

What's Your Hard-Boiled Detective Name?

MONTH YOU WERE BORN

January: Murder

February: Quicksilver

March: Grizzled

April: Tiny

May: Blazing

June: Easy

July: Busy-body

August: Spooky

September: Baby

October: Broken

November: Last

December: Grim

THE FIRST LETTER OF THE NAME OF THE LAST DAME WHO BROKE YOUR HEART

A: Griswald

B: Garbanzo

C: Archer

D: Noir

E: Fatale

F: Daggers

G: Grasky

H: Pistol

I: Irene

J: Hammer

K: Bones

L: Steve

M: Commons

N: Pavement

O: Gun

P: Gray

Q: Night

R: Spade

S: Law

T: Betty

U: Underworld

V: Slasher

W: Scar

X: Dappler

Y: Scorn

Z: Buzz

Can You Answer All These Questions about Your Best Friend?

Check everything you know about your friend. No cheating!

- [ ] The *full* name of everyone they've dated
- [ ] The *full* name of everyone they've slept with
- [ ] The song that will get them on the dance floor every time
- [ ] The movie that will make them cry every time
- [ ] Where they wanna go on their dream vacation
- [ ] The food they are totally disgusted by
- [ ] Both of their parents' first names
- [ ] The name they have picked out for their kid
- [ ] Their middle name
- [ ] Their first childhood celebrity crush
- [ ] Their current #1 celebrity crush

- [ ] If they snore
- [ ] What size pants they wear
- [ ] What size shoes they wear
- [ ] The one piece of clothing they'd save from a fire
- [ ] What their go-to drink is
- [ ] Which drink makes them feel *most* hungover the next day
- [ ] What kind of drunk they are (happy, weepy, loud, etc.)
- [ ] Their most embarrassing moment
- [ ] Which of your other friends they secretly find annoying
- [ ] What time they went to bed last night
- [ ] What time they woke up this morning

- [ ] What they look like naked
- [ ] Their birthday (month, date, and year)
- [ ] Their birthday (month, date, year, and *time of day*)
- [ ] The most recent thing they've Instagrammed
- [ ] Their dream job
- [ ] Their favorite emoji
- [ ] Their current Facebook profile picture
- [ ] The book they've read the most times

If You Checked 0–14:
You're not friends. Oops, y'all thought you were friends, but something does *not* add up.

If You Checked 15–23:
You're friends, but not that tight. You hang out and all, but you're just not as ride-or-die as you thought. Sorry!

If You Checked 24–30:
You're legit best friends. Wow, you *definitely* know your best friend. Props all around for an A+ friendship.

Here's Your Celebrity Soul Mate Based on Your Star Sign: Guys Edition

Pick your sign.

ARIES

CHRIS EVANS (GEMINI)
You're a very charismatic, loving, and passionate person who is constantly on the lookout for your next exciting adventure. And you expect no less from any guy you're interested in. But you also want a man who can deal with your dominant personality and puts you first. And, of course, you love nothing more than putting them first, too. This makes Chris Evans, a Gemini, the ideal adventure-seeking, amorous, and loyal guy for your personality.

CANCER

CHRIS PINE (VIRGO)
While you tend to be someone who is very loyal, loving, romantic, and emotional, that isn't necessarily what you look for in a guy—nope, what you're looking for is someone who can match your intensity. This makes Chris Pine, a Virgo, the reliable and loyal guy who perfectly matches you and will balance out (i.e., hold their own) against your intense personality.

TAURUS

KIT HARRINGTON (CAPRICORN)
You tend to be a quintessential romantic, who is also very chill, and cherishes nothing more than being around loved ones—and these are some of the same qualities you look for in a guy, which makes Kit Harrington, a Capricorn, the perfect chill, sensitive, and romantic guy to connect with your personality on a deep, emotional level.

LEO

RIZ AHMED (SAGITTARIUS)
You're a confident, charismatic, and passionate person, who also happens to have a bit of an adventurous side. But what really makes you YOU is that you don't ever like to settle for second best—you're a natural leader who is full of ambition and drive, which makes Riz Ahmed, a dynamic, excitement-seeking, ambitious Sagittarius, the best match for your personality. And someone who will always bring out the best in you!

GEMINI

JASON MOMOA (LEO)
You're an outgoing, charismatic, and affectionate person with a fun-loving outlook on life. And you tend to look for similar traits in a guy. This makes Jason Momoa, a Leo, the perfect optimistic, playful, and warm-hearted guy to match your personality.

VIRGO

RYAN GOSLING (SCORPIO)
You tend to be very methodical, a little reserved, and fiercely independent when it comes to love. But these aren't necessarily the traits you look for in a guy. What you want is someone who is intensely passionate and is devoted to you, which makes Ryan Gosling, a Scorpio, the perfect profound match for your personality.

LIBRA

CHRIS HEMSWORTH (LEO)

You're all about having peace of mind and happiness in your life, which, of course, also includes your love life. Your ideal guy not only needs to be as charming and as positive as you, but also self-confident. This makes Chris Hemsworth, a Leo, the perfect optimistic, self-assured, magnetic match for your personality.

CAPRICORN

NICK JONAS (VIRGO)

While you tend to be a little more sensible when it comes to life, it doesn't mean that you're boring. In fact, it's the opposite—you're just someone who likes to do things on your own terms. And this is something any guy you're interested in needs to understand, because, hey, you're worth it. This makes Nick Jonas, a practical, loving, and easygoing Virgo, the best match for your personality.

SCORPIO

OSCAR ISAAC (PISCES)

You're a very strong-willed, deeply intense, and passionate person who tends to always be there for those you love. And what you look for most in a guy is someone who is down-to-earth, loyal, and can match (or at least appreciate) your intensity, which makes Oscar Isaac, a Pisces, the ideal down-to-earth, sensitive, and deeply loyal guy who will balance your personality perfectly.

AQUARIUS

DONALD GLOVER (LIBRA)

Okay, so you probably already know this, but you tend to have more than a little bit of an independent streak (which is a good thing), but that doesn't mean that you want to be alone—you're just looking for a guy who is not only loyal but also like-minded, who will recognize you for the fabulous person you are. This makes Donald Glover, a Libra, the perfect peaceful balance to your personality.

SAGITTARIUS

MICHAEL B. JORDAN (AQUARIUS)

You're an awesome mix of enthusiasm, cleverness, and positivity, who also loves nothing more than to stop everything at the drop of a hat so that you can seek out an adventure. What you look for in a guy is someone who can keep up with your spontaneity and won't hold you back. This makes Michael B. Jordan, an Aquarius, the perfect optimistic, impulsive guy to match your personality.

PISCES

HENRY CAVILL (TAURUS)

You're a very loving and loyal person and, at heart, a deep-down romantic. While you seek guys who share those qualities, you also look for them to be dependable and down-to-earth, and to understand that sometimes you can be sensitive and feel misunderstood. This makes Henry Cavill, a Taurus, the ideal stable, easygoing guy to match your personality.

Order a Bougie Meal and We'll Reveal What Percent Marriage Material You Are

Good evening. Can I get you some sparkling water, or is tap okay?

A. I'll take sparkling water

B. Tap's fine, thank you

Anything to drink?

A. A beer

B. A nice cocktail

C. A cider

D. A bottle of red for the table

E. A bottle of white for the table

F. Just water

Can I start you off with some appetizers?

A. Baked Camembert with honey and crostini

B. Oysters

C. Bruschetta

D. Cheese and charcuterie board

E. Arancini

F. Smoked salmon blini topped with caviar

Anything else?

A. Baked Camembert with honey and crostini

B. Oysters

C. Bruschetta

D. Cheese and charcuterie board

E. Arancini

F. Smoked salmon blini topped with caviar

Can I get you a refill?

A. A beer

B. A nice cocktail

C. A cider

D. A bottle of red for the table

E. A bottle of white for the table

F. Just water

And what will you be having for the main?

A. Filet mignon

B. Risotto with shaved black truffle

C. Chicken breast

D. Linguine with pesto

E. Rack of lamb

F. Lobster

Would you like some dessert this evening?

A. Tiramisu

B. Crêpes

C. Chocolate cake

D. Raspberry tart

E. Sorbet

F. Just the check, please

What are you tipping?

A. 5 percent

B. 10 percent

C. 15 percent

D. 20 percent

E. 25 percent

F. More than 25 percent

If You Got Mostly A's:
You're 12% marriage material.
Marriage is the last thing on your mind. You're currently looking out for numero uno!

If You Got Mostly B's:
You're 91% marriage material. You've got the right stuff alright! If you haven't already, you're going to make one lucky person very happy someday.

If You Got Mostly C's:
You're 69% marriage material. Your marriage-material percentage can best be described as "nice."

If You Got Mostly D's:
You're 47% marriage material.
You're, like, down to get married or whatever . . . just not right now. You've got a lot of living to do before then.

If You Got Mostly E's:
You're 73% marriage material.
You're marriage material, but your spouse's uncle will hate you or something.

If You Got Mostly F's:
You're 100% marriage material.
You're what's called in the marriage biz "a steal."

What's Your Hogwarts House?

Start in the center and make your way out of the maze to find out which Hogwarts house you belong in.

RAVENCLAW

GRYFFINDOR

SLYTHERIN

HUFFLEPUFF

Instagram Bingo

Check off or mark the squares that apply to you (things you own, have done, or things that have happened to you). The more you fill out, the more you're obsessed with Instagram! See if you can get five across, down, or diagonally. Then snap a picture and upload online to share your results!

Posted a selfie	Posted a food picture	Been tagged in a picture and a story	Saw a picture of a dog	Posted a candid
Commented on a celebrity's pic	Been guilty of posting a *waaaaay* too long story (over ten bars)	Blocked someone	Followed a recipe account	Accidentally liked someone's picture while you were stalking them
Posted a thirst trap	Got more than ten likes on a picture	**Free Space**	Made a boomerang	Got a DM from a stranger
Liked a picture	Has more than 150 followers	Has entered an IG giveaway	Posted a mirror pic	Posted pictures of your vacation with the sole intention to make people jealous
Won an IG giveaway	Followed a celebrity	Posted an inspirational quote	Has a Finsta	Has story highlights on your profile

This or That: Breakfast Edition

Bacon   or   Sausage?

Cereal   or   Oatmeal?

OJ   or   Apple juice?

Coffee   or   Tea?

English muffin   or   Crumpet?

Scrambled eggs   or   Sunny side up?

Toast with butter   or   Toast with hazelnut spread?

Bagel toasted   or   Bagel untoasted?

Crêpes   or   Pancakes?

Biscuits   or   Biscuits and jam?

Breakfast burrito   or   Breakfast taco?

Croissant   or   Bear claw?

Hash browns   or   Home fries?

Energy bar   or   Nothing?

We Know Your Exact Age by How Many of These Kids' Shows You've Seen

Check off all the TV shows that you've seen at least one full episode of!

- [ ] Blue's Clues
- [ ] Drake & Josh
- [ ] Kim Possible
- [ ] SpongeBob SquarePants
- [ ] Phil of the Future
- [ ] Dora the Explorer
- [ ] Go, Diego, Go!
- [ ] Rolie Polie Olie
- [ ] Maggie and the Ferocious Beast
- [ ] Zooboomafoo

- [ ] Little Bill
- [ ] Brandy and Mr. Whiskers
- [ ] Angelina Ballerina
- [ ] Rugrats
- [ ] Courage the Cowardly Dog
- [ ] The Grim Adventures of Billy and Mandy
- [ ] Dragon Tales
- [ ] Sesame Street
- [ ] Clifford
- [ ] Bob the Builder

- [ ] Maya and Miguel
- [ ] CatDog
- [ ] Ed, Edd 'n Eddy
- [ ] Dave the Barbarian
- [ ] Jay Jay the Jet Plane
- [ ] Lazy Town
- [ ] The Fairly OddParents
- [ ] Jimmy Neutron
- [ ] Danny Phantom
- [ ] Arthur

Continues on next page

- ☐ The Wild Thornberrys
- ☐ The Suite Life of Zack and Cody
- ☐ The Berenstain Bears
- ☐ Fetch! with Ruff Ruffman
- ☐ Teen Titans
- ☐ Buzz Lightyear of Star Command
- ☐ Recess
- ☐ House of Mouse
- ☐ Lilo and Stitch: The Series
- ☐ The Proud Family
- ☐ American Dragon: Jake Long
- ☐ Avatar: The Last Airbender
- ☐ Ben 10
- ☐ Ben 10

- ☐ iCarly
- ☐ Wizards of Waverly Place
- ☐ Dexter's Laboratory
- ☐ Duck Dodgers
- ☐ Foster's Home for Imaginary Friends
- ☐ Hey Arnold!
- ☐ Johnny Bravo
- ☐ My Life as a Teenage Robot
- ☐ Phineas and Ferb
- ☐ The Emperor's New School
- ☐ Samurai Jack
- ☐ Totally Spies
- ☐ What's New, Scooby Doo?
- ☐ Bear in the Big Blue House

- ☐ The Wiggles
- ☐ The Book of Pooh
- ☐ PB&J Otter
- ☐ Madeline
- ☐ Stanley
- ☐ JoJo's Circus
- ☐ Little Einsteins
- ☐ The Legend of Tarzan
- ☐ Life with Derek
- ☐ That's So Raven
- ☐ Cory in the House
- ☐ Hannah Montana
- ☐ Jonas
- ☐ As the Bell Rings

- ☐ Victorious
- ☐ Good Luck Charlie
- ☐ Shake It Up
- ☐ ANT Farm
- ☐ Jessie
- ☐ Rocket Power
- ☐ Austin & Ally
- ☐ As Told by Ginger
- ☐ All Grown Up
- ☐ My Dad the Rock Star
- ☐ The Amanda Show
- ☐ Franklin
- ☐ Teletubbies
- ☐ Wonder Pets

- ☐ The Backyardigans
- ☐ Pokémon
- ☐ 6Teen
- ☐ Baby Looney Tunes
- ☐ The Magic School Bus
- ☐ Elmo's World
- ☐ Sabrina: The Animated Series
- ☐ VeggieTales
- ☐ Yo Gabba Gabba
- ☐ Out of the Box
- ☐ Lizzie McGuire
- ☐ Unfabulous
- ☐ Even Stevens
- ☐ Sister, Sister

If You Checked 0–20:
You're 54! Your kids were too old to watch them, so you didn't watch them either. You missed out on some classics!

If You Checked 21–40:
You're 72! You haven't seen that many of these shows, but the ones you have seen were because you were watching them with your kids or grandkids. You've definitely seen enough to appreciate them!

If You Checked 41–60:
You're 36! You saw some of these shows, but you were too grown-up to see a good chunk of them. That's okay. They've got to be on streaming services somewhere!

If You Checked 61–80:
You're 16! You watched a lot of these shows on the tail ends of their runs or through reruns. You're just lucky that most of these were still on TV while you were growing up!

If You Checked 81–100:
You're 25! You grew up right in the middle of all these shows. You either caught the beginning of the series, the end of it, or you watched a new episode every week. That means you're twenty-five. There's no other explanation!

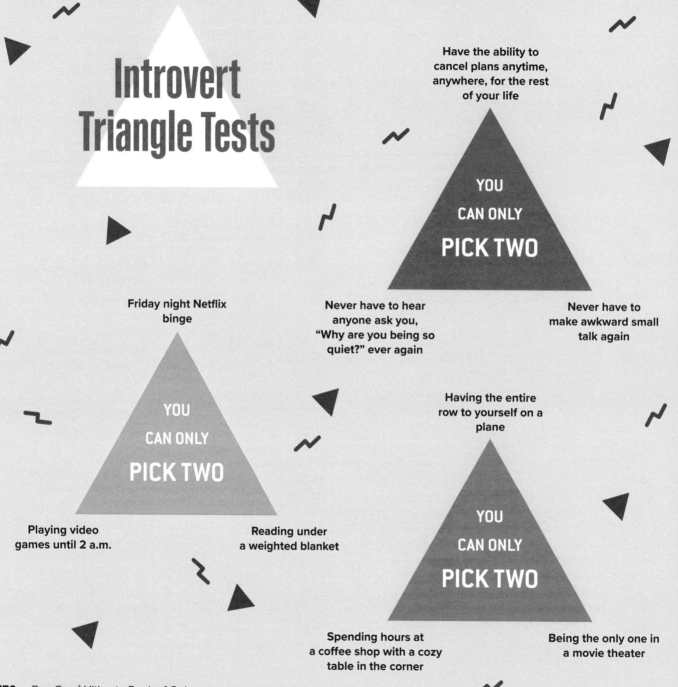

Introvert Triangle Tests

Have the ability to cancel plans anytime, anywhere, for the rest of your life

YOU CAN ONLY PICK TWO

Never have to hear anyone ask you, "Why are you being so quiet?" ever again

Never have to make awkward small talk again

Friday night Netflix binge

YOU CAN ONLY PICK TWO

Playing video games until 2 a.m.

Reading under a weighted blanket

Having the entire row to yourself on a plane

YOU CAN ONLY PICK TWO

Spending hours at a coffee shop with a cozy table in the corner

Being the only one in a movie theater

Let Us Determine Your True Personality

Step 1: Close your eyes and think of a number 2–10
Step 2: Subtract 1 from that number
Step 3: Pick your number below

1 CREATIVE
You are super creative. Whether it's visually or through problem solving, you have an ability to create ideas and find solutions like no one else. If you were trapped in a cage and someone gave you a shoe, a banana, and a paper clip, you could probably figure a way out within minutes.

2 BREEZY
You love warm weather and going to the beach. You know how to relax and stay calm even in crazy situations. People love spending time with you because of your warm and breezy personality.

3 COMPASSIONATE
You are very in touch with people's feelings. You are compassionate, spiritual, and probably a vegetarian (or at least tried to be at some point in your life). You enjoy hikes, hot tea, and a good book. You like both cats and dogs equally.

4 FIERCE
You are calm, cool, and collected, and altogether that makes you one of the fiercest people around. You have a great sense of style—not only in fashion but with home decor. You either have a pet cat or have had one before.

5 RATIONAL
You're very down-to-earth and rational. People respect your opinions and love going to you for advice because of your thoughtful nature. You're very even-keeled and sometimes worry that this makes you boring. But fear not—you are definitely not boring! Also, you like dogs more than cats.

6 DEEP
Your rivers run very deep. You have strong feelings about society and politics. You love loud music and aren't scared to rock out hard at a concert. Your friends are like your family. You're loyal, strong, and resilient.

7 AMBIVERT
You can be equally as shy as you are outgoing, depending on the situation. While you sometimes enjoy socializing, you need time alone in between to recharge or you get worn out. You love binge watching TV shows alone or maybe with one other person.

8 VERY INTELLIGENT
You are extremely intelligent. Whether it's book smart or street smart, you're quick as a whip. You love puzzles, brain teasers, and solving real-life problems. You love solving friends' problems with great advice. With all your brain activity, try not to overthink things.

9 LOYAL
You take being loyal to new levels. Whether it's standing up for family, old friends, or someone you just met and think is great, you're not afraid of anyone or anything. You make an amazing friend because people can always count on you.

We Know Your Relationship Status Based on What You'd Cook for Date Night

Make a pre-dinner app:

A. Bruschetta
B. Cheese plate
C. Guacamole
D. Baked brie
E. Bacon-wrapped dates
F. Um, wine?

What are you two drinking?

A. Margaritas
B. Beer
C. Champagne
D. Coffee
E. Wine
F. Tequila shots

Dinnertime. What are you making for the first course?

A. Caprese salad
B. Grilled vegetables
C. Butternut squash soup
D. Seared scallops
E. Stuffed mushrooms
F. Uh, what's the first course?

What about the main course?

A. Mushroom risotto
B. Steak
C. Lobster
D. Ravioli
E. Lamb chops
F. We're ordering pizza

Finally, what's for dessert?

A. Chocolate-covered strawberries
B. Chocolate soufflé
C. Lemon squares
D. Red velvet cupcakes
E. Ice cream sundaes
F. We're skipping dessert . . .

If You Got Mostly A's:

You're dating up a storm. You have just about every dating app on your phone and you're having the time of your life meeting new people. You're definitely not looking to settle down quite yet.

If You Got Mostly B's:

You're seeing someone, but it's still casual. Sure, you've been seeing the same person for a few weeks or even a few months by now, but it's still totally casual. Maybe one day it'll turn into something more serious, but for now you're just having a good time and taking it slow.

If You Got Mostly C's:

Things are starting to get serious. It's written all over your face: You're in a serious relationship. You've been dating for a few months now, and there's no mistaking you're both in deep. Soon enough you'll be meeting each other's parents, if you haven't already.

If You Got Mostly D's:

You've found the one. There's no denying that you've finally found the person you want to spend your life with. You feel completely comfortable around each other, you make each other laugh—heck, you're pretty much finishing one another's sentences. You're totally in lurve and everyone can tell.

If You Got Mostly E's:

You're married (or basically married). If you haven't officially tied the knot, you might as well. After all, your partner is your best friend who basically knows you better than you know yourself. At this point, you're totally cool keeping things casual every once in a while, like staying in on a Friday night or skipping the fancy Valentine's Day reservation in favor of a cozy night in.

If You Got Mostly F's:

You're single and loving it. You're living the single life and you're crushing it. You don't need anyone to tie you down. You're free to be spontaneous and put yourself first, and that's pretty great.

Can You Ace This AP English Test for 11th Graders?

1. **Which of the following is NOT an oxymoron?**

   A. Breaking news
   B. Definite maybe
   C. Deafening silence
   D. Good grief

2. **What is a rhetorical appeal to the audience's emotions called?**

   A. Ethos
   B. Logos
   C. Pathos

3. **The emotional meaning of a word is its:**

   A. Connotation
   B. Denotation

4. **This is an example of which rhetorical device: "From forth the fatal loins of these two foes"**

   A. Cacophony
   B. Onomatopoeia
   C. Simile
   D. Alliteration

5. **Which logical fallacy is "an attack on an opponent's character, rather than an answer to the contentions made"?**

   A. Post hoc
   B. Non sequitur
   C. Ad hominem
   D. Slippery slope

6. **The "repetition of a word or words at the beginning of successive phrases, clauses, or lines to create a sonic effect" is called:**

   A. Polysyndeton
   B. Anaphora
   C. Metaphor
   D. Synecdoche

7. **The headline "White House announces tariffs on US allies" is an example of:**

   A. Synecdoche
   B. Juxtaposition
   C. Simile
   D. Syllogism

8. Jonathan Swift's "A Modest Proposal," in which he suggests that poor people sell their children as food for the rich, is an example of:

A. Irony
B. Satire
C. Sarcasm

9. "You held your breath and the door for me" is an example of:

A. Hyperbole
B. Allusion
C. Zeugma
D. Asyndeton

10. "The addressing of a usually absent person or a usually personified thing rhetorically" is called:

A. Euphemism
B. Aphorism
C. Simile
D. Apostrophe

1.A; 2.C; 3.A; 4.D; 5.C; 6.B; 7.A; 8.B; 9.C; 10.D

NOW ADD UP YOUR SCORE!

If You Got 0–1 Correct:
You got a 1 on the AP English Language and Composition Exam! Try harder!

If You Got 2–3 Correct:
You got a 2 on the AP English Language and Composition Exam! Okay!

If You Got 4–5 Correct:
You got a 3 on the AP English Language and Composition Exam! Nice!

If You Got 6–7 Correct:
You got a 4 on the AP English Language and Composition Exam! Heck yeah!

If You Got 8–10 Correct:
You got a 5 on the AP English Language and Composition Exam! Get that college credit!

Choose a topic to text your best friend about:

A. Fashion advice
B. Your love life
C. Venting about what happened at work today
D. How your roommates haven't done their dishes in *five* days
E. General catching up and shooting the shit
F. Family drama

When was the last time you and your best friend saw each other in person?

A. Literally right now
B. Within the past week
C. Within the past month
D. 2–5 months
E. 6–11 months
F. 1+ year

This Quiz Will Reveal How Long You and Your BFF Have Known Each Other

Have you met your best friend's family?

A. Yes
B. No
C. Does over FaceTime count?
D. Just the siblings

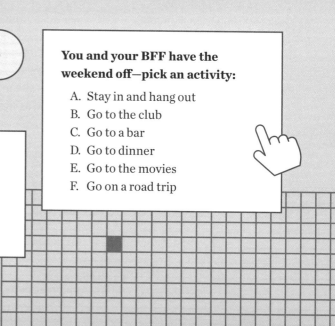

You and your BFF have the weekend off—pick an activity:

A. Stay in and hang out
B. Go to the club
C. Go to a bar
D. Go to dinner
E. Go to the movies
F. Go on a road trip

Has your best friend met your family?

A. Yes
B. No
C. Does over FaceTime count?
D. Just the siblings

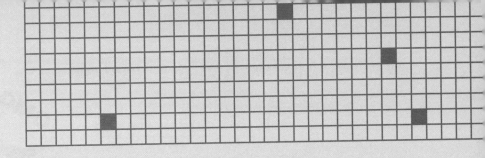

If You Got Mostly A's:

You've known each other for eight years. While some friendships have falling-outs or fade away, yours has been going strong for quite some time, and that won't be changing anytime soon!

If You Got Mostly B's:

You met within the last year. Your connection may be new and blossoming, but it's off to a great start! While you're still learning things about each other's interests, pet peeves, and lives in general, enjoy going on this magnificent journey of friendship together!

If You Got Mostly C's:

You've known each other for two years. Sure, you may not have the lengthy connection that lifelong best friends have, but two years is plenty of time to get to know a person very well! You're in the early years of something special that just might lead to two best friends remaining close as they grow old together!

If You Got Mostly D's:

You've known each other for four years. You are part of a long-running friendship that's growing increasingly comfortable with each passing day! It's obviously something special if the two of you have gone this long without getting sick of each other, so buckle up and enjoy this glorious ride known as friendship for the next several years to come!

If You Got Mostly E's:

You've known each other since you were babies. You can't even remember when the two of you met because you were too young, but you and your best friend have known each other since you were in diapers! You may have your own lives now, but you're practically family and you can pick up right where you left off without a hiccup.

If You Got Mostly F's:

You've known each other for fifteen years. You and your best friend have known each other for so long that at this point you can assume your friendship will last for a lifetime. You may not get to spend time or talk as often as you once did, but that's the beauty of knowing someone for so long. Many things may change, but your friendship remains a connection you can always count on!

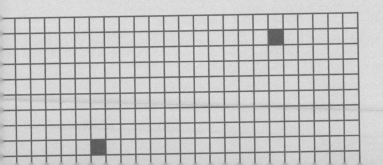

Twilight Characters Word Scramble

DWRAED LUNCEL _____

LABEL AWNS _____

OJABC CLBAK _____

ELIAC ENLUCL _____

SEPAJR AEHL _____

LASEICLR ENCLUL _____

SELOARI ELHA _____

MEES UNLCLE _____

REATLUN _____

LAIERCH NSAW _____

METEMT NLCEUL _____

OAR _____

SCEIJAS NYSELTA _____

LYBLI LKACB _____

MESAJ _____

KEMI WONTNE _____

EEMREENS ELULNC _____

MSA YULE _____

NEAJ _____

HETS WEALTRCARE _____

ORITVICA _____

ALEH ARWECARTLE _____

ERBE ENTRAN _____

USIAC _____

ANSWER KEY

This or That: Condiments

Buffalo sauce   or   Tabasco sauce?

Blue cheese   or   ranch?

Russian   or   thousand island?

Ketchup   or   mustard?

Tartar sauce   or   mayo?

Sriracha   or   chipotle?

Soy sauce   or   wasabi mayo?

BBQ sauce   or   steak sauce?

Maple syrup   or   honey?

Sweet 'n' sour   or   honey mustard?

Tell Us What You're Eating Today and We'll Tell You Where You Should Travel

What are you having for breakfast?

A. Pancakes
B. Yogurt parfait
C. Eggs and bacon
D. Eggs benedict
E. Bagel
F. Croissant

Pick a morning drink:

A. Kale smoothie
B. Espresso
C. Mimosa
D. Cold brew coffee
E. Lemon water
F. Tea

Noon already? What's for lunch?

A. A big salad
B. Pizza
C. Club sandwich
D. Tacos
E. Ramen
F. Lobster roll

You're craving an afternoon snack. What is it?

A. Cheese plate
B. Frozen yogurt
C. Hummus and veggies
D. Chips and guac
E. Pigs in a blanket
F. Kale chips

It's happy hour! What's in your glass?

A. Dirty martini
B. Gin and tonic
C. Sangria
D. White wine
E. Lemonade
F. Ice cold beer

Dinner time. Whatcha ordering?

A. Gourmet burger
B. Lasagna
C. Paella
D. Fried chicken
E. Sushi
F. Linguine with clams

How about some dessert?

A. Tiramisu
B. Ice cream trio
C. Chocolate soufflé
D. Donuts
E. Cheese plate
F. Berry tart

It's 2 a.m. and you're starving. Pick a late-night meal:

A. Poutine
B. Churros and chocolate
C. Pizza
D. Omelet
E. Nachos
F. Mac 'n' cheese

If You Got Mostly A's:

You got France! Ahhh, France. Just imagine the grand boulevards of Paris, the lavender fields of Provence, the renowned wine regions of Burgundy and Bordeaux, and the shimmering coastline of the Côte d'Azur. Prepare to feast on wine and cheese, steak frites, duck magret, escargot, and foie gras in one of the most incredible culinary destinations in the world.

If You Got Mostly B's:

You got California! California, here we come. Whether you visit the quaint towns of Sonoma dotted with wine-tasting rooms, the hilly city of San Francisco, the rugged Big Sur coast, or sunny Los Angeles, you'll find both farm-to-table California cuisine and incredible ethnic food, from burritos to Korean BBQ and everything in between.

If You Got Mostly C's:

You got Argentina! In Argentina you have your pick from the vineyard-clad mountains of Mendoza, the cosmopolitan city of Buenos Aires, and the pristine wilderness of Patagonia. Melt-in-your-mouth Argentinian beef, deep and spicy red wine, and, perhaps surprisingly, some of the best Italian food outside of Italy await you.

If You Got Mostly D's:

You got Australia! There's something for everyone in Australia. Between Sydney, where urban life meets laid-back beach town; Melbourne, a big city with a relaxed vibe; Queensland, with its sandy beaches and coral reefs; and Southern Australia, home to the country's acclaimed wine regions. Plus, Australia has a booming food scene. Breakfast—or ~brekkie~—is not just a start to the day but a way of life, filled with açai bowls and avocado toast. And given Australia's diverse population, you'll find local ingredients get an exotic, creative kick.

If You Got Mostly E's:

You got Japan! Whether you're seeking a bustling metropolis like Tokyo or a more serene city like Kyoto, dotted with gardens and shrines, you'll find the perfect vacation in Japan. Sushi is like an edible art form there, but you'll find more than raw fish. Japan is home to the best ramen, tempura, and comforting Izakaya cuisine you'll ever try.

If You Got Mostly F's:

You got Italy! You have tons of places to choose from in this gorgeous country, from the ancient city of Rome to the rolling vineyards of Tuscany to the storybook cliffs of the Amalfi Coast. But wherever you go, bring an empty stomach and prepare to indulge in all the pizza, pasta, and gelato your heart desires.

What do you typically do on Saturday afternoons?

A. Brunch
B. Uh, I'm still in bed
C. At the gym
D. My to-do list
E. At work
F. With friends

What Kind of Adult Are You?

Which meal sounds the most like your typical dinner?

A. Chick-fil-A
B. Whatever I feel like having delivered
C. Blue Apron
D. Steak and veggies
E. Leftover pizza
F. Whatever microwave dinner is in my freezer

Pick a TV show you'd watch after coming home from work:

A. *The Bachelor*
B. *Parks and Rec*
C. *Fresh Off the Boat*
D. *Scandal*
E. *Law & Order: SVU*
F. *Orange Is the New Black*

You have to be up at 7 a.m. tomorrow. What time will you probably go to bed the night before?

A. 11 p.m.
B. 10:30 p.m.
C. 9 p.m.
D. 8 p.m.
E. 12 a.m. (or later)
F. When I feel like it

If You Got Mostly A's:

You're the imposter adult. Yes, you're TECHNICALLY an adult, but you honestly don't feel 100 percent like one. You have a real job but sometimes still show up to work on Monday hungover. You yell *shit* more often than not for overdrafting your bank account, and you'll wear something even if it should have been washed weeks ago. It's not that you don't care—it's that you'd truly rather spend time and effort doing other things, like live-snapping *The Bachelor* with all your friends.

If You Got Mostly B's:

You're the super carefree adult. You're a pretty mellow, chill, and typically worry-free person. The small hiccups of life don't really give you a reason to freak out. You know things will balance out eventually. You're also someone who typically says yes to new adventures—whether that's trying a new place to eat or exploring a foreign country. You roll with the punches and usually learn a lot along the way.

If You Got Mostly C's:

You're the independent-as-hell adult. You're a pretty self-sufficient person who genuinely doesn't mind doing things alone. Going to a concert and no one can come? Eh, you'll go by yourself—maybe even make some friends! If you don't know how to do something—like jump your car— you're pretty good at figuring it out without help. But while you're fine doing things on your own, you still love being around the people you care about.

If You Got Mostly D's:

You're the old soul adult. You are your age plus ten years—at least that's what people tell you. Levelheaded, mostly responsible, and reliable, you tend to be the parent of your friend group—but that isn't necessarily a bad thing. You'll go out of your way to make sure your friends are hydrating after a long night of drinking, and you always have a piece of gum, charger, *whatever* handy. You're sensitive and caring and your heart is always in the right place. You have a knack for always knowing what to say and giving the advice your friends need.

If You Got Mostly E's:

You're the big dreamer adult. You're passionate, hardworking, and idealistic when it comes to your goals and what you really want. Chances are you're striving toward something creative and fulfilling, but it's also not easy work. You're someone who sacrifices fun nights out to work toward your dream, but you also know when to live a little!

If You Got Mostly F's:

You're the messy adult. You're slightly impulsive, adventurous, and very go-with-the-flow, but your overall adult life is still kind of a mess. As in, most of your clothes are on that random chair you never use and not in your closet—and you're like WTF when it comes to taxes. You're also usually late to social gatherings, but whatever! At least you came. Sure, you can learn how to manage your money better, but you also know you'll get your shit together eventually.

The Hardest Game of Would You Rather for People in Their 20s

Would you rather

have the hangover recovery ability of your early twenties
OR have the furnace-like metabolism of your early twenties?

Would you rather

travel the world for a year right after college
OR have a guaranteed kick-ass job the second you graduate?

Would you rather

see nothing but your friend's engagement photos on your timeline forever
OR read the political opinions from people you went to high school
with forever?

Would you rather

live in an amazing place with terrible roommates
OR live by yourself in an absolute hellhole?

Would you rather

have an early-twenties body
OR have a late-twenties confidence?

Would you rather

go through your entire twenties with no cell phone
OR go through your entire twenties with no internet?

Would you rather

sleep on a twin bed for your entire twenties
OR only eat cafeteria food for your entire twenties?

Would you rather

have a house that's already paid for after college
OR have all your student loans forgiven?

Would you rather

get free, unlimited Starbucks for a year
OR get free iTunes forever?

Would you rather

have a bad relationship with good sex
OR have a great relationship with bad sex?

Would you rather

wear Forever 21 clothes forever
OR relive your twenty-first birthday every day for a year?

Would you rather

find true, permanent love in your early twenties
OR get a lump sum of $5 million and be alone forever?

Would you rather

have an entry-level job you love with terrible pay
OR have an entry-level job you hate with high pay?

Would you rather

have free Netflix, HBO Go, and Hulu accounts
OR only pay happy hour prices anywhere anytime?

Which Dunder Mifflin Employee from *The Office* Would Be Your Best Work Friend?

What would you make out of a piece of paper?

A. A threat to your enemies
B. A fortune-teller
C. Bubble letters
D. An airplane
E. A chain
F. A crumpled ball
G. A crane
H. A poster
I. A greeting card

Which office crime are you guilty of committing?

A. Leaving your belongings on your neighbor's desk
B. Gossiping by the water cooler
C. Coming to work with a contagious disease
D. Gchatting the person who sits next to you
E. "Borrowing" someone's salad dressing
F. Eating a stinky desk lunch
G. Listening to music without headphones
H. Leaving before finishing an assignment
I. Touching the thermostat

What do you keep in the work fridge?

A. A mysterious brown bag that says "do not touch"
B. French Vanilla Coffee-Mate
C. Your world-famous chili
D. Leftover Chinese
E. Salad dressing
F. Tomorrow's lunch
G. An emergency candy bar
H. Your personally labeled nondairy beverage
I. Fruit salad

How many hours of work do you actually get done a day?

A. A full eight—I even work through lunch
B. Six to seven-ish
C. Four probably
D. At least two
E. A solid half hour
F. LOL, none

What do you do right after work?

A. Cook dinner
B. Go on a date
C. Happy hour
D. Go out to dinner
E. Netflix and sweatpants
F. Call my parents
G. Work out
H. Run errands
I. That's private

Which emoticon do you Gchat the most?

A. -___-
B. <3
C. (.)(.)
D. ;)
E. xD
F. >:)

If You Got Mostly A's:
You got Dwight! Dwight would definitely be your work BFF, and together you'd be an unstoppable force that strikes fear into the hearts of your coworkers.

If You Got Mostly B's:
You got Kelly! Yes! Your work BFF is Kelly. She's always there with the hot office goss or to tell you that you look really hot in that button-down.

If You Got Mostly C's:
You got Kevin! The best part of being work BFFs with Kevin is that he always has extra M&M's. Also he's always down to—you know—not work hard, which means more time for friendship!

If You Got Mostly D's:
You got Jim! You and Jim would get into so many shenanigans together. Nothing passes the workday quite like elaborately pranking your coworkers!

If You Got Mostly E's:
You got Andy! As far as work buds go, you can't do much better than Andy Bernard. Just think: the two of you wasting time in the breakroom in perfect harmony.

If You Got Mostly F's:
You got Michael! Being best friends with the boss man certainly has its perks! Like having lunch at Hooters and never having to do any real work. You lucked out!

If You Got Mostly G's:
You got Ryan! Ryan's the kind of BFF who'll ask you to happy hour drinks and then keep you out until 4 a.m. But then the next day at work you get to stand around the watercooler talking about how the hangover was totally worth it. Work BFFs rule.

If You Got Mostly H's:
You got Pam! You and Pam would be total work buds. Whenever you're having a bad day, Pam draws you a doodle to cheer you up. You're so lucky to have her.

If You Got Mostly I's:
You got Angela! You know what really helps lower your stress level? Talking shit on all your coworkers with your BFF Angela in the supply closet. What else are friends for?

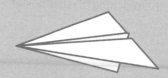

What's Your Cooking IQ?

Answer these questions to find out how much you know in the kitchen.

1. **How many teaspoons are in a tablespoon?**

   A. 2 teaspoons
   B. 3 teaspoons
   C. 4 teaspoons
   D. 5 teaspoons

2. **Which of these knives is the biggest?**

   A. Paring knife
   B. Cleaver
   C. Boning knife
   D. Tourne knife

3. **True or false: Sweet potatoes and yams are the same thing.**

   A. True
   B. False

4. **What is cornstarch mixed with a little bit of water called?**

   A. A roux
   B. A demi-glace
   C. A slurry
   D. A mignonette

5. **Which of these is not a fresh cheese?**

   A. Ricotta
   B. Cottage cheese
   C. Grana Padano
   D. Mascarpone

6. **Which of these ingredients is not typically in mirepoix?**

   A. Carrots
   B. Celery
   C. Garlic
   D. Onion

7. **What is it called to chop food, such as garlic, into very small pieces?**

   A. Zest
   B. Mince
   C. Julienne
   D. Chiffonade

8. **What does it mean to braise something?**

   A. To cook over direct heat
   B. To slowly cook in liquid at a low temperature
   C. To quickly cook something in a small amount of fat
   D. To briefly boil something to soften it, then transfer it into an ice bath

9. **What is a bouquet garni?**

A. A mixture of salad greens cut with fresh herbs
B. A bundle of herbs tied together with string
C. An old-school term for raw vegetables
D. The paper caps that cover the ends of roasted poultry

10. **What does it mean to fold something into a mixture?**

A. To gently incorporate a heavy ingredient into a light one, usually with a rubber spatula
B. To mix two things together with a whisk to incorporate air
C. To quickly add a cold ingredient to a hot one
D. To quickly add a hot ingredient to a cold one

ANSWER KEY

10. **A:** Folding is a stirring technique used to gently incorporate a heavy ingredient into a light one (such as chocolate into whipped egg whites).

9. **B:** A bouquet garni is a bundle of herbs tied together with string. They are usually steeped in a liquid to add flavor without actually adding the physical pieces of herbs to the dish.

8. **B:** Braising is a cooking technique where meat is slowly cooked in liquid at a low heat. This helps break down tough cuts of meat and results in that fall-off-the-bone texture.

7. **B:** Mincing is a knife cut much smaller (and more inconsistent) than a dice.

6. **C:** Garlic is not typically in mirepoix. Mirepoix is made with 50 percent onions, 25 percent carrots, and 25 percent celery.

5. **C:** Grana Padano is not a fresh cheese. The cheese (which is somewhat similar to Parmesan) is aged for about two years.

4. **C:** Cornstarch mixed with a little bit of water is called a slurry. It prevents the cornstarch from clumping up when added to something hot (like a sauce).

3. **B:** Although similar, sweet potatoes and yams are not the same thing. The common orange-fleshed potatoes you see in grocery stores are most likely sweet potatoes while yams are a starchy root vegetable that is less common.

2. **B:** A cleaver is the biggest knife. It's a large, heavy knife that's used to hack through hearty vegetables, bones, and meat.

1. **B:** There are three teaspoons in a tablespoon.

If You Got 0–2 Correct:
You have some work to do. So maybe cooking isn't your thing and that's okay! Keep cooking and studying up on the basics and you'll be a pro in no time.

If You Got 3–5 Correct:
You're a good cook, but you're not pro chef material yet. Keep practicing and honing your skills!

If You Got 6–7 Correct:
You're a pretty talented cook. Well done, chef! Keep cooking and you'll be on your way to culinary stardom!

If You Got 8–10 Correct:
You're a culinary genius. Wait, are you actually a pro already? Because you know A LOT about cooking. Great work, chef!

This or That: Home Edition

City penthouse or Suburban mansion?

Wine cellar or Fitness center?

Infinity pool or Basketball court?

View of the mountains or View of the beach?

Guesthouse or Poolside bar?

Home theater or Bowling alley?

Voice-controlled shower or Voice-controlled toilet?

Automatic curtains or Heated bed?

Lazy river around your pool or Waterfall into your pool?

Conservatory or Rooftop garden?

Library or Music room?

Secret passageways or Between floors?

This Escalating Word Test Will Reveal If You're Logical or Emotional

Pick a two-lettered word:

A. Ox
B. No
C. Yo
D. My

Pick a three-lettered word:

A. Bed
B. Spy
C. Oak
D. Paw

Pick a four-lettered word:

A. Stem
B. Grim
C. Fang
D. Quiz

Pick a five-lettered word:

A. Worry
B. Bacon
C. Stars
D. Extra

Pick a six-lettered word:

A. Resist
B. Marker
C. Wheels
D. Kettle

Pick a seven-lettered word:

A. Fanatic
B. Hipster
C. Puzzles
D. Titanic

Pick an eight-lettered word:

A. Chipmunk
B. Flapjack
C. Maximize
D. Sizzling

Pick a nine-lettered word:

A. Paperback
B. Tortoises
C. Cufflinks
D. Jelly bean

Pick a ten-lettered word:

A. Strawberry
B. Jeopardize
C. Perfection
D. Illuminati

If You Got Mostly A's or D's:

You're more emotional! Your strongest tool is your intuition. You approach challenges and any problems using your heart first and your brain second. Your feelings have a habit of guiding almost all your decisions, which pays off for the most part. But make sure you don't let your emotions exhaust you. Try surrounding yourself with analytical thinkers who can help you see another perspective.

If You Got Mostly B's or C's:

You're more logical! You assess every situation, conversation, and problem with an analytical approach. Unlike most people, you don't get caught up in the drama and can quickly make smart decisions. You have the ability to step away from situations to gain more insight and rarely let your feelings cloud your judgment. However, one of your biggest weaknesses is neglecting your emotional side. Don't forget to tap into that once in a while, especially when it comes to matters of the heart.

Tell Us Your Zodiac Sign and We'll Tell You Where You Should Go on Your Dream Trip

Pick your sign.

TAURUS

FRANCE
Oh, Taurus, always seeking the finer things in life. You'll be happy as a clam in Bordeaux, specifically, among gorgeous châteaus, amazing art, mouthwatering Michelin-star restaurants, and some of the greatest wine in the world.

CANCER

HAWAII
Aloha, Cancer. You're a water sign, and you can't stand being far from the beach. Hawaii is the perfect setting to complement your loving, spiritual, and romantic personality. Think: hidden waterfalls, lush jungles, and fiery sunsets over the Pacific Ocean.

SCORPIO

THAILAND
Scorpio, you're strong-willed, brave, and determined. So when you take a vacation, you go all out. Your ambitious attitude is perfect for exploring Thailand. You'll love the idyllic beaches of Phuket and the bustling city of Chiang Mai, sprawling with ancient Buddhist temples and incredible street food.

GEMINI

ITALY
Gemini, you're multifaceted just like the city of Rome, a mixture of ancient and modern. The plazas, art, and architecture will stimulate your intellectual side, while the spaghetti carbonara and gelato will awaken your youthful nature.

LEO

SPAIN
Leo, you just love being in the spotlight. You're energetic and full of positive vibes, and you treat life like it's a party. You'll feel right at home in the bohemian Mediterranean city of Barcelona, where every day feels like summer.

CAPRICORN

BRAZIL
Don't take this the wrong way, Capricorn, but you're a bit of an overachiever. Your detailed itineraries will do you well in Brazil. There's so much to see and explore, from Christ the Redeemer in Rio to the spectacular beaches in Ipanema.

ARIES

SOUTH AFRICA

Oh hey, Aries! You're adventurous (even a little bit of a daredevil), and you're always seeking out new experiences. You'll adore South Africa, where you can hike Table Mountain, chill with penguins at Boulders Beach, and even go on safari in Kruger.

AQUARIUS

COLOMBIA

Aquarius, you're curious by nature, imaginative, and optimistic. You're a bit of a wanderer, and luckily the colorful old city of Cartagena is the perfect place to get lost. You're eccentric and will love everything from the street art to the salsa dancing.

PISCES

MEXICO

Hola, Pisces. Your sign is a fish, so clearly you've got a thing for the ocean. The slow-paced beach town of Tulum on Mexico's Caribbean coast will bring out your happiest self. Your sign can get a little lazy, and that's okay! A few relaxing days of basking in the sun, eating tacos, and drinking margaritas doesn't sound too bad.

SAGITTARIUS

CHILE

We know people like you, Sagittarius. You love a good challenge and you need freedom to roam. Carefree and good-humored, you'll be enamored by Patagonia's natural beauty and adventure. Hiking in Torres del Paine National Park and climbing glaciers is just what you're looking for.

VIRGO

NEW ZEALAND

We know you, Virgo. You're harmonious and grounded, yet full of energy. But above anything, you love nature and the great outdoors. You'll fall in love with New Zealand's diverse landscape of green, rolling hills, snow-capped mountains, and striking fjords.

LIBRA

DENMARK

Oh, hello, Libra! You're sophisticated and urbane, kind, and easygoing by nature. You'll feel right at home in the playful yet sophisticated city of Copenhagen. You enjoy nice things, so you'll love Denmark's high-end, Nordic culinary scene.

What's your greatest wish in life?

A. To be rich
B. To find love
C. To travel and go on adventures
D. To be famous
E. To be my own boss
F. To land my dream job
G. To have a family
H. To have as much fun as possible
I. IDK, some kind of superpower would be nice

Which Disney Princess Are You, Really?

Which non-princess Disney heroine would be your BFF?

A. Alice
B. Tinkerbell
C. Jane
D. Meg
E. Nala
F. Esmeralda
G. Maid Marian
H. Vanellope
I. Minnie

Picture your dream house. What color is it?

A. Purple
B. Blue
C. Yellow
D. Green
E. White
F. Red
G. Aqua
H. Gray
I. Brown

Choose a Disney-owned franchise:

A. Marvel
B. Pixar
C. *Star Wars*

What kind of queen will you be?

A. Merciful and fair
B. Petty and vindictive
C. Brave and selfless
D. Stylishly spellbinding
E. A damn warrior queen
F. An ambassador for the people
G. A major procrastinator
H. The kind that hooks up with hot foreign princes
I. TBH I'm probably going to leave most of the work to my subordinates

Choose a college major:

A. Creative Writing
B. Theater
C. Journalism
D. Engineering
E. Criminal Justice
F. Psychology
G. Biology
H. Art History
I. Teacher Education

If You Got Mostly A's:

You're Cinderella! Your story is one of rags to riches, even if you're not at the "riches" part yet. You're all about making it in this world, but you probably wouldn't mind having a fairy godmother to help.

If You Got Mostly B's:

You're Ariel! You're a dreamer in every sense, even if it means that your life goals are sometimes a little unrealistic. You're exactly the type of person who, as a kid, probably listed "superhero" as what you wanted to be when you grew up. You just know there's something great out there waiting for you, and you'll sign whichever sketchy documents you have to sign in order to get it.

If You Got Mostly C's:

You're Moana! You're a true adventurer, ready to take on any of life's challenges. You love traveling and seeing new sights, even if sometimes it's just so you can brag about how many places you've been to.

If You Got Mostly D's:

You're Elsa! People think you're cold, but really you just need a little time to yourself on occasion. Don't we all? Basically, you just already have a lot of responsibilities that you're trying to handle and you've learned to ignore everyone's opinions because you know how to do things right.

If You Got Mostly E's:

You're Mulan! If your friends could sum you up in a few words, they would probably choose "fierce AF." You're the first to defend anyone who can't defend themselves, but it's not because you're aggressive or confrontational; it's because you have a big heart. And also maybe because you know you can win a fight.

If You Got Mostly F's:

You're Pocahontas! You're an independent person and your personal freedom is one of your most cherished possessions. Ideally, you'd like to have a life where you don't have to answer to anyone but yourself, even if that means being single for longer than most people.

If You Got Mostly G's:

You're Belle! You're smart and studious, though your love of stories and active imagination can cause you to be a little distracted sometimes. When you're focused, you're unstoppable. Other times, your brain just goes on walkabouts while you try to rein it in.

If You Got Mostly H's:

You're Rapunzel! You're a dreamer, and because of that you hate feeling trapped or confined. Travel is one of your favorite things, but you're also happy staying home as long as you have something fun to do, like painting. Or baking. Or candle-making. Or brushing your hair, even.

If You Got Mostly I's:

You're Jasmine! You're a little dramatic and you're the first to admit it. You're exactly the type who would own some kind of exotic pet if you could, and you've probably gotten in trouble more than once for sneaking out of the proverbial palace walls.

Word Scramble: *Avengers*

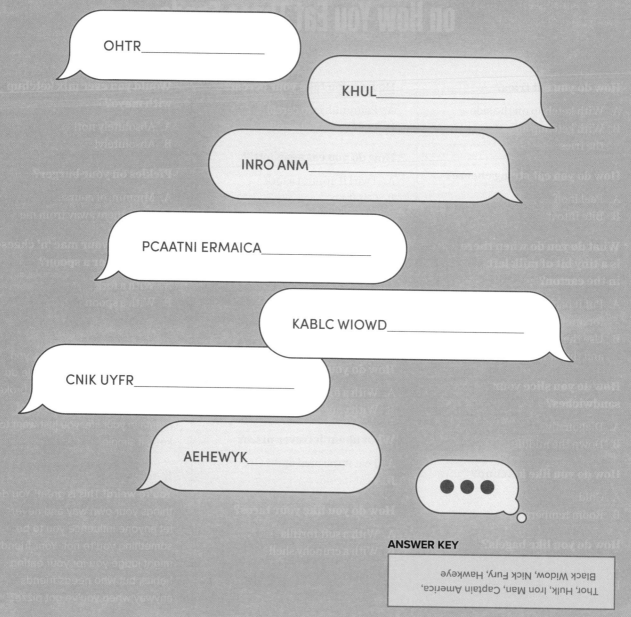

OHTR_____

KHUL_____

INRO ANM_____

PCAATNI ERMAICA_____

KABLC WIOWD_____

CNIK UYFR_____

AEHEWYK_____

ANSWER KEY

Thor, Hulk, Iron Man, Captain America, Black Widow, Nick Fury, Hawkeye

We'll Tell You If You're Weird or Not Based on How You Eat These Foods

How do you eat fries?

A. With ketchup on the side
B. With ketchup all over the fries

How do you eat string cheese?

A. Peel it off
B. Bite into it

What do you do when there is a tiny bit of milk left in the carton?

A. Put it back in the fridge for another time
B. Use the rest immediately and throw it out

How do you slice your sandwiches?

A. Diagonally
B. Down the middle

How do you like ketchup?

A. Cold
B. Room temperature

How do you like bagels?

A. Toasted
B. Not toasted

How do you take your cereal?

A. Pour milk into cereal
B. Pour cereal into milk

How do you eat spaghetti?

A. Twirl it around a fork
B. Cut it up

How do you eat an Oreo?

A. Bite it
B. Twist and lick it

Do you double dip?

A. Nope!
B. Yeah

How do you eat pizza?

A. With a fork and knife
B. With your hands

What about leftover pizza?

A. I eat it warmed up
B. I eat it cold

How do you like your tacos?

A. With a soft tortilla
B. With a crunchy shell

Would you ever mix ketchup with mayo?

A. Absolutely not!
B. Absolutely!

Pickles on your burger?

A. Mmmm, of course
B. Keep them away from me

Do you eat your mac 'n' cheese with a fork or a spoon?

A. With a fork
B. With a spoon

If You Got Mostly A's:

You're not weird! Congrats, you eat food the way most people do. Why fix something that's not broke, ya know? You don't like a lot of drama in your life, you just want to keep it simple.

If You Got Mostly B's:

You're weird! This is great! You do things your own way and never let anyone influence you to be something you're not. Your friends might judge you for your eating habits, but who needs friends anyway when you've got pizza?

Which Celebrity Do You Share Your Height With?

How tall are you? Find your height to reveal your celeb match!

4'9" You're as tall as Snooki!	**4'10"** You're as tall as Danny DeVito!	**4'11"** You're as tall as Kristen Chenoweth!	**5'0"** You're as tall as Ariana Grande!
5'1" You're as tall as Lady Gaga!	**5'2"** You're as tall as Nicki Minaj!	**5'3"** You're as tall as Kim Kardashian!	**5'4"** You're as tall as Britney Spears!
5'5" You're as tall as Lorde!	**5'6"** You're as tall as Kylie Jenner!	**5'7"** You're as tall as Beyoncé!	**5'8"** You're as tall as Rihanna!
5'9" You're as tall as Justin Bieber!	**5'10"** You're as tall as Taylor Swift!	**5'11"** You're as tall as Michelle Obama!	**6'0"** You're as tall as Harry Styles!
6'1" You're as tall as Timothée Chalamet!	**6'2"** You're as tall as Shawn Mendez!	**6'3"** You're as tall as John Mayer!	**6'4"** You're as tall as Jason Momoa!
6'5" You're as tall as Armie Hammer!	**6'6"** You're as tall as Michael Jordan!	**6'7"** You're as tall as Stephen Merchant!	**6'8"** You're as tall as Lebron James!

What is your work schedule like?

A. All over the place
B. Get in late but work late
C. Whatever I want
D. My boss doesn't notice
E. NO ONE OWNS ME
F. I sleep there
G. I'm unemployed, thanks
H. Flexible
I. 9 to 5

Love or money?

A. Love
B. Neither
C. Money
D. Love is the only currency
E. WTF??
F. I'll just buy love
G. Ideally: love. Realistically: money
H. I hate this!
I. Pizza

The highlight of your weekend would be:

A. Having friends over for wine and Netflix
B. Any moment of alone time
C. Reading a really good book
D. Seeing an experimental play or movie
E. Going on a cute date with a crush
F. Flying to a different country
G. Performing onstage
H. Chilling at a dive bar
I. Dancing at a posh club

What Pet Should You Actually Own?

Pick an after-school activity:

A. Fashion club
B. Science club
C. Some kind of team sport
D. Smoking under the bleachers
E. Track team
F. Bowling team
G. Writing for the high school paper
H. Drama club
I. Gym club

At a party, you're the one who is:

A. Telling stories to a group
B. Drinking from a keg or funnel
C. Passed out on the couch
D. Down to do something crazy
E. Playing a video game
F. Snuggling with your SO
G. Helping a drunk person
H. Having an intellectual convo
I. Making out with someone

Continues on next page

It's the first day of nice spring weather. You:

A. Go for a quick stroll
B. Jog in the park
C. Host a picnic
D. Go swimming, DUH
E. Drive with the windows down
F. Switch to a T-shirt and shorts
G. Go on a last-minute road trip
H. Do nothing differently
I. Lie on the grass and read a book

Pick a Coen Brothers movie:

A. *Fargo*
B. *The Big Lebowski*
C. *No Country for Old Men*
D. *True Grit*
E. *Inside Llewyn Davis*
F. *Raising Arizona*
G. *The Ladykillers*
H. *Burn After Reading*
I. *Hail, Caesar!*

When dating someone, your biggest deal breaker is:

A. Coldness
B. Being really boring
C. Being too uptight
D. Shyness
E. Not reading enough books
F. Offensive language
G. Messiness
H. Clinginess
I. Being too independent

How responsible are you?

A. I can be flaky but I'm responsible when it counts
B. Very
C. I'm a FREE SPIRIT, BABY!
D. I'm taking this instead of studying, sooo
E. I am but no one believes me
F. I am very clean, so yes?
G. I'll work on it, Mom
H. I HAVE to be
I. Eh, things work out

Describe where you live:

A. Small
B. Cozy, but I live near lots of parks
C. It's a dorm
D. HUGE
E. Teeny, but it has tons of light
F. Moderately sized
G. 4 x 4 basically
H. A trailer
I. A bungalow

If You Got Mostly A's:
A hedgehog! You may appear guarded, but you have a huge heart and are fairly responsible. No matter how it may look, you always care a lot and you'd make a great hedgie parent.

If You Got Mostly B's:
A fennec fox! You are drawn to anything that is unusual, be it a mysterious local event or a new city. But you're also super responsible and don't go on adventures without taking care of your duties first.

If You Got Mostly C's:
A frog! You're fascinated by what other people may dismiss and have an interest in how the world around you works. You are also mildly nostalgic about elementary school.

If You Got Mostly D's:
A chinchilla! You like soft things, rich minimalist colors, and luxurious baths. Can you think of a better companion?

If You Got Mostly E's:
A bunny! You have a big and *very* forgiving heart—you are willing to deal with a little messiness if it means having a cute li'l cuddle bug to hop through life with!

If You Got Mostly F's:
A garter snake! You like danger . . . but not too much. You're also good at appreciating details that other people do not.

If You Got Mostly G's:
A small fish! You like pretty things and decorating everything you can. But you also have realistic expectations and can be calmed at the end of a long day by the simplicity of a fish.

If You Got Mostly H's:
A horse! You crave the outdoors and love to challenge yourself. You value feeling one with an animal, an essential trait for horse people. Plus, you don't mind spending a little extra on a pet.

If You Got Mostly I's:
A parrot! You *love* to talk. You could talk to a brick wall and become best friends in an instant. This makes you a wonderful host, which helps fill any dreaded silence in your life.

These 7 Questions Will Determine Your Hogwarts House and Patronus

Who would you have the most fun with at the Yule Ball?

A. Harry
B. Ron
C. Cho
D. Lavender
E. Draco
F. Hermione
G. Neville
H. Luna

What subject do you think you'd do well in?

A. Defense against the dark arts
B. Charms
C. Divination
D. Care of magical creatures
E. Transfiguration
F. Potions
G. Herbology
H. History of magic

Which job would you want in the wizarding world?

A. Auror
B. Headmaster
C. Magizoologist
D. Healer
E. Wandmaker
F. Professor
G. Journalist at *The Daily Prophet*
H. Director of magical security

Which Quidditch position would you want to play?

A. Seeker: tries to catch the golden snitch before the other team
B. Keeper: guards the three hoops to prevent the other team from scoring
C. Chaser: controls the quaffle and scores points by getting it through a hoop
D. Beater: uses a bat to keep bludgers away from their team and aim them at the opposing team

Which Educational Decree would bother you most?

A. Nº 26: Boys and girls are not permitted to be within six inches of each other
B. Nº 38: Non-educational toys and games are banned
C. Nº 45: Proper dress and decorum is to be maintained at all times
D. Nº 75: Pets are to be confined to common rooms and dormitories
E. Nº 82: All students will submit to questioning about suspected illicit activities
F. Nº 1: Any student found in possession of a spell-check charmed quill will be severely punished
G. Nº 129: New restrictions regarding library and common room access
H. Nº 46: Any literature by non-wizards or half-breeds is banned forthwith

Which obstacle from *The Philosopher's Stone* would you have handled the best?

A. Facing off with Fluffy
B. Escaping the Devil's Snare
C. Finding the correct key in a swarm of flying keys
D. Playing a game of human chess

Which word do you identify with most?

A. Passionate
B. Adventurous
C. Intelligent
D. Sensitive
E. Ambitious
F. Charismatic
G. Carefree
H. Introverted

If You Got Mostly A's:

You're a Gryffindor with a wolf patronus! You may have had a lot happen in your life and are wary of who to trust, but others shouldn't be deceived by your brave and hard exterior, as you definitely display your softer side once you allow people to get to know you.

If You Got Mostly B's:

You're a Gryffindor with a dolphin patronus! You're definitely an extrovert and love to be around company, with most of the attention on you. You're great at communicating and aren't afraid to take risks to get what you want.

If You Got Mostly C's:

You're a Ravenclaw with a bloodhound patronus! Others would describe you as knowledgeable and resilient. You're not afraid to work hard for what you want and are very patient with those that are close to you.

If You Got Mostly D's:

You're a Ravenclaw with an otter patronus! You're smart and witty and definitely like to show off your skill set. No task is too big for you, especially since you're a master at multitasking and have learned to juggle many responsibilities at once.

If You Got Mostly E's:

You're a Slytherin with a buzzard patronus! You are very good at recognizing a diamond in the rough and have a knack for seeing an opportunity where no one else does. Nothing brings you more joy than seeing others reach their full potential.

If You Got Mostly F's:

You're a Slytherin with a fox patronus! Highly adaptable, you can adjust to most social situations. Some may call you cunning, as you're very good at using your resources to your advantage and always have a vast network of people around you.

If You Got Mostly G's:

You're a Hufflepuff with a hummingbird patronus! Your happy, carefree disposition allows you to get on with what you set your mind to without worrying about what others think. Your perseverance and dedication don't go unnoticed as you serve as an inspiration among your friends.

If You Got Mostly H's:

You're a Hufflepuff with a brown hare patronus! Sometimes sensitive and impatient, you can take things to heart quickly. However, you're known for adapting rapidly to changing situations and don't like to be in one place for too long.

We Know What Type of Person You Are Based on Your Starbucks Order

PIKE PLACE ROAST

YOU'RE A TRUE AMBIVERT!

You perfectly straddle the line between introvert and extrovert. Ambiversion gives you the flexibility to thrive in social situations and enjoy your own company on a quiet night. It's a win-win situation.

ESPRESSO

YOU'RE A THINKING INTROVERT!

You're deeply analytical and you love to solve problems. Because you process most things internally, you tend to come off as a bit quiet. However, you speak when it counts and people always know you're an important person to listen to.

BLONDE ROAST

YOU'RE AN INTUITIVE EXTROVERT!

Not only are you great at reading other people, but you can understand the collective moods and energies of larger groups. Your fantastic instincts don't just work well at parties, but in academic and career settings as well. If they don't already, people will come to trust and rely on you because of it. It's a pretty cool superpower.

PUMPKIN SPICE LATTE

YOU'RE A FEELING EXTROVERT!

Yeah, yeah, people think you're basic, but you know you're much more than that. When you look at the world around you, you try to imagine the positive impact you can have on it. You also tend to see possibilities where others see barriers. Your enthusiasm for life and your fun nature are contagious and people love to spend time around you.

FRAPPUCCINO

YOU'RE A SOCIAL EXTROVERT!

You're a classic extrovert. You thrive on the energy of other people, and because of it you love to throw yourself into large social settings. You're always thinking of new things to do, and if you ever find yourself having a dull moment, well, you just try not to have a dull moment.

PEPPERMINT MOCHA

YOU'RE AN INTUITIVE INTROVERT!

You're deeply in tune with others' feelings and emotions and you tend to understand how people work better than others. When you sense that someone is in pain, you know how to comfort; when someone is happy, you add to their joy. You're more on the quiet side, but your friends and family cherish you all the more because of it.

ICED CARAMEL MACCHIATO

YOU'RE A THINKING EXTROVERT!

Unlike your introverted counterparts, you tend to process your thoughts out loud. You're constantly looking for ways to experiment and try new things and people often view you as bold and unafraid. Though you occasionally act on impulse, for the most part you plan and think ahead.

VERY BERRY HIBISCUS REFRESHER

YOU'RE A SOCIAL INTROVERT!

You're an introvert in disguise, my friend. You enjoy your time alone, but you still thrive in social settings as long as things don't get too wild and crazy. Though most people would be surprised to find out you're an introvert, you know the importance of spending a night in every now and then.

CHAI

YOU'RE A FEELING INTROVERT!

Joy, love, fear, sorrow—you feel these emotions, and many others, on such an intense level compared to the people around you. Because of the intensity of your emotions, you are vivacious and passionate and constantly seeking ways to channel your energy into creative endeavors. There's something spectacular about you and your ability to feel.

You're a

We Can Guess If You're Married or Single from This Short Test

Pick a vacay:

A.  B.  C.

Pick a meal to share:

A.  B.  C.

Pick an animal:

A.  B.  C.

Pick a color:

A. B. C.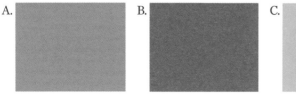

If You Got Mostly A's:

You're single. Congrats! You're single! And if you're not, you should probably break things off with whomever you're with to match this test result.

If You Got Mostly B's:

You're in a relationship. Huzzah! You're in a relationship! Whether that's to a human or with a pizza, I can't say. Either way, hold your loved one near.

If You Got Mostly C's:

You're married. Mazel Tov! You're legally married! Whether it's to your cat, your BFF, or a spouse, I can't say, but what I can say is this test is 100 percent accurate so you are definitely married.

What Movie Genre Is Your Life Based on Your Birth Month?

January: Dramatic Biopic

February: Psychological Horror Movie

March: Romantic Comedy

April: Film Noir

May: Crime Documentary

June: Apocalyptic Sci-Fi

July: Heroic Fantasy

August: Outlaw Western

September: Late-Night Comedy

October: Disaster Movie

November: Legal Thriller

December: Claymation

What Will You Major in, Based on Your Favorite Foods?

It's breakfast.
What are you drinking?

A. Coffee
B. Orange juice
C. Tea
D. Water
E. My fifth shot of espresso
F. Milk

What's on your breakfast plate?

A. Omelet
B. Pancakes and bacon
C. Oatmeal
D. Cereal
E. Fruit and yogurt
F. I'm not a breakfast person

Anything else?

A. Banana
B. Hard-boiled egg
C. Toast
D. Another coffee
E. Trail mix
F. I'm full

Back for lunch.
Whatcha having?

A. Grilled cheese
B. Burger
C. Salad
D. Wrap
E. Soup
F. Cereal . . . again

Something sweet to finish it off?

A. Soft serve
B. Brownie
C. Cookie
D. Granola
E. More coffee . . .
F. None for me

Dinner time already?
Choose a meal.

A. Salad
B. Fish sticks
C. Chicken sandwich
D. Tacos
E. Ramen
F. Pasta

Anything on the side?

A. Fried rice
B. Mac 'n' cheese
C. Mozzarella sticks
D. Onion rings
E. Veggies and hummus
F. Mashed potato

Lastly, some dessert tonight?

A. Cake
B. Apple and peanut butter
C. Waffle sundae
D. Banana split
E. Pie
F. I'm full

If You Got Mostly A's:

You'll major in history. You're fascinated by the past and by different cultures. You love reading, traveling, and even watching movies that give you a lens into a different time period. Whether you go on to be a professor, a journalist, a lawyer, or anything in between, your curious and analytical mind will serve you well.

If You Got Mostly B's:

You'll major in math. You've got a thing for numbers and there's no problem that is too big for you to try to solve. Geometry, trigonometry, algebra, or calculus—it's all fascinating to you. Luckily, there's so many ways to use your math degree, whether you go on to be a doctor, a research scientist, or an entrepreneur.

If You Got Mostly C's:

You'll major in philosophy. If there's one word your friends would use to describe you, it's *curious*. You are never satisfied with what's in front of you, so you're always looking for explanations. You could sit around for hours discussing the meaning of life or the nature of the universe. You should put your inquisitive and abstract mind to use by studying philosophy, looking for answers to all of life's biggest questions.

If You Got Mostly D's:

You'll major in English. You're a creative thinker who loves to get lost in a good book. You've read all the latest novels on the best-seller list, as well as the more obscure titles no one's heard of yet. You're also a great writer, comfortable with words, and excellent at getting your thoughts down on paper. Get your English degree and take advantage of the subjects you love.

If You Got Mostly E's:

You'll major in international relations. You are obsessed with different cultures, exploring new places, and learning new languages. You are a worldly and extremely curious person, always wanting to explore. You want to connect with new people and embrace diversity. You should put those skills and qualities to use by studying international relations. Whether you want to pursue a career in politics, work for an NGO, or even become a journalist traveling around the world, you'll find your niche.

If You Got Mostly F's:

You'll major in engineering. You love a challenge and you've got an analytical mind. You enjoy taking on challenges and you've got a knack for science, math, and technology. You also take your future seriously, which is perfect because an engineering degree will open the door to lots of high-paying career opportunities.

This or That: Dessert Edition

Cupcake   or   Muffin?

Donut   or   Croissant?

Blondie   or   Brownie?

Gelato   or   Tiramisu?

Cake   or   Cheesecake?

Milkshake   or   Banana split?

Churro   or   Funnel cake?

Cherry   or   Key lime pie?

Cookie   or   Fudge?

Ice cream   or   Frozen yogurt?

Candy bar   or   Eclair?

Lemon square   or   Cannoli?

S'mores   or   Oreos?

Crêpe   or   Cinnamon roll?

We Know Your Age Based on the Foods You Hate

Check all that apply.

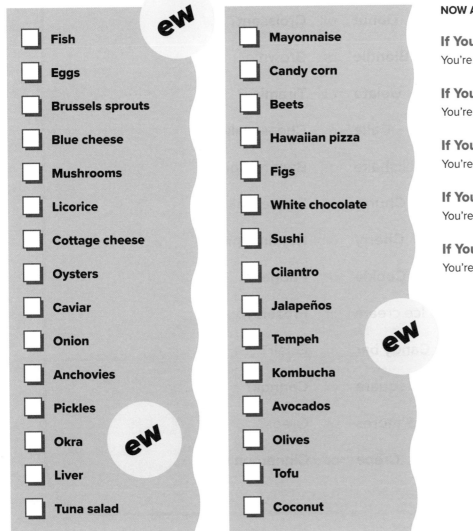

- ☐ Fish
- ☐ Eggs
- ☐ Brussels sprouts
- ☐ Blue cheese
- ☐ Mushrooms
- ☐ Licorice
- ☐ Cottage cheese
- ☐ Oysters
- ☐ Caviar
- ☐ Onion
- ☐ Anchovies
- ☐ Pickles
- ☐ Okra
- ☐ Liver
- ☐ Tuna salad

- ☐ Mayonnaise
- ☐ Candy corn
- ☐ Beets
- ☐ Hawaiian pizza
- ☐ Figs
- ☐ White chocolate
- ☐ Sushi
- ☐ Cilantro
- ☐ Jalapeños
- ☐ Tempeh
- ☐ Kombucha
- ☐ Avocados
- ☐ Olives
- ☐ Tofu
- ☐ Coconut

NOW ADD UP YOUR SCORE!

If You Checked 0–6:
You're actually 35!

If You Checked 7–12:
You're actually 80!

If You Checked 13–18:
You're actually 40!

If You Checked 19–24:
You're actually 25!

If You Checked 25–30:
You're actually 16!

We Know Your Actual Job and Your Dream Job

Where would you first announce your job change?

A. Facebook

B. Instagram

C. Snapchat

D. Twitter

E. LinkedIn

F. From atop the highest mountain

Pick a city to live in:

A. New York City

B. Tokyo

C. Buenos Aires

D. Mumbai

E. Florence

F. Cape Town

Which generic flaw would you give in a job interview?

A. Works too hard

B. Cares too much

C. Tries too hard

D. Too self-critical

E. Spends too much time on details

F. Outdoes coworkers

Pick an office view:

A. Mountains

B. Photo studio

C. Cityscape

D. Residential street

E. The open road

F. A theater

Pick a memoir:

A. *Bossypants* by Tina Fey

B. *Is Everyone Hanging Out Without Me?* by Mindy Kaling

C. *Yes, Please* by Amy Poehler

D. *I'm Judging You* by Luvvie Ajayi

E. *You're Never Weird on the Internet (Almost)* by Felicia Day

F. *Scrappy Little Nobody* by Anna Kendrick

What would you steal from the office on the last day?

A. Stapler

B. Handful of pens

C. The office snacks

D. Packets of tea

E. A mug from the breakroom

F. Your boss's lunch

If You Got Mostly A's:
You're an office clerk, but you want to be a white-water rafting instructor. The office life just isn't for you. You crave excitement and adventure! You want to wake up every morning and have something new to do each day, not trudge along the 9-to-5 life like everyone else.

If You Got Mostly B's:
You're a retail worker, but you want to be a musician. Folding clothes just isn't for you. You want to wow a crowd and have roses thrown at your feet. Maybe you can start practicing in the stockroom while no one is listening. Why waste time, right?

If You Got Mostly C's:
You're a lawyer, but you want to be a professional wine taster. You're fed up with pushing papers. You're ready to sit back, relax, soak in some beautiful vineyard views, and sip on that sweet, sweet grape juice.

If You Got Mostly D's:
You're an accountant, but you want to be a forensics analyst. You want to solve crimes, kick butt, and crack cases. Say goodbye to crunching numbers. The good news is, as a forensics analyst, you can still put that analytical mind of yours to use.

If You Got Mostly E's:
You're a teacher, but you want to be an architect. You want to do more than shape minds—you want to shape buildings! Teaching leaves its mark on the world in numerous ways, but you're ready to create a different kind of mark. Now it's time to whip up those blueprints and make your ideas a reality.

If You Got Mostly F's:
You're a barista, but you want to be an actor. You know what you want, you're just waiting for your big break. Maybe someone ~famous~ will walk into your coffee shop. That could be your big moment! Stay on your toes, because you never know.

We Can Guess Your Favorite Type of Alcohol Based on These 5 Questions

Choose a celebrity:

A. Zayn Malik
B. Miley Cyrus
C. Oprah
D. George Clooney
E. Chris Pratt
F. Mariah Carey
G. Britney Spears
H. Idris Elba

Pick a place to live:

A. New York City
B. Australia
C. France
D. London
E. Dubai
F. Ireland
G. Greece
H. Los Angeles

Pick a movie:

A. *Pineapple Express*
B. *The Dark Knight*
C. *The Sixth Sense*
D. *How to Lose a Guy in 10 Days*
E. *Finding Dory*
F. *The Hangover*
G. *Titanic*
H. *Clueless*

QUIZ

Pick a dog to adopt:

A. German Shepherd
B. Dachshund
C. Golden Retriever
D. Shiba Inu
E. Pomeranian
F. Siberian Husky
G. French Bulldog
H. Maltese

Choose a dessert:

A. Chocolate fudge cake
B. Apple cider donut
C. Fruity gelato
D. Flan
E. Red velvet cupcake
F. White chocolate macadamia cookie
G. Classic cheesecake
H. Vegan ice cream

If You Got Mostly A's:

You love wine! Wine is your absolute fave! Whether it's red or white you are always down for a glass . . . or three.

If You Got Mostly B's:

You love vodka! Simple, sophisticated, classic! Vodka and you go together like pizza and your mouth. YUM!

If You Got Mostly C's:

You love beer! Beer is your favorite alcoholic drink and who can blame you—it's great! There's nothin' like a cool sip on a hot summer's day, am I right?

If You Got Mostly D's:

You love rum! Rum is your #1! While it may be bold, it's perfect to amp up your night on the town.

If You Got Mostly E's:

You love whiskey! You love whiskey, and whiskey loves you right back! It's the perfect drink to help take the edge off and tastes pretty good, too!

If You Got Mostly F's:

You love gin! Gin is your favorite kind of alcohol. It's cool, crisp, and just the drink your taste buds desire!

If You Got Mostly G's:

You love tequila! You know what they say—tequila makes your clothes . . . you know the rest. You're wild and fun and this drink only adds to your crazy personality. Buckle up!

If You Got Mostly H's:

You love Champagne! Classy, elegant, and timeless. Champagne is your favorite and for good reason—it's delicious! There's nothing like a celebratory glass to sip on all night!

This Wedding Quiz Will Reveal Where You'll Get Married

Who would cater your wedding?

A. Panera Bread
B. Chipotle
C. Subway
D. McDonald's
E. Taco Bell
F. El Pollo Loco

Which of these celebs would you invite?

A. Emma Watson
B. Taylor Swift
C. Mindy Kaling
D. Sofía Vergara
E. Beyoncé
F. Amy Poehler

Do you think you'll cry on your wedding day?

A. I'll probably shed a tear or two
B. Just a li'l bit
C. How the hell would I know?
D. It's possible
E. Probably not
F. I'll bawl my eyes out

What does love mean to you?

A. Dedication
B. Paradise
C. Desire
D. It's indescribable
E. Empathy
F. Compromise

Choose a song to walk down the aisle to:

A. "Here Comes the Bride" from Wagner's *Lohengrin*
B. "My Heart Will Go On" by Celine Dion
C. "A Thousand Years" by Christina Perri
D. "I Can't Help Falling in Love with You" by UB40
E. "You're My Best Friend" by Queen
F. "Thinking Out Loud" by Ed Sheeran

How often do you think about marriage?

A. A lot
B. Every other day
C. Occasionally
D. Only if someone brings it up
E. Not often
F. Never

CONGRATS!

If You Got Mostly A's:

You'll get married in a church. You enjoy the more traditional things in life. When you love, you love with your entire heart and spirit. You've always known that a church is the place for you and there's no doubt that your wedding day will be filled with incredible people in an incredible venue.

If You Got Mostly B's:

You'll get married overlooking the beach. Much like the ocean, you're a go-with-the-flow kind of person. You want your special day to be as relaxed as possible and filled with only the people you love most in this world.

If You Got Mostly C's:

You'll get married in a beautiful garden. You are beyond elegant and love to go about your days with your head up high. You try and find the beauty in everyone and everything. A beautiful garden will be the perfect representation of the love you and your partner have blooming.

If You Got Mostly D's:

You'll get married in a country far, far away. You enjoy escaping from the mundane and like to live life to the absolute fullest. You want nothing more than to marry the one you love in a place you'll both appreciate and explore. You'll even save money on a honeymoon!

If You Got Mostly E's:

You'll get married in Vegas. You often live in the moment and realize that life is too short to overthink everything. When you love, you love with all your heart and are willing to do anything to make that love grow even stronger.

If You Got Mostly F's:

You'll get married at City Hall. You're not one for flashy decorations and over-the-top venues. You've found the one you love and that's all you need to make your wedding day special. You prefer to focus on the union over everything else and that'll make your marriage that much stronger.

What Type of Person Will You Marry?

Which sweet treat is better than an SO?

A. Donuts
B. Red velvet cupcakes
C. Ice cream
D. Brownies
E. Cheesecake
F. Cookies

Choose a kissing couple:

A. Ariel and Eric
B. Aladdin and Jasmine
C. Belle and the Beast
D. Pocahontas and John Smith
E. Tiana and Naveen
F. Tarzan and Jane

Describe your ideal spouse in one word:

A. Loyal
B. Smart
C. Ambitious
D. Hot
E. Honest
F. Funny

Which habit is a total turnoff?

A. Belching
B. Scratching themselves
C. Spitting
D. Openly farting
E. Making crotch adjustments
F. Picking their nose

Which city would you love to honeymoon in?

A. Rio de Janeiro
B. Paris
C. New York City
D. Sydney
E. Tokyo
F. Cape Town

What outfit would you most want to see the person you're attracted to in?

A. A tailored head-to-toe outfit
B. A fitted pair of jeans
C. A crisp white shirt
D. A bathing suit
E. A uniform
F. A birthday suit

Would you rather have your groom/bride be great in bed, or great at cooking?

A. Great in bed
B. Great at cooking

If You Got Mostly A's:

You should marry Mr./Mrs. Big Shot. You are sophisticated, ambitious, and a go-getter. You deserve a partner who is at the top of their game and who knows how to call the shots. Together you'll be a true power couple and totally take the world by storm.

If You Got Mostly B's:

You should marry The Perfect Specimen. You have high standards and like it when things are just right. You need to be married to someone who takes care of themselves and knows that all bodies are sacred temples. You're a total catch and deserve to spend your life with nothing but the best.

If You Got Mostly C's:

You should marry Mr./Mrs. Tall, Dark, and Beautiful. You have classic tastes and know a good thing when you see it. The person by your side should always fit the textbook standard of desire. You're totally worth it.

If You Got Mostly D's:

You should marry The Foreign Goddess/Adonis. You're cultured, have a penchant for travel, and know a good thing when you see it. You need a dashing partner from a distant land. You love the locals, but a foreign individual is what you need in your lifelong plan.

If You Got Mostly E's:

You should marry The Funny Person. You have a good sense of humor and love a good time. For you, nothing is a bigger turn-on than someone who can make you laugh. If you're going to be with them forever, you might as well have a good chuckle along the way.

If You Got Mostly F's:

You should marry The Bad Boy/Girl. You have a wild side that refuses to be tamed. You need a spouse who can keep you on your toes but knows how to appreciate you. After all, it takes two lions to rule a jungle.

What Kind of Dog Are You?

DAY YOU WERE BORN

1: Golden Retriever

2: Corgi

3: Schnauzer

4: German Shepherd

5: Pit Bull

6: Poodle

7: English Bulldog

8: Beagle

9: Yorkshire Terrier

10: Rottweiler

11: French Bulldog

12: Yellow Labrador Retriever

13: Chocolate Labrador Retriever

14: Black Labrador Retriever

15: Australian Shepherd

16: Boxer

17: Chihuahua

18: Dachshund

19: Siberian Husky

20: Great Dane

21: Doberman Pinscher

22: Pug

23: Boston Terrier

24: Cavalier King Charles Spaniel

25: Pomeranian

26: Bichon Frise

27: Shih Tzu

28: Basset Hound

29: Shiba Inu

30: Dalmatian

31: Italian Greyhound

MONTH YOU WERE BORN

January: with one eye

February: who carries their own leash because they're independent

March: with three legs

April: named Big Mama

May: who always carries around a teddy bear

June: dressed up as a taco

July: who's ripping the stuffing out of a plush pillow

August: who can carry five tennis balls in their mouth at once

September: with orange booties

October: who pees territorially

November: who makes weird noises that sometimes vaguely sound like they're saying "I love you"

December: in a stroller

Can You Unscramble These Breakfast Foods?

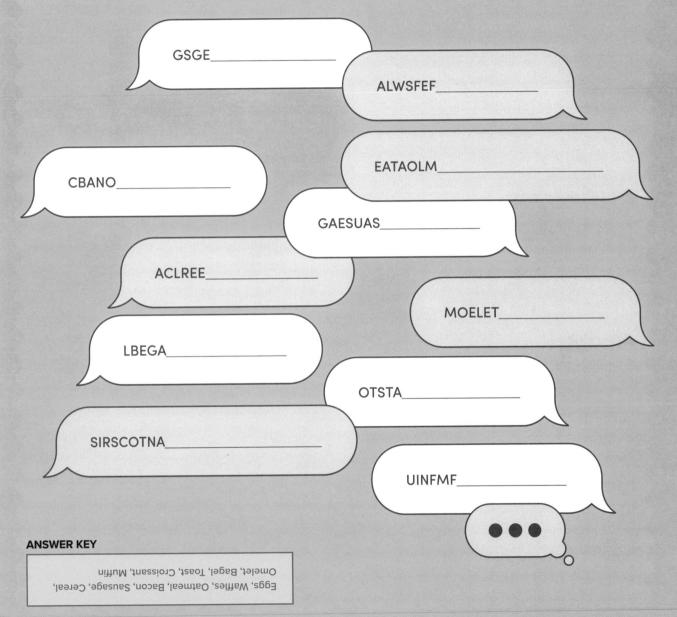

GSGE_____

ALWSFEF_____

CBANO_____

EATAOLM_____

GAESUAS_____

ACLREE_____

MOELET_____

LBEGA_____

OTSTA_____

SIRSCOTNA_____

UINFMF_____

ANSWER KEY

Eggs, Waffles, Oatmeal, Bacon, Sausage, Cereal, Omelet, Bagel, Toast, Croissant, Muffin

201

We Know Your Exact Age Based on Your Taste in French Fries

What's your favorite style of fries?

A. Curly fries
B. French fries
C. Crinkle fries
D. Waffle fries
E. Shoestring fries
F. Sweet potato fries

Now pick the best condiment for your fries:

A. Ketchup
B. Chili cheese
C. Ranch dressing
D. Hot sauce
E. Mayo
F. Chipotle aioli

What's your go-to fast food variety of fry?

A. Burger King
B. Arby's
C. McDonald's
D. Chick-fil-A
E. Wendy's
F. In-N-Out

What meal is accompanying your fries?

A. Milkshake
B. Hot dog
C. Burger
D. Ribs
E. Sandwich
F. Steak

If you couldn't have fries (God forbid), which potato would you eat?

A. Tater tots
B. Chips
C. Potato skins
D. Baked potato
E. Mashed potatoes
F. Potato salad

If You Got Mostly A's:
You're 18! You're slightly picky when it comes to fries, but that may be because your tastes are simplistic. You're not one to go *crazy* overboard with your fry experience and that's okay.

If You Got Mostly B's:
You're 21! TBH, you'll eat *almost* any fry that's put in front of you—*especially* if it's free. Your adventurous tastes match your go-with-the-flow attitude about life. But you do have a certain way you like them, because you're not a complete monster.

If You Got Mostly C's:
You're 14! You have a very youthful taste in French fries, which may mean you haven't branched out to your full fry potential. You know what you like and you tend to stick to it, but don't miss out on other ~adventurous~ options.

If You Got Mostly D's:
You're 35! You're basically a French fry professional, TBH. You've taste-tested enough to know what works and what doesn't, and you're *never* going to settle for shitty fries again. In fact, you're the one recommending the absolute best fry options to all your friends.

If You Got Mostly E's:
You're 41! You're a fry connoisseur who has been around long enough to know what you like! You have a refined taste when it comes to your fries and won't settle for anything less than the best.

If You Got Mostly F's:
You're 26! You've lived on this earth long enough to know there *is* a perfect type of fry-and-condiment combination that exists. However, your tastes are not close-minded. While you're not the pickiest when it comes to fries, you still enjoy trying new things.

If You Can Tell the Popular Disney Character from These Simple Drawings, You Deserve a Medal

1.

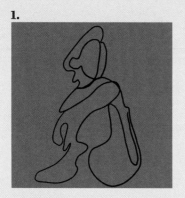

A. Simba
B. Prince Eric
C. Aladdin
D. Prince Charming

3.

A. Queen Elinor
B. Elsa
C. Jasmine
D. Moana

5.

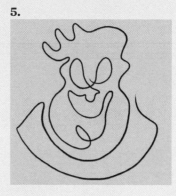

A. Oogie Boogie
B. Hades
C. Ursula
D. Queen of Hearts

2.

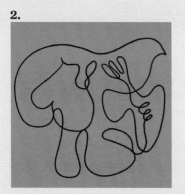

A. Belle
B. Cinderella
C. Rapunzel
D. Ariel

4.

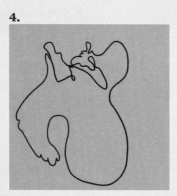

A. Jafar
B. Baymax
C. Genie
D. Baloo

6.

A. Aurora
B. Tiana
C. Ariel
D. Maid Marian

7.

A. Cruella de Vil
B. Stepmother
C. Evil Queen
D. Maleficent

9.

A. Thumper
B. Stitch
C. Lilo
D. Simba

8.

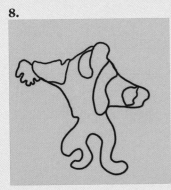

A. Evil Queen
B. Beast
C. Prince Naveen
D. Prince Charming

10.

A. Genie
B. Baymax
C. Ursula
D. Quasimodo

NOW ADD UP YOUR SCORE!

If You Got 0–3 Correct:
Tough break! It's pretty difficult recognizing the characters you see in animated form from sloppy single lines, but that doesn't mean you're not still a massive Disney lover!

If You Got 4–6 Correct:
Wow, great job! It's not easy identifying one of many Disney characters drawn in a single line, but you did a phenomenal job considering the challenge! Kudos to you, Disney fanatic!

If You Got 7–10 Correct:
Whoa, you're a Disney expert! Not only are you knowledgeable in all things Disney, but you also just have a really good eye that allows you to recognize characters from the slightest hint of their appearance. Respect!

What's Your Most Attractive Quality?

Tell us, what's your best physical feature?

A. Your butt
B. Your hair
C. Your smile
D. Your arms
E. Your legs
F. Your skin

Choose a caring Disney parent:

A. King Triton
B. Sarabi
C. Sultan Hamed
D. Eudora
E. Tarzan's father
F. Queen Elinor

What personality trait turns you off?

A. Arrogance
B. Hypocrisy
C. Dishonesty
D. Rudeness
E. Vanity
F. Jealousy

What's your biggest driving pet peeve?

A. Tailgating
B. Erratic stop lights
C. Not using a turning signal
D. Slow drivers
E. Texting while driving
F. Backseat drivers

Choose a Canadian celebrity:

A. Ryan Gosling
B. Rachel McAdams
C. Ryan Reynolds
D. Ellen Page
E. Hayden Christensen
F. Elisha Cuthbert

What's your favorite type of TV show?

A. Reality shows
B. News
C. Cooking shows
D. Soap operas
E. Sitcoms
F. Game shows

What high school superlative would you win?

A. Most artistic
B. Most beautiful/handsome
C. Too cool for school
D. Most likely to succeed
E. Class clown
F. Most popular

If You Got Mostly A's:
Your adorable awkwardness. You're quirky in the most adorable way and your kinks are one of the reasons people love you. You have your own unique way of doing things, but that's what makes you awesome. Your eclectic nature and special ways are sexier than you'll ever know.

If You Got Mostly B's:
Your well-rounded intelligence. You've always been one of the sharper knives in the drawer and everyone knows brains are sexy. Your intelligence has many layers—you're book smart and have tons of common sense as well. When it comes to attractiveness, smart is always a good start.

If You Got Mostly C's:
Your upfront honesty. You've always been blunt and prefer to tell it like it is. People appreciate your honesty and you always give the best advice since you never sugarcoat things. You've never been afraid to speak your mind, and with you, honesty is always the best policy.

If You Got Mostly D's:
Your amazing sarcasm. You are witty by your very nature and are a master of verbal timing. You know what to say and when to say it in a way that cleverly conveys a point. People love your wit, because when it comes to the language of sarcasm your fluency is never in question.

If You Got Mostly E's:
Your awesome sense of humor. You're the class clown and life of the party. You can be funny on purpose or unintentionally and you're always a riot to be around. You're never at a loss for friends, because everyone loves a jokester.

If You Got Mostly F's:
Your independent nature. Some people become leaders, but you were born one. You're driven, ambitious, know what you want, and know how to get it. You've always done things on your own terms and you're a BO$$ in your own right.

What House Will You Live In?

What did you eat for breakfast?

Eggs: California bungalow

Bagel: Modern mansion

Cereal: Haunted house

Oatmeal: Beach house

Coffee: Tiny house

Yogurt: Penthouse

Fruit: Treehouse

Nothing: Log cabin

Can You Find All 19 *Friends* Characters?

Ross
Rachel
Monica
Joey
Phoebe
Chandler
Gunther
Emily
Carol
Susan
Ben
Tag
Richard
Janice
Ursula
Mr. Heckles
Marcel
Barry
Estelle

```
G B U P V T W V D G N R N L X
K D I W R A C H E L D E M Y T
M I W I R G T V V E C K O L P
Z P N N S U S A N E T B N H G
R G M D M E F R E F J T I G U
N P E Q R E S T E L L E C W N
W H K O H Z I P N V S Q A Q T
J O E Y E T B P Y J Y U W O H
B E N A C R H D P A P H X W E
U B B Q K U M M B N A O C U R
X E A E L G E P R I C H A R D
U R R M E C M A R C E L R S U
T O R I S N F E F E Z D O U I
S S Y L X L G M Z S W H L L G
B S H Y C H A N D L E R B A T
```

Answers on p. 310

What's Your Dominant Character Trait?

What factor has the biggest influence on your life?

A. Your friends
B. Your parents
C. Your job
D. Your level of education
E. Where you live
F. Your SO

Choose a Disney villain with a distinct personality:

A. Ursula
B. Yzma
C. Hades
D. Jafar
E. The Queen of Hearts
F. Madam Mim

What do you connect to on a spiritual level?

A. Pizza
B. Wine
C. Coffee
D. Chocolate
E. Cheese
F. Guacamole

What's the best way to put your mind at ease?

A. Read a book
B. Go for a walk
C. Cuddle with a pet
D. Smoke some weed
E. Meditate
F. Talk to a friend

What do people like most about you?

A. Your sharp wit
B. Your adorable awkwardness
C. Your IDGAF attitude
D. Your silly nature
E. Your compassion
F. Your limitless intellect

What's your biggest fear?

A. Pain
B. The unknown
C. Being alone
D. Failure
E. Death
F. Rejection

Do you have more regret for the things you've done, or the things you haven't done?

A. I have more regret for the things I've done
B. I have more regret for the things I haven't done

If You Got Mostly A's:

Your intelligence! You've always been on the bright side. You pick up on things quickly and have a razor-sharp wit. You're also deep and introspective, because you know how to read into things better than most people.

If You Got Mostly B's:

Your humor! You are an absolute riot! Whether it's unintentional or on purpose, you know how to get a good laugh out of people. Whenever anyone is around you, they can't help but smile.

If You Got Mostly C's:

Your introversion! You're thoughtful, creative, and analytical. Sometimes you prefer a night in and don't mind a little time to yourself. You are also a great listener and observer, and there is so much more to you than meets the eye.

If You Got Mostly D's:

Your creativity! You have a broad mind and an active imagination. You see the world differently and have a unique way of expressing yourself. You find inspiration and your mind is always active, no matter what.

If You Got Mostly E's:

Your sensitivity! You're in touch with your emotions and are not afraid to show them. You are kind and have an uncanny ability to recognize what others are feeling as well. You're so great to be around 'cause you wear your emotions on your sleeve and never lack sincerity.

We Can Guess Which Decade of Life You're in with This Movie Test

Check off the movies you've seen and we'll guess if you're in your teens, 20s, or 30s.

- ☐ The Shawshank Redemption
- ☐ The Godfather
- ☐ The Dark Knight
- ☐ The Godfather: Part II
- ☐ Pulp Fiction
- ☐ Schindler's List
- ☐ The Lord of the Rings: The Return of the King
- ☐ The Good, the Bad and the Ugly
- ☐ 12 Angry Men
- ☐ Avengers: Infinity War

- ☐ Inception
- ☐ The Lord of the Rings: The Fellowship of the Ring
- ☐ Forrest Gump
- ☐ Fight Club
- ☐ Star Wars: Episode V— The Empire Strikes Back
- ☐ The Matrix
- ☐ Goodfellas
- ☐ One Flew Over the Cuckoo's Nest
- ☐ The Lord of the Rings: The Two Towers
- ☐ Seven Samurai

- ☐ Interstellar
- ☐ The Silence of the Lambs
- ☐ Se7en
- ☐ Léon: The Professional
- ☐ Star Wars: Episode IV— A New Hope
- ☐ Léon: The Professional
- ☐ Saving Private Ryan
- ☐ The Usual Suspects
- ☐ Spirited Away
- ☐ City of God

- [ ] Life Is Beautiful
- [ ] It's a Wonderful Life
- [ ] City Lights
- [ ] Coco
- [ ] The Lion King
- [ ] The Departed
- [ ] Back to the Future
- [ ] Raiders of the Lost Ark
- [ ] Gladiator
- [ ] The Green Mile

- [ ] The Prestige
- [ ] Whiplash
- [ ] Alien
- [ ] Psycho
- [ ] Apocalypse Now
- [ ] Terminator 2
- [ ] American History X
- [ ] Memento
- [ ] The Intouchables
- [ ] Casablanca

NOW ADD UP YOUR SCORE!

If You Checked 0–22:
You're in your teens. You've got some work to do when it comes to hunkering down and watching a classic flick, but these movies just aren't your thing—and that's okay. Keep living that teen life!

If You Checked 23–41:
You're in your twenties. You've seen around half of these well-known movies and that's a lot for just being in your twenties. Keep up the good work!

If You Checked 42–50:
You're in your thirties. You're a total movie buff and have spent a large amount of your life just watching epic films—go you!

What's an ideal first date?

A. Dinner and a movie
B. Grabbing drinks
C. A walk on the beach
D. Staying in
E. A picnic
F. Coffee

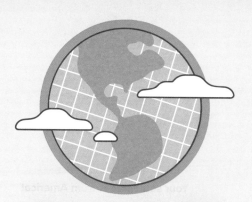

What Country Will Your Soul Mate Come From?

Choose a Disney character with magical powers:

A. King Triton
B. Madam Mim
C. Jafaar
D. Fairy Godmother
E. Merlin
F. Elsa

What's your fantasy honeymoon destination?

A. Narnia
B. Mount Olympus
C. Neverland
D. Middle Earth
E. Hogwarts
F. Atlantis

Describe your love life in one word:

A. Active
B. Weird
C. Chaotic
D. Dull
E. Normal
F. Extinct

Choose a gorgeous British celebrity:

A. Emily Blunt
B. Theo James
C. Thandie Newton
D. Idris Elba
E. Keira Knightley
F. Chiwetel Ejiofor

What's the best way to meet somebody?

A. At a bar
B. At school
C. At the gym
D. Through a dating app
E. At work
F. Through a friend

Which couples vacation spot is totally underrated?

A. Ireland
B. Bali
C. South Africa
D. Egypt
E. Costa Rica
F. Argentina

If You Got Mostly A's:

Your soul mate is from America!
You are free-willed and independent. You're an absolute boss and have always had an unbridled spirit. A true American classic is what you need in your life of badassery.

If You Got Mostly B's:

Your soul mate is from Japan!
You are a person of integrity and hold your values high. You're regularly commended for your character and your future love is bound to be Japanese.

If You Got Mostly C's:

Your soul mate is from Brazil!
You have a wild spirit and are extremely charismatic. Your energy and glow absolutely light up a room, and with you there is never a dull moment. Someone from Brazil is what you need to make your life whole indeed.

If You Got Mostly D's:

Your soul mate is from Great Britain!
You are refined and have sophisticated tastes. You are all class and are as clever as they come. Only a real Brit can keep up with your wit.

If You Got Mostly E's:

Your soul mate is from Australia!
You are rugged, tough, and dreadfully good-looking. There is nothing you can't handle and you're always up to take on any challenge. An Aussie is who you'll meet and the rest of your life will be a treat.

If You Got Mostly F's:

Your soul mate is from Canada!
You make friends easily and have always had a pleasant disposition. Your friendliness is contagious and people love being around you. Only a true Canadian can match your warm heart, 'cause you have a lot of love to give.

What Was Your Nickname in High School?

MONTH YOU WERE BORN

January: Big

February: Mister

March: Commando

April: Queen

May: Stinky

June: T-

July: Slim

August: Doctor

September: Kid

October: Teeny

November: Professor

December: Princess

COLOR OF SHIRT YOU'RE WEARING

White: Whiz

Red: Eggs

Orange: Knuckles

Yellow: Flip-flop

Blue: Tank

Black: Cheddar

Green: Dawg

Pink: Pigeon

Purple: Reckless

Gray: Worm

This or That: Movie Villain Edition

Pet cat   or   Pet snake?

Spooky mansion   or   Sleek lair?

Shark tank   or   Plank?

Swanky yacht   or   Expensive car?

Evil laugh   or   Crooked smile?

Cheap disguise   or   Tailored suit?

Tons of henchmen   or   I work alone?

World domination   or   Dismantling society?

Tragic backstory   or   Agent of chaos?

What's Your Celebrity Dog Name and Personality?

LAST LETTER OF YOUR FIRST NAME

B: Boom Boom

C: Diamond Nymph

D: Joyful Noise

E: Department Store

F: Zootopia

G: Nancy Reagan

H: Bubble Bath

I: Novella

J: Rumble Tumble

K: Lollipop Blitz

L: Bergdorf Baby

M: Dirt Licker

N: Millionaire

O: Pleather Honey

P: Jade Roller

Q: Sweetie McSugar

R: Skirt Suit

S: Handsome Prince

T: Crusher

U: Library Card

V: Musk

W: Leopard Print

X: Booboo Bear

Y: Left-on-Fifth

Z: Grease 2

LAST DIGIT OF YOUR PHONE NUMBER

0: You have a passion for fashion

1: You love to dig holes

2: You have serious RBF

3: You're always learning new tricks

4: You know everyone in town

5: You hate when the grass is wet

6: You love to strut your stuff

7: You just want to snuggle

8: You live for the limelight

9: You want to be left alone

What Kind of Cat Are You?

How do you feel about Mondays?

A. Great! I love seeing people!
B. Eh
C. I'm cool with whatever
D. Screw manmade schedules
E. I'm freelance so it's all the same to me
F. Love a break from family!
G. Hate hate hate!
H. !!!!
I. Better than Hump Day

What would be the name of your first album?

A. *How Do You Like Me Now?*
B. *Punkadilly Circus*
C. *Days on Days*
D. *The Woods Are Callin'*
E. *Tru$t I$$ue$*
F. *Southern Comforts*
G. *Food for Thought*
H. *Dance for the Revolution*
I. *Small Explosion*

Would you ever be found in a club?

A. The club comes to me
B. Only themed ones
C. If you carried me there
D. There are no clubs where I live
E. I could never get in
F. I'm too comfy here at home
G. Is there food?
H. HAHA NO
I. Sure, I like to boogey!

What kind of milk do you prefer?

A. Almond
B. Where did it come from?
C. Milk is for babies
D. Nonfat
E. Any, as long as it's served with a straw
F. Soy
G. Whatever you have!
H. Chocolate
I. Coconut

Continues on next page

Pick a winter accessory:

A. I need them all
B. Your warm embrace
C. Winter boots
D. Anything I can find
E. The heater my assistants follow me with
F. My own layer of fat
G. I don't go outside
H. Mittens or a hat!
I. An infinity scarf

What were you made fun of for as a kid?

A. My general appearance
B. My hair
C. Being lazy
D. Being too serious
E. My clothes
F. My lunch
G. Never going out
H. Being short
I. Oh, I never paid any attention to that!

What would your gravestone say?

A. "I proved them wrong!"
B. "Here I lay, as I laid in life"
C. I'll be cremated
D. "Lived, loved, mostly didn't give a fuck"
E. "Lived well, tolerated family"
F. "Found the meatloaf"
G. "Up for anything, including the Great Beyond"
H. "Little one, big heart"
I. "Misunderstood"

How do you feel about dogs?

A. Not as cute as me
B. Ugh, we are at war
C. They're cool
D. As long as they don't take my food, I like
E. I love annoying them
F. Indifferent
G. Don't trust 'em
H. LOVE THEM SO MUCH!!
I. They are scary, but I know they mean well

If You Got Mostly A's:

You're a famous cat! What's so great about you is that what makes you the most unique is also what makes you so lovable. Maybe you were self-conscious about that at some point, but now you own it! Some people may call you a diva, but really, you just know how to get stuff done. Plus, you meet everyone with a gracious, warm heart, which makes you a winner.

If You Got Mostly B's:

You're hairless! You love the simple things in life and this can sometimes make you misunderstood. You're actually really sweet, which can make it infuriating when people judge you right off the bat. You keep doing you!

If You Got Mostly C's:

You're a Maine Coon! You certainly are a wild one, which draws people to you. However, you are loyal and pragmatic. You love the outdoors and never do anything you don't want to. Basically, you're the Ron Swanson of cats.

If You Got Mostly D's:

You're a feral cat! So, you can be a little rough around the edges, but it's all part of your charm. You have so much love to give but sometimes have a hard time trusting others with your heart. (Who can blame you? The world can be rough.) However, you make the most loving and loyal companion once you establish trust and that is invaluable.

If You Got Mostly E's:

You're a *fat* indoor cat! All right, so this isn't your specific body type as much as it is a mind-set (your bod is hot). You know you have it made in life and kind of have a more laissez-faire attitude, which can be refreshing in a high-stress world. Sometimes people ask, "Are you stoned?" to which you respond, "I'm just enjoying life, man." Cheers to that!

If You Got Mostly F's:

You're a Scottish Fold! Are you a dog? Basically, you are outgoing and cheerful and love having a good time. Yeah, you have your introvert moments (who doesn't??), but that doesn't mean you don't love experiencing life at its fullest! Your mix of introvert and extrovert makes you empathetic, drawing all kinds of people to you.

If You Got Mostly G's:

You're an indoor cat! Everyone loves you, even though you want your space sometimes. You're introverted for the most part, but will tolerate those you love and give them the affection they absolutely need. You're a daydreamer, mainly because you can daydream from the comfort of a plush couch.

If You Got Mostly H's:

You're a Munchkin! You are adorable and maybe the sweetest person you know. Sometimes you get scared of big things, but you can pull out that bravery when you need it. Your spunky personality makes you an asset to any environment!

If You Got Mostly I's:

You're a Ragdoll! You apply the motto "go with the flow" to most of your activities. You're down-to-earth and are open to new experiences, as long as you don't have to put in too much effort. You probably give the best hugs and that's downright magical.

What's key to making a relationship last?

A. Trust
B. Making time for each other
C. Similar values
D. Communication
E. Sexual chemistry
F. Being able to compromise

Let's Settle This: What's Your Actual Type?

What physical feature do you find most attractive?

A. Full lips
B. Sexy eyes
C. Luscious hair
D. Well-maintained eyebrows
E. Clear skin
F. A bright smile

What mountainous region would you like to visit with a partner?

A. The Rocky Mountains
B. The Swiss Alps
C. The Fjords of Norway
D. The Andes
E. The Himalayas
F. The Hindu Kush

Describe your personality in one word:

A. Fun
B. Social
C. Deep
D. Reserved
E. Loyal
F. Bookish

What's an ideal food to have on a date?

A. Sushi
B. Spaghetti
C. Fondue
D. Tacos
E. Pho
F. Steak

Which personality trait is a total turnoff?

A. Dishonesty
B. Vanity
C. Selfishness
D. Cockiness
E. Terrible manners
F. Aloofness

What's better to have in a relationship?

A. A lot of food
B. A lot of good sex

If You Got Mostly A's:

You got the creative type! You like someone with an expansive mind, but it also doesn't hurt if they're *fiiine*. Nothing turns you on more than someone who is expressive and knows a thing or two about the arts. For you, brains and creativity are the ultimate turn-on.

If You Got Mostly B's:

You got the comedian! You like someone who can always make you laugh and keep you on your toes. A good joke and witty remarks are the quickest way to your heart. It's true what they say; nothing is sexier than a good sense of humor.

If You Got Mostly C's:

You got the total babe! You'd love to have someone who is easy on the eyes. You are a connoisseur of beauty and you know exactly what you want. Eye candy makes you feel dandy.

If You Got Mostly D's:

You got the thinker! Nothing turns you on more than intelligence. You like someone who is cultured, well educated, and can carry on a conversation. To you, nothing is sexier than someone with brains.

If You Got Mostly E's:

You got the athlete! Your type is someone who loves sports. Whether it's playing or watching them, athletics is part of your aesthetics. To you, someone active is always attractive.

If You Got Mostly F's:

You got Mr./Ms. Perfect! You like someone who truly has it all. You need someone who is well rounded in all aspects of life. When it comes to looks and personality, only perfection receives your affection.

What's Your Race Car Driver Name?

YOUR ZODIAC SIGN

Aries: Silver

Taurus: Speedy

Gemini: Flying

Cancer: Red

Leo: Silent

Virgo: Young

Libra: Neon

Scorpio: Captain

Sagittarius: Flaming

Capricorn: Detective

Aquarius: Iron

Pisces: Major

WHAT YOU ATE FOR LUNCH

Sandwich: Big Toe

Salad: Granola

Soup: Eagle

Pasta: Pony

Sushi: Phantom

Grain bowl: Lizard

Just a bunch of little snacks: Cheeto Dust

Leftovers: Whoopie Cushion

I didn't eat lunch yet: Hammer

What Color Should You Dye Your Hair?

Enter Here

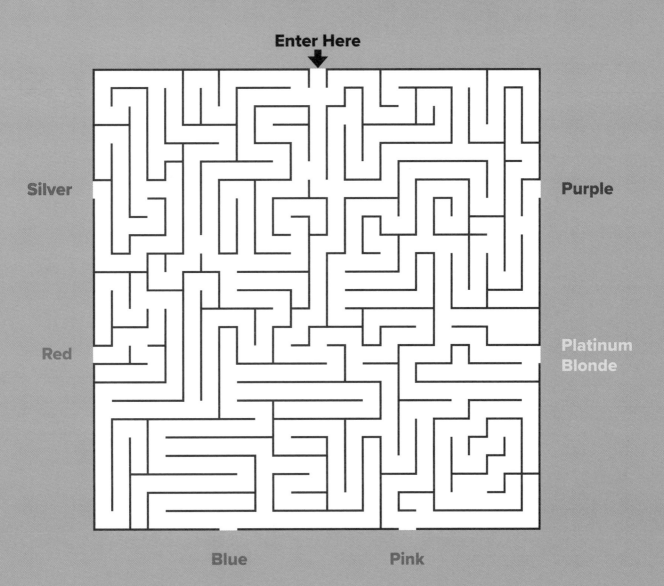

Silver

Purple

Red

Platinum Blonde

Blue

Pink

We Know Your Age and State Based on Your Mani

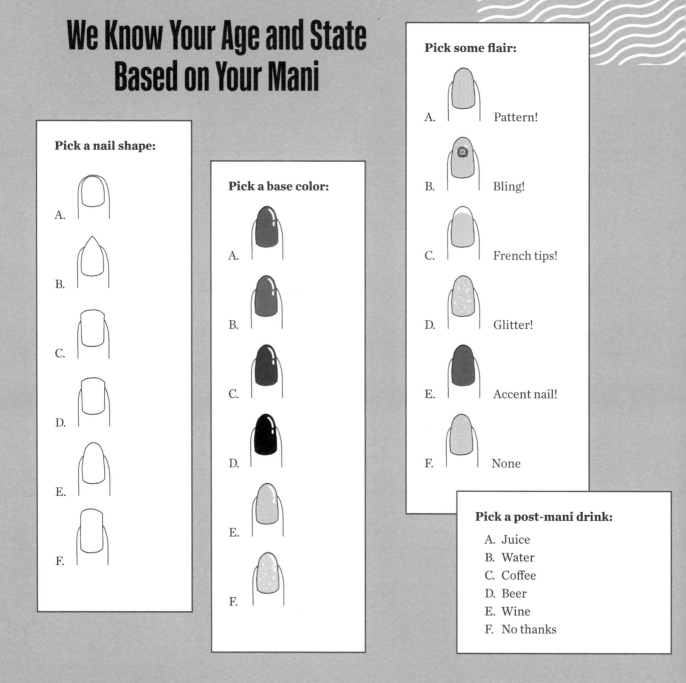

Pick a nail shape:

A.

B.

C.

D.

E.

F.

Pick a base color:

A.

B.

C.

D.

E.

F.

Pick some flair:

A.   Pattern!

B.   Bling!

C.   French tips!

D.   Glitter!

E.   Accent nail!

F.   None

Pick a post-mani drink:

A. Juice
B. Water
C. Coffee
D. Beer
E. Wine
F. No thanks

If You Got Mostly A's:
You are sweet sixteen and living like a celeb in Cali.

If You Got Mostly B's:
You are thirteen years old and living it up in Ohio.

If You Got Mostly C's:
You're a solid forty-two years old and settled down in Arkansas.

If You Got Mostly D's:
You're a twenty-four-year-old enjoying life in Texas.

If You Got Mostly E's:
You are a mature thirty-one, living and working in New York.

If You Got Mostly F's:
You're a wise seventy-one and living large in Colorado.

What Does Your Frozen Yogurt Order Say about You?

Pick a frozen yogurt flavor:

A. Tart
B. Mango
C. Cake batter
D. Chocolate

Do you mix flavors?

A. Always
B. Sometimes
C. Only if there are two I really want
D. Never

Pick a fruit topping:

A. No fruit
B. Strawberries
C. Bananas
D. Pineapple

Pick a second fruit topping:

A. I said no fruit!
B. Peaches
C. Mango
D. Kiwi

Pick another topping:

A. Gummy bears
B. Reese's Peanut Butter Cups
C. M&M's
D. Coconut shavings

Pick another topping:

A. Cherries
B. M&M's
C. Reese's Peanut Butter Cups
D. None of these

Pick another topping:

A. Chocolate chips
B. Yogurt chips
C. Rainbow sprinkles
D. Chocolate sprinkles

And another:

A. Cookie dough
B. Peanuts
C. Almonds
D. Fruity pebbles

Keep going:

A. Mochi
B. Granola
C. Cap'n Crunch
D. Fruit pearls

One more—you know you want to:

A. Cheesecake bites
B. Graham crackers
C. Oreos
D. Brownie bites

Pick a sauce:

A. Chocolate syrup
B. Hot fudge
C. Caramel sauce
D. Strawberry sauce

wow **win**

If You Got Mostly A's:
You're intelligent and thoughtful! Wow. Just wow. You really know what you're doing. In frozen yogurt but also in life. You have it together. (Even if it doesn't feel like it sometimes, you're ahead of the game compared to most people.)

If You Got Mostly B's:
You're a creative genius! Everyone needs to step aside because you're yogurt royalty. Your yogurt choices prove that your creativity knows no bounds. You don't play by the rules and it pays off.

If You Got Mostly C's:
You're life-experienced! You're wise. You've seen some things. You've lived through some tough stuff and now you know what's up. You're good at picking the right toppings, but you also surround yourself with the right people.

If You Got Mostly D's:
You're a smart risk-taker! You're not scared to take a risk, but you're not reckless—you're smart about it. And you're never boring. You go after what you want. Some haters can't handle that, but you don't even care.

Which *Friends* Character Are You?

Pick a New York landmark:

A. Statue of Liberty
B. Central Park
C. Central Perk
D. Empire State Building
E. Times Square
F. Grimaldi's Pizza

Pick a '90s toy:

A. Polly Pocket
B. Legos
C. Moon shoes
D. Ninja Turtles
E. Barbie
F. Super Soaker

Choose your fave boyfriend:

A. Dr. Richard
B. David
C. Mike Hannigan
D. Joshua
E. Paolo
F. Fun Bobby

What were you like in high school?

A. Quiet
B. The Class Clown
C. Quirky
D. Kinda nerdy
E. Popular, TBH
F. A little lazy

What's your dream Friday night?

A. Partying
B. Watching a movie
C. Chilling out and just listening to music
D. Reading
E. Catching up on chores
F. Eating ice cream

How do you take your coffee?

A. Black
B. With milk or cream
C. Latte
D. Okay, fine, frappuccinos
E. As dessert :)
F. I don't drink coffee

What's your sense of humor like?

A. Dark
B. Sarcastic
C. Idiosyncratic
D. Goofy
E. Witty
F. I'm not really that funny

What really ticks you off?

A. Bad drivers
B. Tardiness
C. Men
D. Stupid people
E. Lint
F. When you run out of beer

If You Got Mostly A's:

You're Rachel! You're fashion-forward, outgoing, and maybe . . . a little bit spoiled. You're a true romantic who believes everyone finds their lobster at the end.

If You Got Mostly B's:

You're Chandler! Could you *be* any more hilarious? You're a constant jokester with a witty mind to boot, but deep down you're a huge softie who loves spending time with your friends and loved ones.

If You Got Mostly C's:

You're Phoebe! You're quirky, bubbly, and really, really talented (maybe not musically). You may have not had the easiest past, but you love to daydream about a totally rad future.

If You Got Mostly D's:

You're Ross! You're a total smarty-pants who works hard on your career. While you have drive and ambition, your friends always come first.

If You Got Mostly E's:

You're Monica! You're definitely a type-A personality who thrives on neatness and organization, but that doesn't mean you don't know how to let loose! You can enjoy the party as much as the next person and you love taking care of your friends and family.

If You Got Mostly F's:

You're Joey! You're the life of the party and always ready to get the fun going, but you're also a loyal friend who will, uh, always be there for your besties. And let's be real—you *love* to eat.

Which Decade Were You Meant For?

What modern necessity can you not live without?

A. Hot showers
B. Central air
C. Social media
D. GPS
E. Microwaves
F. Cell phones

Choose a movie about the future:

A. *Back to the Future Part II*
B. *Mad Max: Fury Road*
C. *Blade Runner*
D. *The Terminator*
E. *The Hunger Games: Catching Fire*
F. *The Divergent Series: Insurgent*

Would you rather have your life come with a pause button or a rewind button?

A. Pause button
B. Rewind button

What old-timey English phrase needs to make a comeback?

A. Tickle one's innards
B. Bitch the pot
C. Beer and skittles
D. Tallywags
E. Crinkum-crankum
F. Shoot into the brown

Which throwback toy reminds you of your childhood?

A. Gak
B. Cabbage Patch Dolls
C. Teddy Ruxpin
D. Troll Dolls
E. Game Boy
F. Talkboy

Would you risk time travel knowing you might never return?

A. Yes, send me back to the future
B. No, I wouldn't risk not coming back

If You Got Mostly A's:
You were meant for the '50s. You appreciate when life was simple and love a good sock hop. The '50s was a happy time full of doo-wop music and milkshakes. There is a joy in simplicity and the '50s is where it's at.

If You Got Mostly B's:
You were meant for any decade in the Renaissance. You're a forward thinker and have a creative side. There is nothing you enjoy more than artistic expression. You're ahead of your time and are a classy and creative bo$$!

If You Got Mostly C's:
You were meant for the 1920s. You have a personality that's larger than life and you belong in an era of lax rules, great dancing, and even better music. Whether it's flapper fashion or legendary gangsters, there was never a dull moment in this decadent decade.

If You Got Mostly D's:
You were meant for the '60s. You're all about peace, love, and knowing what you're made of. From bell-bottoms to Woodstock, the '60s truly had it all. So jump in your Volkswagen van and enjoy the glory that was the swinging '60s.

If You Got Mostly E's:
You were meant for the '80s. You are full of energy and love good music, big hair, and even bigger fashion. Whether it's teasing your hair or watching a John Hughes movie, you were meant for this decade. Get those acid-wash jeans and shoulder pads on and enjoy the ride.

If You Got Mostly F's:
You were meant for the '90s. Your place is in arguably the greatest decade of all time. Whether it's playing your Nintendo or jamming out on your Walkman, the '90s is the place for you. Strap on your Reebok pumps and don't ever forget to rewind your VHS tapes—the '90s rocks!

Which Disney Animal Are You?

Choose a Disney princess:

A. Rapunzel
B. Cinderella
C. Ariel
D. Belle
E. The Ugly Stepsisters
F. Mulan
G. Pocahontas
H. Anna
I. Sleeping Beauty

Choose a Disney dude:

A. Prince Eric
B. Flynn Rider
C. Hercules
D. Tarzan
E. Peter Pan
F. Aladdin
G. The Beast
H. Prince Hans
I. Prince Naveen

What's your favorite kitchen appliance?

A. Microwave
B. Keurig
C. Toaster
D. Blender
E. I don't really cook for myself
F. This is such a dumb question
G. Crock-Pot
H. Tea kettle
I. Knife sharpener

What's your ideal vacation spot?

A. Give me a beach and I'm happy
B. A nice cabin in the woods, away from worries and cares
C. Disney World!
D. Paris
E. Inside an active volcano
F. Vegas, baby!
G. Anywhere but here, honestly
H. Anywhere new! I love adventures!
I. I'm too busy to even *think* about vacation

What is your general reaction to free samples at the grocery store?

A. I'm all about free samples
B. HELL YEAH FREE SAMPLES I'LL TAKE TWELVE
C. I would take one and politely thank the sample giver-outer
D. I'd light the table on fire even if it was my favorite food
E. It's hit or miss with free samples, so I don't get too excited
F. Whoop-dee-doo, free samples, no big deal, whatever
G. I probably won't like any of them, so I'd just keep walking
H. I love trying new things! Sample tables are so *fun*!
I. Free samples? That's a thing?

Choose the celebrity most like yourself:

A. Kanye West
B. Ellen DeGeneres
C. Keanu Reeves
D. Timothée Chalamet
E. Mahershala Ali
F. Julie Andrews
G. Amy Schumer
H. Ryan Gosling
I. Zoë Kravitz

What do you look for in a suitor?

A. Kindness
B. Good looks
C. Honesty
D. Confidence
E. Intelligence
F. A knack for devising evil plans
G. Nothing, I'll be single forever
H. Humor
I. A good sense of sarcasm

If You Got Mostly A's:
You're Simba! You are a confident and hardworking individual whom people admire and look up to. You're down-to-earth and friendly and you probably got really hot after your awkward teenage years.

If You Got Mostly B's:
You're Sebastian! Although you're a bit of a worrywart, you are incredibly caring and responsible. You work hard and you have a dedication to what you love. You also sometimes sing incredibly catchy songs to prove a point to rebellious teenage mermaids.

If You Got Mostly C's:
You're Bambi! You are too precious for this world. You can be a little naive, but you're genuinely excited about life and everyone loves having you around. You're friendly and cute and a little drop of sunshine in this cold world.

If You Got Mostly D's:
You're Perdita! You are elegant, polite, and confident. Although you are very well-mannered, you can be fierce when you need to be and will do anything to protect the ones you love. Also, you tend to fall in love with ~rascals~.

If You Got Mostly E's:
You're Mushu! You've got *a lot* of swagger. Although your attitude can get you into trouble, you love adventures and are very courageous. And sometimes you mistake horses for cows.

If You Got Mostly F's:
You're Scar! You are straight-up evil.

If You Got Mostly G's:
You're Eeyore! You can be a Debbie Downer, but you still recognize when you've got good friends and adventure ahead. You are a hard worker and you have a devotion to whatever you put your mind to. Keep your head up!

If You Got Mostly H's:
You're Dory! You are so much fun! Although you can be forgetful and scatterbrained, you are super friendly and caring and everyone loves to be around you. Just keep swimming!

If You Got Mostly I's:
You're Iago! You're sarcastic and cynical, but at least you're funny about it. Even though you may complain, you work hard and are very ambitious. You'll get the job done!

Make Dinner for $20

Circle the items you want to purchase. The goal is to try to not go over your budget.

$10	Steak	Lobster	Truffles	Scallops
$8	Chicken	Hamburger	Tofu	Shrimp
$6	Kale	Avocado	Beans	Tomatoes
$4	Pasta	Avocado	Potatoes	Cheese
$2	Hot sauce	Ketchup	Rice	Parsley

What Does Your Name Look Like in Morse Code?

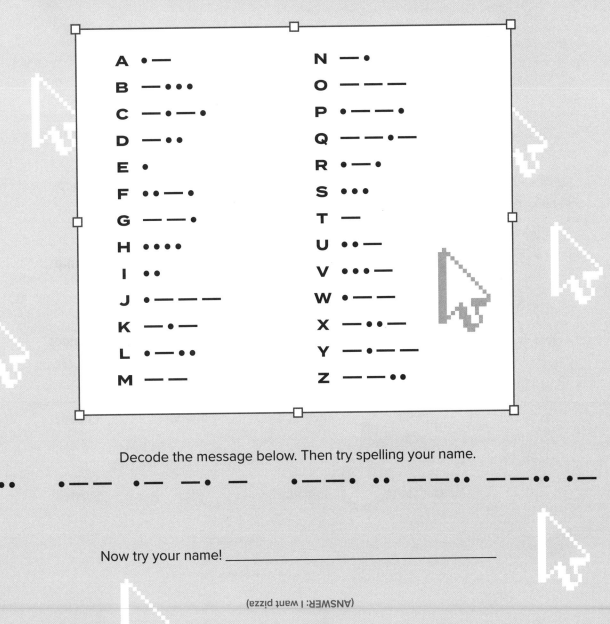

A	•—	N	—•
B	—•••	O	———
C	—•—•	P	•——•
D	—••	Q	——•—
E	•	R	•—•
F	••—•	S	•••
G	——•	T	—
H	••••	U	••—
I	••	V	•••—
J	•———	W	•——
K	—•—	X	—••—
L	•—••	Y	—•——
M	——	Z	——••

Decode the message below. Then try spelling your name.

•• •——— ——• —• ——— •——• •• ———•• —••• •—

Now try your name! _____

(ANSWER: I want pizza)

How long have you been friends for?

A. 1 to 2 years
B. 2 to 3 years
C. 3 to 5 years
D. 5 to 10 years
E. 10 to 15 years
F. Literally forever

Which Food Pair Perfectly Matches You and Your Best Friend?

What activity do you enjoy doing the most together?

A. Eating
B. Karaoke
C. Hiking
D. Going to a bar
E. Shopping
F. Just chilling

Which animal sums you both up?

A. An owl
B. A bird
C. A lion
D. A horse
E. An elephant
F. A bear

Finally, choose the word that best describes your friendship:

A. One-of-a-kind
B. Inseparable
C. Loyal
D. Hilarious
E. Comforting
F. Deep

If You Got Mostly A's:

You're pizza and ranch! Though the internet is split on whether or not pizza and ranch go together, you two know WITHOUT A DOUBT that you're a pair that's meant to be best friends for life. There's just something magical about your friendship that you can't quite explain, which makes you a duo like no other. Snap a pic of this quiz for your BFF to see if they get the same thing!

If You Got Mostly B's:

You're chicken and waffles! Savory *and* sweet? Yeah, you two are a match made in heaven. You were basically destined to be BFFs because you completely balance each other out with the best of both your personalities. No one would ever dare split you up because they know how well you work together. Snap a pic of this quiz for your BFF to see if they get the same thing!

If You Got Mostly C's:

You're cookies and cream! Yeah, you guys are ULTIMATE best friends in that your two foods have melded into one. There's not one situation you've ever been in where you didn't know exactly how your BFF would react, which means you know them basically better than anyone in the entire world. Whether you've been best friends your whole life or just a few years, you're meant to be. Snap a pic of this quiz for your BFF to see if they get the same thing!

If You Got Mostly D's:

You're tequila and lime! LOL. Not only do you guys know how to have a good time, but everyone else knows it about you, too. You're the life of any party because, when you're together, straight-up magic happens. Snap a pic of this quiz for your BFF to see if they get the same thing!

If You Got Mostly E's:

You're macaroni and cheese! You knew carbs were going to be involved, didn't you? You and your BFF are as comforting and classic as they come. When you boil everything down to the basics, you're both still there cheering each other on and supporting one another. You'll always be the perfect pair! Snap a pic of this quiz for your BFF to see if they get the same thing!

If You Got Mostly F's:

You're wine and cheese! Well, well, well—look at you two classy BFFs. The best part about your friendship is that you appreciate each other more and more with age. As each year passes, you grow closer and your bond grows stronger. There's basically no other pair out there who could beat your friendship. Snap a pic of this quiz for your BFF to see if they get the same thing!

Which Avenger Are You Destined to Date?

How do you show someone that you love them?

A. Tease them
B. Give them gifts
C. Anticipate their needs
D. Cook for them
E. Tell them
F. Act awkward
G. Ignore them
H. Talk about your future with them
I. Show them affection

Justice is . . .

A. Simple
B. Complex
C. Pointless
D. A lie
E. A goal
F. A long game
G. Imperative
H. Never gonna happen
I. A tween clothing brand

How do you resolve conflict?

A. Talk it out
B. Make a joke
C. Wage emotional warfare
D. Sulk
E. Silent treatment
F. Apologize a lot

What's your tragic flaw?

A. I care too much
B. I'm kinda mean
C. I brood a lot
D. I'm insecure
E. I don't care enough
F. I have a bad temper
G. I'm a little messy
H. I'm passive-aggressive
I. I have too many clothes

How do you defeat your enemies?

A. With your natural charm and good looks
B. Cool gadgets
C. Mental games
D. Magic
E. Diplomacy
F. Brute strength
G. Snarky one-liners
H. Teach them right from wrong
I. Blackmail

What kind of kiss is the most romantic?

A. Kiss on the lips
B. Kiss on the neck
C. Kiss on the wrist
D. Hot, heavy make-out session
E. Kiss on each finger
F. Kiss on the cheek
G. Kiss on the forehead
H. Kiss on the nose
I. A surprise kiss

If You Got Mostly A's:

You're destined to date Captain America! You might be sensible and logical on the outside, but, like Cap, you're a true romantic at heart. You're both very loyal people who commit to others 100 percent and would never turn your back on a friend in need. Cap's your match in every way except for the fact that he's definitely *waaay* older than you, but whatever, you'll make it work.

If You Got Mostly B's:

You're destined to date Iron Man! You're a confident and successful person who needs a partner who matches your ambition. Like Tony Stark, you can sometimes come off as brash or impatient, but you're both brilliant and don't have time for nonsense. Together, you'd make an unstoppable pair.

If You Got Mostly C's:

You're destined to date Black Widow! You're capable and cunning and you're always one step ahead of the game. You need someone who's just as quick on their feet—both literally and figuratively—which is why you and Natasha would make a smashing pair. You want someone who will both commit to and challenge you on a daily basis, so dating a spy with a secret heart of gold is just the ticket.

If You Got Mostly D's:

You're destined to date Scarlet Witch! Much like Wanda, you're a low-key goth who secretly longs for true love. That icy facade can keep people at a distance, but what they don't know is that you're just trying to save yourself from getting hurt. Together, you and Wanda could learn the value of letting someone else into your deep and rich inner emotional life.

If You Got Mostly E's:

You're destined to date Black Panther! Like T'Challa, you find someone you love and devote yourself to them entirely. You're probably a bit of a serial monogamist and put a lot of time and effort into making your romantic relationships work. You'd make a great pair because you both prioritize your love lives and make an effort to make sure your partner feels appreciated.

If You Got Mostly F's:

You're destined to date Thor! He may be the God of Thunder, but above all, Thor is super fun. He's become the funniest and most chill Avenger and you need a superhero who's as fun as they are powerful, ya know? He's confident, super hot, and can wield lightning. *Sooo* congrats and enjoy!

If You Got Mostly G's:

You're destined to date Ant-Man! We're all suckers for superheroes, but you need someone who appreciates humor way more than you need someone with superpowers. Scott Lang is one of the few Avengers who can keep up with your razor-sharp wit and go toe-to-toe with you in pop culture trivia. Sure, it helps that he's a handsome, devilishly charming member of earth's coolest clique, but you're here for the jokes.

If You Got Mostly H's:

You're destined to date Doctor Strange! You're usually the smartest person in most rooms, so you need someone who can challenge you intellectually. Doctor Strange, with his Time Stone and reality-bending powers, will definitely challenge you, but even better, you're one of the few people who can challenge him back. Most people might find a constant battle of wits exhausting but not you two—you need that kind of rapport to stay interested in a person.

If You Got Mostly I's:

You're destined to date Winter Soldier! You and Bucky both have a tendency toward melancholy, but that's not a bad thing. You're similarly broody creatures, but the few people you let into your inner circle know they can rely on you for anything. Together, you'd be able to finally let your guards down and embrace the comfort of trusting someone else for once.

How would you most likely find someone to date?

A. On a dating app
B. At a bar/club
C. In a friend group
D. At work

This Love Test Will Reveal the Exact Age When You'll Get Married

What is your ideal first date?

A. Just drinks
B. Dinner and drinks
C. Dinner and a movie
D. Coffee

When is it appropriate to have a first kiss?

A. On the first date is fine
B. Second or third date
C. At least five dates
D. Not until we're in a committed relationship

When is it appropriate to have sex?

A. On the first or second date
B. On the third or fourth date
C. It'll take you months before we have sex
D. I'm waiting until marriage

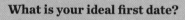

What is the point of marriage?

A. To show someone how much you love them
B. Tax purposes
C. To please your family
D. There is no point

Someone says "I love you" after a month of dating. What do you say?

A. "I love you, too!"
B. "I really like you a lot."
C. "What does love even mean?"
D. "I love spaghetti."

If You Got Mostly A's:

You got 21! You have someone in your life who you're certain is ~the one~. People will tell you it's a mistake to get hitched at such an early age, but you know what? You do you. If you feel it's the right time, then do it. If it doesn't work out, then you'll learn from your mistakes and move on.

If You Got Mostly B's:

You got 30! At thirty, you've left behind all the juvenile and adolescent stuff. You've made mistakes through your teens and twenties (A LOT OF THEM), you learned from them, and you've become a better person. At thirty, you're looking to settle down with someone and start a new chapter in your life.

If You Got Mostly C's:

You got 40! You made it a priority to live your life. You wanted to focus on you and only you and YOU MADE THE RIGHT DECISION. At forty, you've done it all. You've seen it all. You've fucked around, dated, broken hearts, and had your heart broken. But now you're done with all that at forty. A new phase in your life is starting out and what better way to ring in your fortieth year of life than by getting married? It's perfect.

If You Got Mostly D's:

You got never! That's right. You're never gonna get married. And that's a *great* thing. You can go out with whomever you choose, you can date whomever you want to date, you can love whomever you want to love. But marriage is not for you. You'll see the world and experience life to its fullest without having someone to anchor you down. You might even find the love of your life, but you won't marry them. You don't need marriage to show someone you love them. Go you!

What Kind of Potato Are You?

Pick your favorite style of potato.

FRENCH FRY

You make your bed every single day.

You have a fire Instagram aesthetic.

You studied abroad and still won't shut up about it.

BAKED POTATO

You always have the best snacks.

You love to chill with the homies.

You press the snooze button ten times every morning.

CURLY FRIES

You stage-managed the spring musical.

You love water parks.

You can't fall asleep without *The Office* playing in the background.

MASHED POTATOES

You skipped the party to sleep.

You call your mom multiple times a day.

You always made excuses to get out of P.E.

WAFFLE FRY

You're chaotic but in a cute way.

You have best friends in multiple states.

You drink iced coffee in the winter.

POTATO SALAD

You pay for your own Netflix account.

You get all your memes from Facebook.

You think minions are absolutely adorable.

What Would Be the Title of Your Autobiography?

COLOR OF THE SHIRT YOU'RE WEARING

White: My Tremendous

Red: My Bold

Orange: My Beautiful

Yellow: My Confusing

Blue: My Surprising

Black: My Secret

Green: My Fabulous

Pink: My Impressive

Purple: My Intoxicating

Gray: My Exhilarating

MONTH YOU WERE BORN

January: Struggle

February: Obsession with Slime

March: Love Affair with Mac 'n' Cheese

April: Stamp Collection

May: Overactive Sweat Gland

June: Attempt at Becoming a Reality TV Star

July: Fascination with Baby Ducklings

August: Addiction to Tater Tots

September: Story about How I Was Abducted by Aliens

October: Criminal Record

November: Story about How I Was a Celebrity Personal Assistant

December: Journey to Becoming a Dog Psychic

Which Kardashian-Jenner Are You?

On a scale of 1–10, how much do you love drama?

A. One
B. Ten
C. Eh, around the lower end of that spectrum
D. Somewhere between five and ten
E. I'm pretty neutral
F. One million
G. I stay out of the drama completely
H. I only *pretend* not to love it

Who would you rather date?

A. Kanye West
B. Corey Gamble
C. Scott Disick
D. Tyga
E. Travis Scott
F. Rob Kardashian
G. Tristan Thompson
H. Lamar Odom

Pick a product to endorse:

A. Ride-sharing app
B. Hair vitamins
C. Detox tea
D. Skin-care product
E. Makeup product
F. Teeth-whitening product
G. Shapewear
H. Your own app

Pick a career path:

A. Model
B. Manager
C. Mom
D. Singer
E. Designer
F. Actress
G. Brand ambassador
H. Photographer

If you had to name your kid one of these names, which would you pick?

A. Saint
B. Stormi
C. Penelope
D. North
E. Mason
F. Dream
G. Chicago
H. True

If You Got Mostly A's:
You're Kim Kardashian-West! You're the one who started it all and you'll be damned if anyone thinks they're going to claim your throne.

If You Got Mostly B's:
You're Kris Jenner! You're the matriarch of this whole friggin' empire.

If You Got Mostly C's:
You're Kourtney Kardashian! You're the most down-to-earth member of your whole family, TBH.

If You Got Mostly D's:
You're Caitlyn Jenner! After years in the shadows you're finally able to be your true self.

If You Got Mostly E's:
You're Kylie Jenner! You're the real star of the family now, with nowhere to go but up.

If You Got Mostly F's:
You're Angela Renée Kardashian! You came from nothing, only to beat these biotches at their own game.

If You Got Mostly G's:
You're Kendall Jenner! You stay out of most of the drama. You're focused on carving out your own lane.

If You Got Mostly H's:
You're Khloé Kardashian! You've never been afraid to say what you're thinking, even if it means stirring the pot every once in a while.

Zodiac Sign Word Scramble

ELO_____

SERIA_____

GORVI_____

RATGASSUITI_____

SATURU_____

CESSPI_____

RANCORCIP_____

RANCEC_____

BARLI_____

ROOPICS_____

MENIIG_____

SQUARAUI_____

You're a True Southerner Only If You've Eaten 20/28 of These Foods

Check off all the Southern food that you've tried.

- ☐ Fried okra
- ☐ Fried chicken
- ☐ Country ham
- ☐ Moon pie
- ☐ Buttermilk biscuit
- ☐ Fried green tomatoes
- ☐ Pecan pie
- ☐ Jambalaya
- ☐ Red beans and rice
- ☐ Po' boy
- ☐ Pulled pork
- ☐ Cornbread muffin
- ☐ Black-eyed peas
- ☐ Collard greens

- ☐ Fried catfish
- ☐ Cobbler with ice cream
- ☐ Hush puppies
- ☐ Mashed potatoes and gravy
- ☐ Succotash
- ☐ Grits
- ☐ Sweet tea
- ☐ BBQ beef brisket
- ☐ Peach pie
- ☐ Deviled eggs
- ☐ Boiled peanuts
- ☐ Kimchi
- ☐ Nachos
- ☐ Chitlins

NOW ADD UP YOUR SCORE!

If You Checked 0–10:
You've dabbled in Southern food, but I gotta tell ya, you're really missing out! There's so much good food left to try!

If You Checked 11–19:
You know your way around a big Southern buffet, but you haven't tried everything there is to try. Keep going—you're almost there!

If You Checked 20–28:
You're a tried-and-true Southerner! From fried chicken to fried green tomatoes, you love it all!

What Would Your Food Name Be Based on Your Birthday?

MONTH YOU WERE BORN

January: Hard-Boiled

February: Charred

March: Poached

April: Fried

May: Brûléed

June: Baked

July: Roasted

August: Sautéed

September: Dried

October: Frozen

November: Melted

December: Grilled

DAY YOU WERE BORN

1: Popcorn

2: Salad

3: Meatloaf

4: Potatoes

5: Granola Bar

6: Pudding

7: Cheesecake

8: Cereal

9: Trail Mix

10: Jell-O Shot

11: Yogurt

12: Beef Stew

13: Egg Rolls

14: Salmon

15: Pizza

16: Spaghetti

17: Fruit Salad

18: Popsicle

19: Ramen

20: Licorice

21: Pumpkin Pie

22: Cheese Wheel

23: Birthday Cake

24: Cappuccino

25: Chili

26: Cookie Dough

27: Pancakes

28: Lasagna

29: Ice Cream

30: Nachos

31: Eggs

Which Country Is Best Suited to Your Personality?

What do you appreciate most about a culture?

A. The food
B. Holiday traditions
C. The architecture
D. The music
E. The art
F. The fashion

yaaass

What activity puts your mind at ease?

A. Reading a book
B. Hanging out with a good friend
C. Taking a nap
D. Going on a walk
E. Cuddling with a pet
F. Talking to family

What's your biggest pet peeve while traveling abroad?

A. Crappy exchange rates
B. Jet lag
C. Food that's too exotic
D. Traveler's diarrhea
E. The language barrier
F. Obvious tourist traps

What's your most dominant trait?

A. Ambition
B. Sarcasm
C. Humor
D. Honesty
E. Intelligence
F. Sassiness

What word best describes your favorite food?

A. Sweet
B. Spicy
C. Tart
D. Savory
E. Salty
F. Cheesy

Would you rather live in your home country permanently or live abroad forever?

A. I'd rather stay in my home country
B. I would love to spend the rest of my life abroad

If You Got Mostly A's:

You got Japan! You are disciplined but also have a wild and creative side. You love a place teeming with energy and life. You should plan a move to Japan.

If You Got Mostly B's:

You got Brazil! You are charismatic and have infectious energy. People love you and love being around you. You are friendly, talkative, and proud, so Brazilians should be part of your crowd.

If You Got Mostly C's:

You got England! You are sophisticated and dapper. You're one of the sharpest people around and have a lightning-quick wit and a penchant for sarcasm. For you, being a Brit is the shit!

If You Got Mostly D's:

You got Australia! You're friendly and easygoing and you don't have a hard time making friends. You love a land of great beaches and even greater people. You'll never blunder if you're down under.

If You Got Mostly E's:

You got America! You're confident and very self-assured. You put freedom above everything else and love a place with a ton of variety. There is no better place for you than the land of the red, white, and blue.

If You Got Mostly F's:

You got Italy! You carry yourself with pride and flair and you've always had a passion for fashion. You're well-suited for a place with rich food and an even richer history. Italy should be your home and your heart will no longer roam.

What's Your Hippie Name?

Select a flower:

A. Daffodil
B. Rose
C. Peony
D. Tulip
E. Sunflower
F. Gardenia

Everyone should be a little:

A. Nicer
B. Richer
C. Hotter
D. Smarter
E. Calmer
F. Higher

Pick a music festival:

A. Coachella
B. Bonnaroo
C. Warped Tour
D. Lollapalooza
E. Woodstock
F. Lilith Fair

Pick a scent of incense:

A. Patchouli
B. Euphoria
C. Orange clove
D. Frankincense
E. Sandalwood
F. Chai spice

Put something in your hair:

A. Flower crown
B. Butterfly clips
C. A red ribbon
D. Baseball cap
E. Sock bun
F. Something sparkly

Pet a baby animal:

A. Baby deer
B. Baby duck
C. Baby elephant
D. Baby goat
E. Baby pig
F. Baby tiger

If You Got Mostly A's:

Your name would be Rain. You're calm and self-assured and you always reassure your friends when they're feeling down.

If You Got Mostly B's:

Your name would be Heaven. You're a dreamer who's always on the hunt for something new. You bring light and inspiration everywhere you go.

If You Got Mostly C's:

Your name would be Daisy. You're the happy-go-lucky one in your friend group. You're always wearing a sunny smile and you have a pure inner sweetness.

If You Got Mostly D's:

Your name would be Echo. You're a deep, wise spirit who looks for the true meaning in life. Your friends always count on you for real, truthful advice.

If You Got Mostly E's:

Your name would be Sunshine. You light up the room with your cheery personality and warm spirit. You have a large group of friends who cherish your presence in their lives.

If You Got Mostly F's:

Your name would be Rebel. You never go with the grain and always dance to the beat of your own bongo drum. A true individual, you think for yourself and never let anyone keep you from being who you really are.

Theater Kid Bingo

Check off or mark the squares that apply to you (things you own, have done, or things that have happened to you). The more you fill out, the more you're a theater kid! See if you can get five across, down, or diagonally. Then snap a picture and upload online to share your results!

Would die for Sutton Foster	Has a drawer full of show shirts you never wear but won't get rid of	Attempted and failed to explain the significance of techweek to other students	"Thank you five"	Ate lunch in the chorus room
Feels personally victimized by Sondheim's rhythm choices	Has gone to an Applebee's for a cast party	Hoped for an onstage kiss with your crush	Stood around a corkboard waiting for the cast list to go up	Extra at karaoke
Friends with your theater teacher on Facebook	Knows every word to "La Vie Bohème"	**Free Space**	Has gotten really stressed and yelled at someone during a quick change	Owns tap shoes
Made your parents listen to soundtracks in the car	Has made friends take headshots for you	Has broken into song in a Denny's	Still laughs about *Spiderman the Musical*	Tears up whenever you hear "Defying Gravity"
Has seen the TV show *Smash*	Knows how to do unconvincing old people stage makeup	"May-me-mah-mo-moooo"	Knew about Lin-Manuel Miranda before *Hamilton*	Has tried to sing both parts of "The Confrontation" at once

Everyone Is a Combination of a Character from *The Office* and *Parks and Recreation*–What's Yours?

Pick a hangout:

A. Snakehole Lounge
B. Cooper's Seafood
C. Tom's Bistro
D. Alfredo's Pizza Cafe
E. JJ's Diner
F. Poor Richard's
G. The Bulge Bar
H. Chili's
I. Lake Scranton

Pick a word to describe you best:

A. Lazy
B. Loving
C. Ambitious
D. Goofy
E. Sensitive
F. Rude
G. Sassy
H. Practical
I. Lucky

Pick a sitcom:

A. *Brooklyn Nine-Nine*
B. *Veep*
C. *The Good Place*
D. *Broad City*
E. *Black-ish*
F. *Fresh off the Boat*
G. *Unbreakable Kimmy Schmidt*
H. *Silicon Valley*
I. *Modern Family*

Pick a supporting character:

A. Darryl Philbin
B. Mona-Lisa
C. Jan Levinson
D. Jean-Ralphio
E. Toby Flenderson
F. Tammy 2
G. David Wallace
H. Bobby Newport
I. Mose Schrute

Pick an iconic quote:

A. "Dwight, you ignorant slut!"
B. "Give me all the bacon and eggs you have. Do you understand?"
C. "Bears. Beets. *Battlestar Galactica*."
D. "I love you and I like you."
E. "Number one. How dare you?"
F. "Time is money. Money is power. Power is pizza and pizza is knowledge."
G. "Did I stutter?"
H. "I'm allergic to sushi. Every time I eat more than eighty sushis, I barf."
I. "Well, happy birthday, Jesus. Sorry your party's so lame."

If You Got Mostly A's:

You're Kelly Kapoor and April Ludgate! You're a tough cookie on the outside but a softie on the inside. Your sass is legendary and you will do anything it takes to bring down the people you hate . . . even if it doesn't always work out. People are slightly afraid of you, but as soon as they get to know you they know how lovable you are.

If You Got Mostly B's:

You're Ryan Howard and Garry/ Jerry/Larry/Lenny/Terry/Barry/Gerry Gergich/Gengurch/Girgich/ Gergrench! You get lucky very easily and no one knows how. You have struggled your way through, but no one really sees it. You're a dark horse and while people may not notice you, you always make a mark.

If You Got Mostly C's:

You're Dwight Schrute and Andy Dwyer! You don't ask for much in life. That said, in your mind, you are the hero no one else expects you to be. You think you're a legend and that makes you the butt of all jokes. But it doesn't stop you from dreaming anyway.

If You Got Mostly D's:

You're Jim Halpert and Ben Wyatt! You're an ideal partner and a total nerd. There is so much you will do for the people you love. You're also a prankster who doesn't always know where life is headed. But as long as you have the ones you love, you have your center in life.

If You Got Mostly E's:

You're Michael Scott and Leslie Knope! You are a leader, but not one without problems. You are always delivering the results that are required of you, but you take your time, learning along the way. You are idealistic and some might think you're crazy. But you're actually someone people aspire to be.

If You Got Mostly F's:

You're Kevin Malone and Ron Swanson! You have basic needs; your passion for music and food might surprise some because you don't say much. But when you do, you say enough to make an impact.

If You Got Mostly G's:

You're Creed Bratton and Donna Meagle! No one really knows who you are because you are shrouded in mystery. That said, you have had the most fun life anyone could ever imagine. You put your joy above all else and never sweat the small stuff.

If You Got Mostly H's:

You're Angela Martin and Ann Perkins! You care for the people you love immensely. While you are mostly conservative, you have often broken the rules. You can be unpredictable like that. You're loyal, almost to a fault, but you don't take shit from people, either.

If You Got Mostly I's:

You're Pam Beesly and Tom Haverford! You are a kind soul with ambition. You have so many plans and such little time. Around people, you're a prankster and a lover at heart. You know you deserve more than the life you're in and you're always working to find a way out.

Your Proposal Preferences Will Reveal When You'll Get Engaged

What do you want to wear when you get proposed to?

A. Something *super* fancy
B. Pajamas
C. Whatever I wear to work
D. Something cute
E. Matching outfits
F. Ehhh, I'm not sure

Where do you want the proposal to happen?

A. At a restaurant
B. In the comfort of my own home
C. Some sort of landmark like the Grand Canyon
D. A completely different city
E. Somewhere outside like a beach or park
F. Somewhere significant to our relationship

Do you want the proposal to be public?

A. Yes, I want random people around
B. Yes, but I want it to be people we actually know
C. No, I want it to be just us
D. No, but I do want it to go online
E. I don't care, I just want it to happen
F. It honestly will depend on my mood

Pick a ring that you want:

A. A pearl encrusted in diamonds
B. A straight-up rock
C. A precious jewel
D. Pear-shaped/tear drop diamond
E. It will actually be a family ring
F. I don't care what it looks like

Pick something extra to have at your proposal:

A. A photographer
B. Puppies!
C. A flash mob
D. A live band
E. Tons of flowers
F. Candles everywhere

Finally, will you marry me?

A. Yes!
B. OMG, I didn't see this coming! Yes!
C. This seems a little sudden
D. Can I think about this?
E. Umm . . . okay?
F. No

If You Got Mostly A's:
You'll get engaged in six months.
Wow! So sudden. Your next six months are going to be like heaven for your love life! Enjoy it!

If You Got Mostly B's:
You'll get engaged in five years.
You'll be getting engaged in five years! That gives your love a chance to grow and flourish into something wonderful!

If You Got Mostly C's:
You'll get engaged in three months.
I know it's a little sudden but when true love comes a-knockin', you gotta answer the door! (Also, consider this a blessing because now you'll know when to get your nails done!)

If You Got Mostly D's:
You'll get engaged in a year.
Here's to your next year full of adventure and love!

If You Got Mostly E's:
You'll get engaged in two years.
There is absolutely no rush when it comes to your engagement! You've got two years to do you and live your best life!

If You Got Mostly F's:
You'll get engaged in ten years.
So, this engagement is a little far off, but that's completely okay! That gives you a chance to figure out what you want, and it gives you a chance to enjoy your life before you truly have to settle down!

Which Candy Matches Your Personality?

Take this totally random quiz and we'll tell you what candy your personality is.

What's your dream?

A. To be rich
B. To be rich and famous
C. To find love
D. To find love and be rich
E. Love, fame, $$$
F. To be the best in my field
G. To just be happy
H. None of these!
I. You'll never understand my dream!

What's your nightmare?

A. Apocalypse
B. Everyone's dead
C. Bugs everywhere
D. Being chased
E. Monsters
F. Falling
G. Naked in public
H. None of these!
I. You'll never understand my nightmare!

Pick a beverage:

A. Green juice
B. Water
C. Cappuccino
D. Beer
E. Red wine
F. White wine
G. Cocktail
H. Milkshake
I. Soda

What's the max number of dogs you think you could take care of?

A. Zero
B. One
C. Two
D. Three
E. Four
F. Five
G. Six
H. Seven plus
I. Infinite!

What's the max number of cats you think you could take care of?

A. Zero
B. One
C. Two
D. Three
E. Four
F. Five
G. Six
H. Seven plus
I. Infinite!

What's the max number of lizards you think you could take care of?

A. Zero
B. One
C. Two
D. Three
E. Four
F. Five to thirty-one
G. Thirty-two
H. Thirty-three plus
I. Infinite!

If you had the option to be famous, would you be?

A. Yes!!!
B. No way!
C. Not sure
D. Only if I'm more famous than Taylor Swift
E. Only for a good reason
F. Only medium famous
G. Don't look at me!
H. I'm already famous
I. I want to be less famous

How do you feel about mushrooms?

A. Love them
B. They're okay
C. I eat them sometimes
D. Depends on the situation
E. They are garbage
F. Used to like them
G. They are not food
H. I hate them
I. My favorite food

If You Got Mostly A's:
You're Skittles! You're so wild and free. No one tells you what to do. YOU TELL THEM WHAT TO DO. AND THEY DO IT. Because you're the boss.

If You Got Mostly B's:
You're licorice! You're both classic and fun, old-timey and fun-timey. You're addictive. You work your magic and no one can get enough of you.

If You Got Mostly C's:
You're pink Starburst! You're the only flavor of Starburst that's celebrated, loved, and respected. And that's because you're better than other people. You're just a really quality person and everyone likes you best.

If You Got Mostly D's:
You're gummy candy! That includes gummy bears, worms, sour cola, all the gummy things. Everyone loves you and you work well in pretty much any situation. But you're too cool to care what other people think. You're king of your own gummy empire—such a versatile candy genre.

If You Got Mostly E's:
You're chocolate! You make the world a better place just by existing. Thank you for just being you. In fact, everyone in your life should thank you because you're just that amazing.

If You Got Mostly F's:
You're a Kit Kat! You don't follow the rules—you make your own rules. And everyone steps aside because Kit Kat is coming through, dominating the scene.

If You Got Mostly G's:
You're M&M's! You're bright, colorful, and you project an aura of fun wherever you go. The people around you can't help but feel joy in your presence. And you can be anything you want to be: plain, peanut, even birthday cake (???). The world is your candy-coated oyster, which is a good thing.

If You Got Mostly H's:
You're Twix! You came here to party. Trick-or-treaters want you. Hell, everyone wants you. You're the cool candy with an attitude. There's a decent chance there are cookies inside you.

If You Got Mostly I's:
You're a peanut butter cup! You're basically perfect. All your qualities complement each other. You have a power deep within—a power that will take you places. (That power is called peanut butter.)

How Do These Inkblots Make You Feel?

This inkblot personality test is frighteningly accurate. For each image, circle the emotion that it evokes in you and total up your results to find out your true personality.

A. Happy
B. Sad
C. Angry
D. Content
E. Curious
F. Nothing

A. Happy
B. Sad
C. Angry
D. Content
E. Curious
F. Nothing

A. Happy
B. Sad
C. Angry
D. Content
E. Curious
F. Nothing

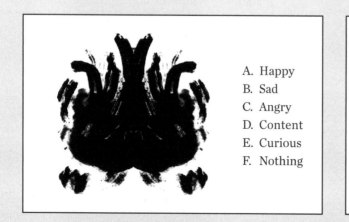

A. Happy
B. Sad
C. Angry
D. Content
E. Curious
F. Nothing

A. Happy
B. Sad
C. Angry
D. Content
E. Curious
F. Nothing

A. Happy
B. Sad
C. Angry
D. Content
E. Curious
F. Nothing

A. Happy
B. Sad
C. Angry
D. Content
E. Curious
F. Nothing

If You Got Mostly A's:
You are incredibly thoughtful and considerate, almost to a fault. When other people don't match your level of thoughtfulness you find yourself very frustrated. Try to be more compassionate to others' deficiencies—people show they care in different ways. Unrelated, you *love* animals.

If You Got Mostly B's:
You're a realist. Your feet are planted firmly on the ground, even if sometimes you can come off as a little "head in the clouds." You love the ocean and, well, water in general. You're drawn to nature and nothing lifts your spirits like a bright blue sky. Unrelated, you *love* dogs.

If You Got Mostly C's:
You're passionate and opinionated. You don't shy away from disagreeing with others, but that's okay because you're usually right. You love fiercely and are loyal to a fault. Nobody messes with your loved ones. Unrelated, you have a *major* sweet tooth.

If You Got Mostly D's:
You're a natural peacekeeper. The levelheaded one in most situations, people come to you for perspective and clarity. You're incredibly genuine and nice. You believe in helping others before yourself. Unrelated, you *love* cats.

If You Got Mostly E's:
You're creative, imaginative, and extremely clever. You excel in environments where you're free to experiment. You are selective socially and only open up around certain people. The lucky ones who see the real you are dazzled by your charm. Unrelated, you *love* to travel.

If You Got Mostly F's:
You're honest and care deeply about society. You're particularly apt at seeing the good in others and understanding different perspectives. While sometimes the world gets you down, you have a deep-rooted optimism that carries you through life's ups and downs. Unrelated, you *love* cheese.

Which Dog Should You Adopt?

DAY OF THE WEEK

Sunday: A Dalmatian

Monday: A Pug

Tuesday: A Golden Retriever

Wednesday: A German Shepard

Thursday: A Boston Terrier

Friday: A Bulldog

Saturday: A Great Dane

LETTER YOUR NAME STARTS WITH

A: Named Charlie

B: Named Harley

C: Named Molly

D: Named Stella

E: Named Penny

F: Named Winston

G: Named Ruby

H: Named Luna

I: Named Scout

J: Named Daisy

K: Named Hulk

L: Named Tiny

M: Named Lady

N: Named Paul

O: Named Oscar

P: Named Willow

Q: Named Oreo

R: Named Ziggy

S: Named Petunia

T: Named Titan

U: Named Oliver

V: Named Kiwi

W: Named Fiona

X: Named Beans

Y: Named Blue

Z: Named Max

The Serious Ariana Grande Fan's Crossword Puzzle

ACROSS

3 Type of dancing Cat does in *Victorious*

6 Surprise single released Nov. 3, 2018

7 State where she has a penthouse

8 A YouTube star + fanboy calls himself _____ Grande

9 Arianator slang for "yes" or "yeah"

12 SNL cast member ex

15 "Problem" collaborator

16 Fitness class in "Side to Side" video

DOWN

1 She's from Boca _____

2 There are seven of these

3 Her beagle-chihuahua mix

4 She posted one of these on Twitter about mangoes

5 Family on her father's side

10 "Borderline," "Bang Bang," "No Tears Left to Cry," etc.

11 Her lifestyle (dietary)

13 Mom

14 Home state, abbreviated

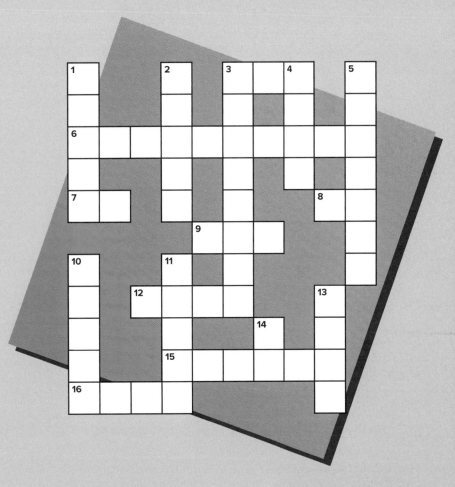

Answers on p. 310

You Won't Score a 20/20 on This Quiz Unless You've Seen Every Pixar Movie

1. **What's the name of the dinosaur from *Toy Story*?**
   A. Rex
   B. Jeff
   C. Lucas
   D. Tito

2. **In *A Bug's Life*, the bugs that Flik mistakes for warriors actually worked where?**
   A. The theater
   B. The circus
   C. The mall
   D. The farm

3. **In *Toy Story 2*, what's the name of the 1950s puppet show in which Woody was the star?**
   A. *The Woody Hour*
   B. *The Cowboy Hour*
   C. *Woody and the Gang*
   D. *Woody's Roundup*

4. **When *Monsters, Inc.* opens up, who's the "Top Scarer" at the company?**
   A. Mike
   B. Sulley
   C. Randall
   D. Frank McCay

5. **In *Finding Nemo*, what type of fish are Marlin and Nemo?**
   A. Goldfish
   B. Clownfish
   C. Pink anemonefish
   D. Saddleback fish

6. **In *The Incredibles*, what's Frozone's actual name?**
   A. Lucas
   B. Lewis
   C. Lucius
   D. Loomis

7. **In *Cars*, the Piston Cup is being held at what venue?**
   A. Los Angeles International Speedway
   B. Daytona International Speedway
   C. Texas Motor Speedway
   D. Talladega Superspeedway

8. **The chef in *Ratatouille* has a pretty large role—what's his name?**
   A. Chef Peeler
   B. Chef Slicer
   C. Chef Mincer
   D. Chef Skinner

9. **In *WALL-E*, what does EVE visit earth in search of?**
   A. Oil
   B. Plant life
   C. Friendship
   D. Anything of value

10. **In *Up*, where is Paradise Falls located?**
    A. Costa Rica
    B. Chile
    C. Guatemala
    D. Venezuela

11. **Which character *doesn't* make an appearance in *Toy Story 3*?**

A. Slinky
B. Bo Peep
C. Rex
D. Mrs. Potato Head

12. **In *Cars 2*, where is the first race of the World Grand Prix held?**

A. London
B. Hong Kong
C. Tokyo
D. Paris

13. **In *Brave*, what's the name of Merida's mother?**

A. Elinor
B. Merida
C. Maudie
D. Victoria

14. **What's the name of Monsters University's rival school in *Monsters University*?**

A. Fear University
B. Scare Tech
C. Scare State
D. Fear Tech

15. **Which of the following is *not* one of Riley's five emotions in *Inside Out*?**

A. Disgust
B. Angst
C. Anger
D. Joy

16. **What's the main character's name in *The Good Dinosaur*?**

A. Arlo
B. Marlo
C. Harlow
D. Arnold

17. **What kind of fish is Dory (from *Finding Dory*, of course)?**

A. Blue clownfish
B. Blue saddleback
C. Blue baby
D. Blue tang

18. **What's the name of Lightning McQueen's rival in *Cars 3*?**

A. Timmy Speed
B. Ron Fast
C. Jackson Storm
D. Luther Lightning

19. **In *Coco*, what does Miguel's family make for a living?**

A. Hats
B. Shirts
C. Jackets
D. Shoes

20. **Finally, in *The Incredibles 2*, which of the following is *not* one of Jack-Jack's known superpowers?**

A. Telepathy
B. Telekinesis
C. Superhuman strength
D. Polymorphing (shape-shifting)

NOW ADD UP YOUR SCORE!

If You Got 0–5 Correct:
You've never seen a Pixar movie in your life!

If You Got 6–10 Correct:
You clearly didn't study.

If You Got 11–15 Correct:
Not bad! You've seen most of these!

If You Got 16–19 Correct:
NICE WORK! You're a Pixar expert!

If You Got 20 Correct:
PERFECT SCORE!

ANSWER KEY

1. A; 2. B; 3. D; 4. B; 5. B; 6. C; 7. A; 8. D; 9. B; 10. D; 11. B; 12. C; 13. A; 14. D; 15. B; 16. A; 17. D; 18. C; 19. D; 20. A

What's Your Patronus, Based on Your Zodiac Sign?

Pick your sign.

AQUARIUS

PHOENIX
You're an individual, unique thinker—someone with big ideas, whose role is often to inspire others. You may be soft-spoken and occasionally hard to read, but a bright flame burns within you.

TAURUS

JACK RUSSELL TERRIER
You're down-to-earth, reliable, and stubborn as all get-out. You're loyal to your friends and a hard worker with a good heart. Everyone wants you on their team.

PISCES

HARE
You're compassionate, creative, and introspective. Sometimes people think you're a bit odd, but you simply have a unique way of looking at things. You're bright and love animals.

GEMINI

CAT
You're sharp, cunning, and mysterious. You may come off as serious and intimidating, but in reality you have a rather playful, witty nature. Maybe a bit of a prankster.

ARIES

STAG
You're a go-getter, extremely ambitious, and driven to succeed. You know what you must do and you'll always make sure it gets done. You carry a lot of responsibility on your shoulders.

CANCER

SWAN
You're sensitive, family-oriented, and emotional. You need a lot of alone time and prefer to socialize in small, tight-knit groups. You have an artist's soul.

LEO

FOX
You're the class clown, a sharp wit, and a bit of a troublemaker. You love attention more than most and feel left out when you're not getting enough of it. You're a quick, fun conversationalist.

SCORPIO

GOAT
You're mysterious, cunning, and quiet. People can't quite figure you out, and you prefer it that way. You need lots of alone time and have a hard time trusting others.

VIRGO

OTTER
You're meticulous, detail-oriented, and brilliant. You may be a bit of a worrywart, but you're highly skilled, a great multitasker, and an extremely reliable friend.

SAGITTARIUS

HORSE
You're fun, strong-willed, and free-spirited. You have a difficult time with authority and prefer to do things your own way. You're likely very active and good at sports.

LIBRA

WOLF
You're a fair-minded, loyal person, determined to seek justice and do what's right. You're also fun, a bit of a performer, and someone who loves to make a statement with your appearance.

CAPRICORN

DOE
You're a strong, determined worker, happiest when working toward a goal and taking care of yourself and others. You're resilient and dependable.

This *Friends* Quiz Will Determine Which Two Characters You're Most Like

What word describes you best?

A. Lazy

B. Goofy

C. Friendly

D. Quirky

E. Dorky

F. Well-rounded

G. Cynical

H. Likable

What's your dream job?

A. Cartoonist

B. Fashion designer

C. Eating champion

D. Professional dancer

E. Pianist

F. Actor

G. Teacher

H. Any job where I'm the boss

Pick a type of food:

A. Pizza

B. Fried chicken

C. Chinese takeout

D. Sandwich

E. Cheesecake

F. Trifle

G. Fajitas

H. Jam

What sounds like it would make you say, "Me at a party."

A. Getting heated in an intense game of beer pong

B. Trying to be the best host ever and making sure everyone is having fun

C. Flirting with everyone

D. Judging everyone. Literally everyone.

E. Making out with someone

F. Taking a shot

G. Loving someone from afar

H. Drinking in a corner with a friend while pretending to narrate other guests' conversations

What sounds like a good time to you?

A. Playing football

B. Debating anyone about anything

C. Looking at photos of high school friends on Facebook

D. Eating a lot of food

E. Prank calling people

F. Having an argument that ends in sex

G. Reading a magazine

H. Watching TV

Choose your favorite boyfriend/girlfriend:

A. Mike
B. Tag
C. David
D. Janice
E. Richard
F. Julie
G. Mona
H. Ethan

Choose your least favorite boyfriend/girlfriend:

A. Paolo
B. Paul
C. David
D. Janice
E. Pete
F. Kathy
G. Elizabeth
H. Charlie

If You Got Mostly A's:

You're most like Chandler and Joey! You're the life of the party and everyone knows it. When someone is feeling down, they know they can come to you to be cheered up. (Oh, and did we mention that you're super charming?)

If You Got Mostly B's:

You're most like Chandler and Monica! Just like the marriage that is Chandler and Monica, you know how to balance yourself out. You like things to go your way, but your day isn't ruined if things don't turn out perfectly. And, yeah, some people might be surprised, but you have a joke or two up your sleeve.

If You Got Mostly C's:

You're most like Joey and Phoebe! Quick question: Has anyone ever called you goofy or unique before? Probably. You're a good person who likes to have a good time and you don't need much to make you happy. Your soul is as pure as they get.

If You Got Mostly D's:

You're most like Monica and Rachel! You're a loyal friend with an amazing sense of confidence and self-worth. You're going places in life, but you don't want to go anywhere if it's not filled with those you care about and those who care about you.

If You Got Mostly E's:

You're most like Monica and Ross! Oh, boy. You are a handful. You know what you want and then you go and get it. Sure, you might rub some people the wrong way, but, hey, their problem, not yours.

If You Got Mostly F's:

You're most like Rachel and Ross! You can definitely be described as an ambivert. You love being surrounded by friends and family, but you also love some good alone time. You have high expectations of yourself, but, yeah, you know how to have fun.

If You Got Mostly G's:

You're most like Joey and Rachel! You're a strong, endearing, and enthusiastic person who knows how to use your strengths to your advantage. You tend to attract the company of others with your outgoing and lovable personality!

If You Got Mostly H's:

You're most like Phoebe and Chandler! You, my friend, are as fun as they get. Sure, you can be sarcastic and a tad dry, but it's all balanced out with your love of life. Ain't nothin' gonna get you down.

What's Your Amateur Magician Name?

MONTH YOU WERE BORN

January: The Great

February: The Mysterious

March: The Legendary

April: The Illustrious

May: The Magical

June: The Mystical

July: The Distinguished

August: The Renowned

September: The Famed

October: The Unparalleled

November: The Notorious

December: The Wondrous

DAY YOU WERE BORN

1: Pete

2: Libby

3: Guy

4: Sara

5: Stew

6: Meg

7: Bob

8: Jessica

9: Rick

10: Tara

11: Josh

12: Rachel

13: Jim

14: Angela

15: Tom

16: Jennifer

17: Johnathan

18: Viv

19: Billy

20: Ellen

21: Stanley

22: Jessica

23: Harry

24: Becky

25: Lenny

26: Karen

27: Christopher

28: Suzy

29: Andy

30: Jan

31: Steve

Make a Cup of Coffee and We'll Guess What Season You Were Born In

Pick a blend:

A. Light roast
B. Medium roast
C. Dark roast
D. Decaf

Add a flavor:

A. Caramel
B. Hazelnut
C. None
D. Vanilla

Pick a sweetener:

A. White sugar
B. Raw sugar
C. None
D. Artificial sugar

Choose something to pour in:

A. Regular milk
B. Creamer
C. Almond milk
D. None

How do you take your coffee?

A. Over ice
B. Piping-hot
C. Latte
D. Frapp

What are you drinking it out of?

A. Iced coffee cup
B. Hot coffee cup
C. Mug
D. Anything with a Starbucks logo

Where are you usually found drinking coffee?

A. At home
B. At work
C. Indie coffee shop
D. Starbucks

If You Got Mostly A's:

Summer! Your coffee choices are just like the season you were born in—exciting. There's no denying that summer is the most fun season, and your coffee order is just one of the many ways that your exuberant personality shines through. So, go grab an iced coffee or a cold brew, you crazy kid you, and keep ordering coffees that are as fun and lovable as you.

If You Got Mostly B's:

Winter! When the weather gets colder, winter babies know how to turn up the heat. Their coffee orders may seem pretty normal, but that's because winter babies are risk takers in all other facets of their life and know how to perfectly balance work and play.

If You Got Mostly C's:

Spring! Spring babies are a crazy combination of all seasons' personalities. They have their chill moments, their crazy moments, and everything in between. Like their coffee order they tend to be a bit unpredictable, but that makes them all the more exciting to be around, just like the ever-changing but fun season they were born in.

If You Got Mostly D's:

Fall! People born in fall are nice and relaxed, just like their coffee order. There's no better time to sit back and relax with a hot latte than in autumn, and the easygoing nature of fall babies makes them all-around admirable people—the kind of people we need when the warm weather's ending and the chilly weather's starting.

What about you is most animal-like?

A. Your appetite
B. Your loyalty
C. Your sex drive
D. Your temper
E. Your playfulness
F. Your innocence

Choose a truly terrifying deep sea creature:

A. Goblin shark
B. Blobfish
C. Viperfish
D. Anglerfish
E. Stargazer
F. Gulper eel

What's your preferred habitat?

A. Land
B. Air
C. Sea

Which Animal Matches Your Personality?

Choose a Disney cat:

A. Cheshire Cat
B. Lucifer
C. Rufus
D. Dinah
E. Duchess
F. Figaro

What's your biggest pet peeve?

A. Shedding
B. Picky eating
C. Scratching
D. Pooping indoors
E. Spontaneous noises
F. Refusing to bathe

Which animal adjective describes your love life?

A. Wild
B. Playful
C. Domestic
D. Nocturnal
E. Shy
F. Extinct

Do you prefer the company of animals or people?

A. Animals
B. People

If You Got Mostly A's:

You're a lion! You're a leader and a person others look up to. You seldom follow others and like to set your own path. You're a damn royal and carry yourself with enviable prestige.

If You Got Mostly B's:

You're an owl! You are intelligent and wise beyond your years. Your intelligence is vast and you have common sense along with book smarts. Above all, you have perspective that always allows you to see the bigger picture.

If You Got Mostly C's:

You're a shark! You're aggressive and goal-oriented but also looked up to. People admire you not only for who you are but for what you've done. Your greatness is sometimes feared but always respected.

If You Got Mostly D's:

You're a wolf! You are driven and focused. You can tackle almost any problem that comes your way and you welcome a good challenge. You always have your eyes on the prize and will achieve much just through patience and perseverance.

If You Got Mostly E's:

You're a sloth! You are super chill and easygoing. You like to take life one day at a time and never sweat the small stuff. You're also relaxed and know how to keep a level head in any situation.

If You Got Mostly F's:

You're a panda! You are playful and energetic. You're cute and always the life of any party you go to. People like your attitude and always want to be around you.

We Dare You to Try This Disney vs. *Harry Potter* Would You Rather

Would you rather
have your own wand (you'll be able to use it, obviously, you're not a Muggle or a Squib) OR have three wishes from a genie? (you can't wish for a wand and the genie will be freed after your third wish)

Would you rather
have a magical portrait that prevents people from entering your room OR have a magical tattoo of yourself that moves around?

Would you rather
live at Hogwarts OR live at the Beast's castle?

Would you rather
travel by broom OR travel by magic carpet?

Would you rather
have Rapunzel's magical hair and be able to heal anyone OR have the Peverell invisibility cloak and be able to sneak around?

Would you rather
be part of the Parr family (you get a superpower, of course) OR be part of the Weasley family?

Would you rather

eat grubs for dinner for a week OR have detention with Umbridge every Saturday for a year?

Would you rather

have Ursula steal your voice for a year OR have a lightning-shaped scar that gives you headaches every time you watch your favorite show?

Would you rather

have Dobby as your BFF OR have Baymax as your BFF?

Would you rather

have brunch with Ursula and Hades and sassily judge people OR go out drinking with Hagrid and Dumbledore?

Would you rather

be an international Quidditch superstar OR have ice powers and rule your own kingdom?

Would you rather

have Mary Poppins as your nanny OR have Sirius Black as your uncle?

Would you rather

have Remy as your personal chef OR eat every meal in the Great Hall?

Would you rather

never watch a Disney movie ever again OR never read a *Harry Potter* book ever again?

How Adventurous of a Pizza Eater Are You?

Check off every topping you'd eat.

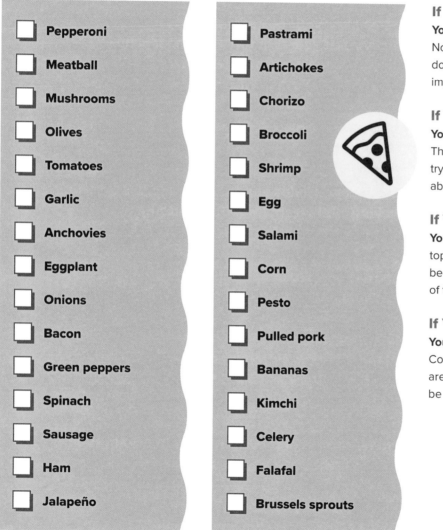

- ☐ Pepperoni
- ☐ Meatball
- ☐ Mushrooms
- ☐ Olives
- ☐ Tomatoes
- ☐ Garlic
- ☐ Anchovies
- ☐ Eggplant
- ☐ Onions
- ☐ Bacon
- ☐ Green peppers
- ☐ Spinach
- ☐ Sausage
- ☐ Ham
- ☐ Jalapeño

- ☐ Pastrami
- ☐ Artichokes
- ☐ Chorizo
- ☐ Broccoli
- ☐ Shrimp
- ☐ Egg
- ☐ Salami
- ☐ Corn
- ☐ Pesto
- ☐ Pulled pork
- ☐ Bananas
- ☐ Kimchi
- ☐ Celery
- ☐ Falafal
- ☐ Brussels sprouts

If You Checked 23–30:
You are a fearless pizza legend!
No one loves the pizza the way you do—you're up for anything! We're impressed!

If You Checked 15–22:
You are a serious pizza fan!
There are some toppings you won't try, but mainly you're game for just about anything on a pizza!

If You Checked 7–14:
You like what you like! A lot of toppings scare you off, but that's just because you've found the handful of toppings you love!

If You Checked 7 or less:
You are a total pizza wimp!
Come on, branch out a little! There are more pizza flavors waiting to be discovered!

Instagram @ Hunt: Disney Edition

*Take a pic of this page on your phone, upload to your Instagram story,
and start tagging your friends to cast your Disney movie!*

YOU'RE THE LEAD OF A DISNEY MOVIE!

@S = YOUR TRUE LOVE

@T = YOUR ANIMAL SIDEKICK

@M = THE VILLAIN WHO'S JEALOUS OF YOUR LOOKS

@Z = THE VILLAIN'S DUTIFUL ACCOMPLICE

@A = THE PERSON YOU'D DO A MUSICAL NUMBER WITH

@_ = YOUR FAIRY GODMOTHER

@R = YOUR TRUSTY STEED

1. We'll start off easy. Which celebrity name can be deciphered from this clue?

2. Which celebrity name can be deciphered from this clue?

3. Which celebrity name can be deciphered from this clue?

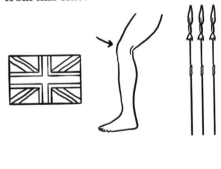

If You Can Name Each of These Celebrities, You're an Expert at Brainteasers

Each of the picture clues below can be deciphered into a celebrity name. Don't focus on the spelling of the words—only focus on the sounds of the words!

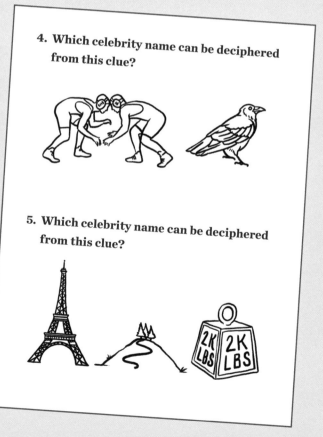

4. Which celebrity name can be deciphered from this clue?

5. Which celebrity name can be deciphered from this clue?

6. Which celebrity name can be deciphered from this clue?

7. Which celebrity name can be deciphered from this clue?

8. Which celebrity name can be deciphered from this clue?

NOW ADD UP YOUR SCORE!

If You Got 0–3 Correct:
Whaaaaat? You were not on board with this whole picture-clue thing. You just want your brainteasers written out. I get it! These are tricky.

If You Got 4–6 Correct:
Casual celeb fan! You like following celebrities so you knew a good portion of these, but that part of your brain that was fired up trying to figure out the brainteasers is a little rusty. No worries! It'll warm up soon.

If You Got 7–8 Correct:
Expert celeb decoder! You're great at solving riddles, puzzles, and brainteasers. If you were Nicolas Cage in *National Treasure*, the movie would've been so much shorter because you would have figured out all the clues right away!

What's the Perfect Dog for You, Based on Your Zodiac Sign?

Pick your sign.

ARIES

AUSTRALIAN SHEPHERD

A herding dog by nature, Aussies are determined, confident, and full of energy, just like an Aries. But watch out—if your little buddy doesn't get enough exercise or attention, they can get a little moody. (Hey, sounds like someone else we know.)

CANCER

YORKSHIRE TERRIER

Cancer, you're one of the most difficult signs to get to know, given your multifaceted personality, so it makes sense that your dog should have the same traits. The adorable Yorkie may be small, but they've got a lot of personality. On the one hand, Yorkies are lively and perfect companions, but on the other hand, they can be stubborn and difficult to train.

TAURUS

BERNESE MOUNTAIN DOG

Taurus, you need a pet like a Bernese Mountain Dog that is down-to-earth and easygoing. We know you can be a bit sensitive, so this dog's easily trainable and affectionate nature will bring out the best in you. And don't take this the wrong way, Taurus, but you can get a little lazy from time to time. No worries—the Berner can also be quite the couch potato.

LEO

SIBERIAN HUSKY

Leo, you're passionate and dominating, so you need a hound who also wants to be the star of the show. Huskies are warmhearted and friendly, just like you. But be warned: This breed can be self-centered and stubborn if they don't get their way. You can relate to that though, Leo, can't you?

GEMINI

CHIHUAHUA

Gemini, your sign is known for being two personalities in one. Given your multifaceted nature, you'll instantly connect with a Chihuahua (and you'll sympathize with this tiny dog's mood swings). They may be entertaining and lively one minute, but possessive and suspicious of others the next.

VIRGO

SHIBA INU

This Japanese breed is keen and introspective, the perfect companion for the intelligent but soft-spoken Virgo. Just like its owner, a Shiba loves using their mind to work through tough problems. So don't be surprised if they find a way into your sock drawer no matter how many times you make sure it's closed.

LIBRA

POODLE MIX

Libra, you'll instantly fall in love with a poodle mix (think: goldendoodle, cavapoo, or Labradoodle). Like you, these dogs are charming and intelligent. They crave socializing and affection, but they're also super chill. They're happy playing fetch for hours or just curling up on your lap. Sounds like a perfect fit, huh?

CAPRICORN

FRENCH BULLDOG

Capricorn, you're dependable and a great companion, which is why your loyal, attention-loving Frenchie will become your instant best friend. Plus, this slightly mischievous, silly dog will bring out the more playful side of your naturally routine-oriented personality.

SCORPIO

GERMAN SHEPHERD

Like Scorpios, German Shepherds are curious, confident, and natural leaders. The breed is also one of the most devoted and courageous of all. Scorpio, you can be a little distrusting and skeptical of others, but you'll always feel safe and loved with your German Shepherd by your side.

AQUARIUS

CHOW CHOW

Aquarius, two of your strengths are that you're independent and original, so every once in a while you crave some alone time. A Chow Chow, with its loyal but aloof personality, is a perfect complement for your sign. This breed is a great companion, but it also seeks independence.

SAGITTARIUS

GOLDEN RETRIEVER

Just like a Sagittarius, this loyal dog breed is energetic, curious, and charming. Your Golden Retriever wants nothing more in the world than to make you happy and feel loved, and is ideal for your extroverted, generous personality type. The two of you live for exploring and seeking adventure—what a perfect match!

PISCES

CAVALIER KING CHARLES SPANIEL

Pisces, you spend so much time caring about others and taking their needs into account, it's time you let someone else shower you with affection. The Cavalier is the definition of a lap dog, which makes it a perfect companion for the empathetic and caring Pisces. This pup is lovable and loves nothing more than nuzzling up on your lap.

Which US State Should You Live in Based on Your Fast Food Preferences?

What's your McDonald's breakfast order?

A. Egg McMuffin

B. Hotcakes

C. Sausage McGriddle

D. Oatmeal

What type of bread are you getting at Subway?

A. Monterey Cheddar

B. 9-Grain Wheat

C. Italian

D. Flatbread

Choose a fast food fry:

A. McDonald's

B. Arby's

C. Wendy's

D. Chick-Fil-A

Where do you want your chicken from?

A. Bojangle's

B. Church's Chicken

C. KFC

D. Popeyes

What's for dessert?

A. McFlurry from McDonald's

B. Frosty from Wendy's

C. Reese's Peanut Butter Cup Pie from Burger King

D. Pineapple Sundae from Sonic

Which pizza is the best pizza?

A. Pizza Hut

B. Papa John's

C. Domino's

D. Little Caesars

Who's got the best burger?

A. McDonald's

B. Wendy's

C. Burger King

D. In-N-Out

Drive Thru

If You Got Mostly A's:

You should live in New York! You are an extremely organized and efficient person, which is why you would thrive in the fast-paced lifestyle of New York City. You were born to be a boss; it's obvious by the way you can command anyone's attention and everyone around you values your opinion. So make your way to the Big Apple and take a big bite—you'll be there to stay.

If You Got Mostly B's:

You should live in Ohio! You have a laid-back and chill personality, which would fit right in in the Midwest. You enjoy the quieter things in life, but are also up for a great adventure now and again. Ohio has it all. What are you waiting for? You know what they say—the Midwest is best.

If You Got Mostly C's:

You should live in Texas! Texas is the perfect mix of beauty and brawn, just like you. You're kind of weird, in the best way possible. People look to you for inspiration and are constantly in awe of your creative side. Texas is the perfect place for you.

If You Got Mostly D's:

You should live in California! You're the type of person who likes to be outdoors and loves the unexpected. That's why California is the perfect state for you. You need sunshine and adventure to survive. And in California, you get both, and an ocean. So when are you moving?

Go to Prom for $1,000

Circle the items you want to purchase. The goal is to try not to go over your budget.
Can you go to prom for $1,000 or less?

	Get ready with a . . .	Wear a . . .	Arrive in a . . .	Eat some . . .	Dance to a . . .
$500	Professional makeup artist	Floor-length gown	Horse and carriage	Chocolate fondue fountain	Special appearance by Robyn
$250	Mani + pedi	Designer tuxedo	Stretch limo	Steak and potatoes	Live orchestra
$100	Nice Sephora associate	Top hat and bow tie	Parents' convertible	Chicken parm	Cover band
$75	Quick spray tan	Vintage dress	Carpool with friends	Sliders	Mediocre DJ
$50	YouTube tutorial	Corsage you made yourself	Motorcycle side car	Pizza	Student council playlist

Which Pokémon Go Team Is Right for You?

Choose a Gen-One starter:

A. Charmander
B. Bulbasaur
C. Squirtle
D. Pikachu

Are you more influenced by nature—your innate qualities—or nurture—the experiences that have shaped who you are?

A. Nature
B. Nurture

Do you think of yourself more as an introvert or as an extrovert?

A. Introvert
B. Extrovert
C. Can be a bit of both

You've got a beloved Pikachu and Thunderstone. Do you evolve your friend into a Raichu, or keep him as a Pickachu?

A. Raichu
B. Pikachu

Do you worry about a lot of things, or are you more laid-back?

A. Worrier
B. Laid-back

Do you have an active imagination?

A. Yes
B. No
C. Depends on my mood

Pick a gym leader:

A. Lt. Surge
B. Sabrina
C. Giovanni

If you had something you had to get done, when would you do it?

A. Right away
B. I'll get to it tomorrow
C. Not until I absolutely have to

If You Got Mostly A's:

Team Mystic! "I am Blanche, leader of Team Mystic. The wisdom of Pokémon is immeasurably deep. I am researching why it is that they evolve. With our calm analysis of every situation we can't lose!" —Blanche, Team Mystic Leader

If You Got Mostly B's:

Team Instinct! "Hey! The name's Spark—the leader of Team Instinct. Pokémon are creatures with excellent intuition. I bet the secret to their intuition is related to how they're hatched. You never lose when you trust your instincts!" —Spark, Team Instinct Leader

If You Got Mostly C's:

Team Valor! "I'm Candela—Team Valor's leader! Pokémon are stronger than humans and they're warmhearted, too! I'm researching ways to enhance Pokémon's natural power in the pursuit of true strength. There's no doubt that the Pokémon our team have trained are the strongest in battle!" —Candela, Team Valor Leader

20 Questions

Take a photo of the page. Fill it out on your phone.
Share it with your friends!

WHO ARE YOU?

Name:_____

Age:_____

Eye color:_____

Zodiac sign:_____

Hogwarts house:_____

WHAT'S YOUR FAVORITE?

Musical artist:_____

Disney movie:_____

TV show:_____

International city:_____

Fro-yo flavor:_____

WHAT'S YOUR LEAST FAVORITE?

Food:_____

School subject:_____

Musical genre:_____

Season:_____

Reality TV show:_____

DO YOU PREFER . . .

Dogs or cats:_____

Rom-coms or thrillers:_____

Baths or showers:_____

Beach or ski mountain:_____

Instagram or TikTok:_____

What Will You Be Famous For?

What time did you go to bed last night?

8 p.m.: Starring in a movie

9 p.m.: Writing a book

10 p.m.: Starring in a musical

11 p.m.: Recording a rap album

12 p.m.: Breaking a world record

1 a.m.: Being a self-made millionaire

2 a.m.: You don't want to be famous

What Is Your Celebrity Baby Name?

YOUR FAVORITE COLOR

Red: Bry

Green: Ky

Blue: Jay

Purple: Mae

Pink: Brax

Yellow: Pay

YOUR FAVORITE ICE CREAM

Vanilla: la

Chocolate: lynn

Cookie dough: den

Cookies 'n' cream: leigh

Mint chocolate chip: ler

Coffee: son

What Zodiac Sign Are You Really?

Which phrase(s) truly speaks to you?

A. "Is it okay if I pet your dog?"

B. "Listen, I have a meticulous skin-care routine."

C. "You guys, I think I'm in love. No, really, this time I mean it."

D. "Just checking in . . ."

E. "Let's go shopping!"

F. "Look at my new plant!"

G. "Just to play Devil's advocate . . ."

H. "I'm a Slytherin."

I. "When I studied abroad . . ."

J. "As per my last email . . ."

K. "I had the weirdest dream last night . . ."

L. "BRB astral projecting."

What's your favorite pastime?

A. Letting people know that you participated competitively in a Little League sport

B. Naps

C. Advocating for your friends to dump their deadbeat SOs

D. Scrapbooking

E. Watching music videos from the '90s

F. Color-coding your Google Cal

G. Pinning things to your *secret* Pinterest boards

H. Watching serial killer documentaries

I. Actively dodging the "So, what are we?" chats

J. Giving rational life advice

K. Hanging out with the cat at every party

L. Scrolling through the 100+ animal accounts you follow on Instagram

Continues on next page

Who are you in your friend group?

A. The dad (aka the DD)
B. The one who talks about how important it is to get eight hours of sleep a night
C. The one who knows all the gossip all the time
D. The intuitive one
E. The ringleader of the group text
F. The Mom Friend
G. The one who is *actually* good at adulting
H. The listener
I. The one who's here for a good time, not a long time
J. The one who divides up the birthday brunch bill
K. The one who calls planets "celestial bodies"
L. The one who texts their ex after 1.5 glasses of wine

What's your defining character trait?

A. Bad tattoos
B. Buys athleisure wear that's never seen the gym
C. Could hold a lively and riveting conversation with a napkin
D. Nostalgic for anything that happened, ever
E. Winged eyeliner
F. Loves anything with a sleek, modern design
G. Romantic AF
H. Only wears black
I. Loud AF
J. Only wears pantsuits to fancy occasions
K. Has dyed hair blue at some point
L. Knows the moon calendar like the back of their hand

Choose a vacation:

A. Gambling in Monaco
B. Wandering the canals in Amsterdam
C. A wine tour in Napa
D. Staying at The Ritz in Paris
E. Surfing in Hawaii
F. Getting lost in Rome
G. Doing a walking tour of Japan
H. Exploring Mayan ruins in Mexico
I. Partying in Rio de Janeiro
J. Camping in a national park
K. Ecotourism in Costa Rica
L. Romantic getaway in Tahiti

If You Got Mostly A's:

You're really an Aries! Aries are ambitious leaders with independent tendencies—they want success and may put themselves under a lot of pressure to achieve it. They can be aggressive and impatient, but they're also super fun because they're adventurous.

If You Got Mostly B's:

You're really a Taurus! A Taurus is one who is both cautious and determined. You take your time easing into things in relationships. Similarly, you won't spend your money until you're sure it's the right choice. (But you're not frugal; you just like nice things.)

If You Got Mostly C's:

You're really a Gemini! Geminis are smart, independent people who usually have a lot going on at once. Concentrating on one project is difficult. These people have many thoughts and emotions constantly running around and changing, so you'll never know what idea they'll come up with next.

If You Got Mostly D's:

You're really a Cancer! Cancers are family-oriented folks who like to take care of others. They can be extremely sensitive, though. One bad comment can cause them pain and withdrawal, but it's just because they have so many feelings!

If You Got Mostly E's:

You're really a Leo! Leos love to live life big. They are confident and magnetic personalities who prefer being surrounded by company to being alone. They're always down to make plans and initiate the fun.

If You Got Mostly F's:

You're really a Virgo! Virgos are perfectionists, constantly nit-picking the details and analyzing their surroundings. Their wheels are constantly turning: They live in their heads and are always creating plans for their future.

If You Got Mostly G's:

You're really a Libra! Libras are passionate, artistic types who seek peace and balance. Seeking balance can be tricky, however, because they tend to have a harder time making decisions. They're more the person *behind* the idea rather than the person who *actually made* the idea happen.

If You Got Mostly H's:

You're really a Scorpio! Fearless and thirsty for knowledge, Scorpios are powerful forces to be reckoned with. They're extremely creative, can be *super* intense, and tend to fiercely guard their secrets.

If You Got Mostly I's:

You're really a Sagittarius! Sagittarius individuals possess a magical mix of adventure, smarts, loyalty, and charm. They're more philosophical than other signs, having a zest for knowledge, exploration, and understanding. They're outgoing people who are natural entertainers.

If You Got Mostly J's:

You're really a Capricorn! Capricorns are ambitious people. They are often workaholics (but love it) and make great managers. They like to remain strong in their relationships and get around conflict by making others think the resolution was their idea in the first place. Clever!

If You Got Mostly K's:

You're really an Aquarius! Aquarius doesn't want to be chained down and may never feel the need to get married. They never follow the crowd and may express their beliefs in interesting ways, especially through random acts of kindness.

If You Got Mostly L's:

You're really a Pisces! Pisces have brilliant, creative minds. The problem is they're a bit disorganized and aren't always big-picture thinkers. They tend to do better with someone keeping them in check, yet they are whimsical, and happiest when inspired.

Which Alcohol Matches Your Zodiac Sign?

Choose your zodiac sign and we'll tell you what booze or spirit best matches your personality.

ARIES

VODKA

As an adventurous Aries who brings thrills into everyone's lives, your drink personality is vodka. You're dynamic, bold, and you adapt well to any situation.

CANCER

GIN

As a mysterious and moody Cancer, your drink personality is just as mysterious as you are. Enter: gin. What's its deal? It tastes like a pine tree, but it's just as refreshing and endearingly eccentric as you are.

TAURUS

BEER

You're a chill Taurus. You can just kick back with a beer like a real cool dude. Just keepin' it real.

LEO

RED WINE

You're a classy Leo, destined for greatness, much like an old fermented grape. You're charismatic and a leader, just like a bold red wine.

GEMINI

TEQUILA

You're a Gemini on the move. You like to really grab life by the butt, thirsty for knowledge and new experiences.

VIRGO

WHITE WINE

You're a caring, compassionate Virgo. Your inner light shines like the light through a glass of white wine. You love *love*, like a grape loves bein' smooshed up into wine.

LIBRA

WHISKEY
As a no-drama Libra, your personality
warrants a no-drama drink. You're charming and
destined for success, just like a
strong whiskey.

CAPRICORN

SCOTCH
You're a powerful achiever, Capricorn, just
quietly sippin' your scotch. Waiting. Watching.
A true winner.

SCORPIO

MOONSHINE
As the most powerful sign, your personality
should reflect a powerful drink. You're
wise beyond your years and you always triumph.
You're hard-core, like moonshine.

AQUARIUS

BOXED WINE
As someone who understands life's
mysteries, you're unpretentious and non-judgmental—
like wine in a box. You're unique and
a trendsetter, so it doesn't matter if you're
like a box of wine.

SAGITTARIUS

CHAMPAGNE
You classy, Sagittarius. You have great taste and
you live your best life. You tend to just
go for it, Champagne-style.

PISCES

ABSINTHE
You're a creative genius, Pisces.
And your original ideas and fantasies are
a lot like an absinthe-fueled night of
debauchery anyway.

Which Disney Character Is Your Dad?

Pick a Disney princess:

A. Esmeralda
B. Pocahontas
C. Jasmine
D. Mulan
E. Ariel
F. Tiana

Pick a Disney villain:

A. Hades
B. Maleficent
C. Jafar
D. Ursula
E. Gaston
F. Scar

Are you easily embarrassed?

A. Yes
B. I'm never embarrassed
C. In certain situations
D. I used to be
E. Kind of
F. Not really

Pick something to complain about:

A. Sports
B. The roads
C. Kids
D. Bacon crispness level
E. Things that are too expensive
F. Bad drivers

If You Got Mostly A's:
Your new dad is Genie from *Aladdin*! Your new dad is fun! He can give you whatever you want, kind of.

If You Got Mostly B's:
Your new dad is Mufasa from *The Lion King*! What a kind, majestic dad who really believes in you.

If You Got Mostly C's:
Your new dad is Sebastian from *The Little Mermaid*! You have a new singing, dancing dad who wants to tell you about life under the sea.

If You Got Mostly D's:
Your new dad is the Beast from *Beauty and the Beast*! Wow, your new dad is complicated. He has a dark side, but his heart is still there.

If You Got Mostly E's:
Your new dad is the fox from *Robin Hood*! Wow, hot dad.

If You Got Mostly F's:
Your new dad is Jiminy Cricket from *Pinocchio*! That's a tiny dad! But he's very wise and has a cool top hat.

Can You Find All the Quotes from Well-Known Movies?

ACROSS

2 "Here's Johnny!"
4 "That'll do, pig. That'll do."
7 "The things you own end up owning you."
9 "There's no place like home."
14 "We'll always have Paris."
15 "My mama always said life was like a box of chocolates."
16 "Ogres are like onions."
18 "Are you not entertained?"
20 "I feel the need, the need for speed."
21 "Shall we play a game?"

DOWN

1 "I see dead people."
3 "May the force be with you."
5 "You're gonna need a bigger boat."
6 "To infinity and beyond!"
8 "Wakanda forever!"
10 "I'll be back."
11 "Say hello to my little friend!"
12 "Take your stinking paws off me, you damn dirty ape!"
13 "You had me at hello."
17 "I want you to draw me like one of your French girls."
19 "You is kind. You is smart. You is important."

Answers on p. 310

We Know How Smart You Are Based on How You Take Your Eggs

HOW DO YOU TAKE YOUR EGGS?	HOW SMART ARE YOU?
Scrambled	**STREET SMART** Okay, so school isn't or wasn't your thing. But that doesn't mean you aren't smart AF. You're calm, cool, and collected—and that makes you the first person someone would call with a problem to solve.
Poached	**BOOK SMART** You are smart with a capital S. You love to read and are a great student. That said, just because you get good grades doesn't mean you always make the best decisions in life!
Sunny-Side Up	**EMOTIONALLY SMART** You have great emotional intelligence. You can tell what someone is feeling just by looking at them. This makes you an amazing friend.
Soft-Boiled	**HUMOR SMART** To be truly funny, you must be extremely intelligent. Your comedic timing and jokes are perfect and could make anyone laugh and you do.
Over Easy	**LOGICAL SMART** You are extremely rational and logical. Your logic always leads you to the right answer—nothing gets by you.

Sweet vs. Savory Bracket

*Pick your favorite contender from each pairing on the left and right.
An item that's not selected gets eliminated. The winner takes on the winning item from
the next pairing and so on until you have one final winner. You can fill out as you go,
snap a pic and share online, and compare your results with friends.*

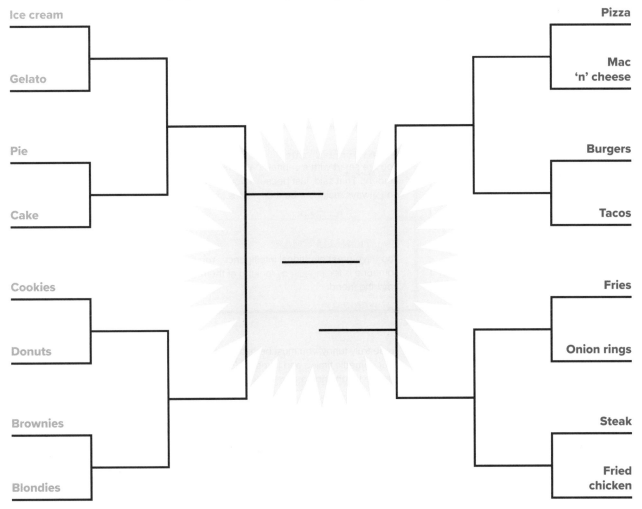

Ice cream

Gelato

Pie

Cake

Cookies

Donuts

Brownies

Blondies

Pizza

Mac 'n' cheese

Burgers

Tacos

Fries

Onion rings

Steak

Fried chicken

Your Opinions about Pizza Will Determine How Rich You'll Be

Pick a crust:

A. Thin crust
B. Thick crust
C. Deep dish
D. Stuffed crust
E. Gluten-free crust

Pick a sauce:

A. Tomato
B. Pesto
C. Olive oil and garlic
D. Bechamel sauce
E. No sauce!

Pick a cheese:

A. Mozzarella
B. Buffalo mozzarella
C. Parmigiano-Reggiano
D. Goat cheese
E. Gorgonzola

What's better?

A. Homemade pizza
B. Delivery pizza

Pick a controversial pizza topping:

A. Pineapple
B. Olives
C. Shrimp
D. Anchovies
E. Raw sliced tomatoes

Do you ever fold your pizza like a taco?

A. Yes
B. Depends on the pizza
C. No

Pick a veggie:

A. Jalapeño
B. Mushroom
C. Onion
D. Red pepper
E. Garlic

Pick a meat:

A. Pepperoni
B. Chicken
C. Bacon
D. Meatballs
E. No meat!

And finally, do you ever use a knife and fork?

A. Yes
B. Depends on the pizza
C. No
D. There's no other way to eat it!
E. Who eats pizza with a knife and fork?!

If You Got Mostly A's:

You'll be ridiculously rich! You will become so rich that it'll be hard to fathom. We're not going to get into the numbers, but just know that you won't need to worry about paying your phone bill ever again. You'll spend your riches on flights around the world and treating your family and friends. Cha-ching!

If You Got Mostly B's:

You'll be stinkin' rich! Oh, hot damn! You'll be pretty damn rich. You're going to hit the jackpot and spend the rest of your days living in luxury. You'll surround yourself with glitter and gold and celebrities and dogs and can we have your life? Seriously. Want to trade?

If You Got Mostly C's:

You'll be not only rich but famous! You'll beat the odds! I mean, sure, anyone can be rich, but not everyone can be famous! You'll do both! You'll use your money to launch yourself into celebrity stardom. You'll probably get a reality show filled with cheesy taglines and fake friends, but you know what? You'll earn even more money from that. Just don't forget to give back once in a while!

If You Got Mostly D's:

You'll be so-rich-that-people-follow-you-on-Instagram-because-of-it rich! You're going to sleep on a bed of money. And then you're going to buy a regular mattress because that's not very comfortable or practical. You'll have a huge social media following just because you're swimming in cash. Your feed will be packed with photos of you chillin' on tropical islands and hanging with celebs. Live your life!

If You Got Mostly E's:

You'll be bored because you're so rich! Bow down! You'll be hella rich. So rich, in fact, that you've grown tired of being rich. There's just nothing to do when you have everything! You'll blow some cash on Jacuzzi boats and other insanely dumb things and you'll donate some to charity. Way to go, champ!

Which US City Should You Live in, Based on Your Zodiac Sign?

Pick your sign.

AQUARIUS

NEW ORLEANS

Idealistic, unconventional, and artistic, you would enjoy living in New Orleans, Louisiana, among like-minded spirits and a relaxed pace of living. You, like the city, are extremely fun and memorable.

TAURUS

PORTLAND

You're stable, reliable, and grounded—much like Portland, Oregon. There you can be your reserved, peace-loving, and compassionate self, and still have plenty of energy and space to get outdoors and commune with nature.

PISCES

SEATTLE

You're spiritual and imaginative, and would therefore likely enjoy living in Seattle, Washington. Your penchant for periods of introspective melancholy are also well-suited to the city's rainy climate, and your artistic, creative nature is a good match for the culture.

GEMINI

CHICAGO

You're versatile and adaptable—traits that will serve you well in the Windy City. You're youthful, witty, and love to talk, and will find much to celebrate (and agonize over) in Chicago sports. Here you will find a natural home for your idealistic, lively self.

ARIES

NEW YORK CITY

You're a go-getter with a driven, me-first personality. You're ambitious, blunt, and energetic. Where better for you to live than the nonstop, relentless, ever-striving New York City?

CANCER

DALLAS

You're sensitive, nurturing, and loyal. As a family-oriented individual, you'll be at home in a city known for its family-friendly nature like Dallas, Texas, consistently ranked in the top five American cities for families.

LEO

LOS ANGELES

You're confident, attention-seeking, and warm—where better to land than Los Angeles? You want to be a *star*, or at least live among them. And in the meantime, Los Angeles appeals to your interests in holistic health, sunshine, and gossip.

SCORPIO

ALBUQUERQUE

You're mysterious, intense, and complex—a natural match for somewhere out in the desert. You might like Albuquerque, New Mexico, where isolation is always close at hand and you won't be overwhelmed by too many people.

VIRGO

MINNEAPOLIS

As a meticulous, detail-oriented, and health-conscious Virgo, why not consider Minneapolis, consistently ranked as one of the US's top three healthiest cities? The culture suits your practical, hardworking, and reserved nature, and the bike trails, rivers, and lakes give you plenty of space to get out and be active.

SAGITTARIUS

HONOLULU

You're fun-loving and adventurous with a childlike spirit, and would probably enjoy living somewhere like Honolulu, Hawaii. You love being outdoors and daydreaming, both of which are best accomplished in a hammock on the beach.

LIBRA

DENVER

Charming and socially poised, you should live in Denver. The Libra, a diplomat ever in search of balance and harmony, would be grounded and soothed by the city's beautiful surroundings, particularly the nearby mountains.

CAPRICORN

MILWAUKEE

As a Capricorn, you're disciplined, calm, and reserved—all traits that make you well-suited to Milwaukee, Wisconsin. You're also an optimistic opportunist, which will help you do well in Milwaukee winters, as well as at any one of its six Fortune 500 company headquarters.

What Did Your High School Notebook Doodles Say about You?

Pick the doodle you doodled the most in class.

BORED AF
You almost dropped out you were so bored in high school. You mastered the art of sleeping with your eyes open and powered through. Congrats on not flunking out!

SOCIAL BUTTERFLY
You were quite the social butterfly—most likely getting separated from friends in class for talking too much. But that didn't stop you from communicating—you just passed notes instead.

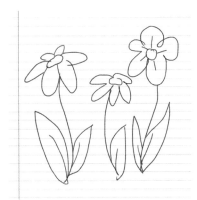

CUTIE
Hey cute thing, aren't you cute? You were very cute in high school; it was hard to find romantic prospects when you looked like a second grader. That ended up working out for you, though, because you didn't end up dating lots of losers.

TROUBLEMAKER
Uh-oh. You were a troublemaker. You were quiet but funny, and your classmates appreciated your sense of humor, even if your teachers didn't.

SUPERSTAR
You were planning big things in high school and many of those dreams probably came true! Maybe not in the exact way you expected (like Britney Spears), but you're still a star in your own right.

DAYDREAMER
You daydreamed through most of high school. You appreciate good art, books, music, and movies. You're a little shy, but once you warm up to someone you're an amazingly loyal and fun friend.

ROBOT
Cool, you're a robot and probably had perfect grades.

CREATIVE CAT
You were super creative. You are now most likely involved in the visual arts or fashion design (even if it's just as a hobby).

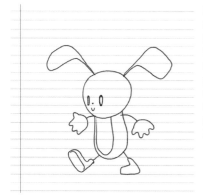

LONER
Okay, so you weren't the MOST POPULAR kid in school. But that's just because you were busy being awesome by yourself. You most likely blossomed after high school.

Tv vs. Movies Bracket

Pick your favorite contender from each pairing on the left and right.
An item that's not selected gets eliminated. The winner takes on the winning item from
the next pairing and so on until you have one final winner. You can fill out as you go,
snap a pic and share online, and compare your results with friends.

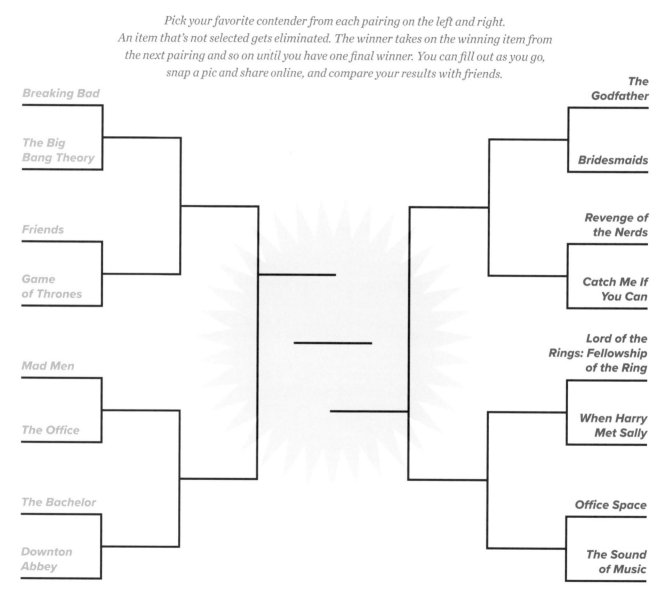

Breaking Bad

The Big Bang Theory

Friends

Game of Thrones

Mad Men

The Office

The Bachelor

Downton Abbey

The Godfather

Bridesmaids

Revenge of the Nerds

Catch Me If You Can

Lord of the Rings: Fellowship of the Ring

When Harry Met Sally

Office Space

The Sound of Music

Zodiac Sign Word Search

Can you find all twelve zodiac signs?

```
G M N T C Q X V I R G O S
N X T E A T A U R U S I R
A J F R P Y U I N A S I L
G C O A R I E S D Q A L B
C Q W O I B J P P U G Q M
Y P V C C Z S A L A I D G
P Z L N O Y X M Z R T P J
I S J M R W G K C I T J P
S O C A N C E R G U A U O
C H Z U Q A M V I S R Y D
E X B L Q L I B R A I Y K
S V T E Y N N F U K U K M
Q S C O R P I O Q L S C T
```

Aries
Taurus
Gemini
Cancer
Leo
Virgo
Libra
Scorpio
Sagittarius
Capricorn
Aquarius
Pisces

Answers on p. 310

Which Zodiac Sign Should You Be With?

Pick your sign.

ARIES

GEMINI
Aries and Geminis are a great match.
You're both charming extroverts and have a lot in common. Being fire and air signs, you drive each other and can be a passionate pairing. You both get bored easily, seek excitement, need personal space and freedom, and like to do everything at one hundred miles per hour.

CANCER

SCORPIO
Cancer and Scorpio do well together because their water-sign compatibility makes it easy for them to find things in common. This is a highly emotional pairing, and as long as everyone is honest and keeps their jealousy in check (here's looking at you, Scorpio), then you have the makings of a truly cosmic connection.

TAURUS

CAPRICORN
Taurus and Capricorns seem like an odd pairing because they're both so rigidly practical, but their similarities make it very easy for them to let go with each other; their love and affection cancel out their need for control and they let their relationship become a safe place where they can unwind.

LEO

ARIES
As a Leo, you should date an Aries. Since you're both fire signs, your attraction and chemistry will be immediate. The passionate connection of an Aries and a Leo does stand a chance of getting competitive, so rely on your mutual respect for each other to keep that element of your relationship in check.

GEMINI

AQUARIUS
Aquarians are the most rebellious and free-spirited of the air signs, which can be tempered by the Gemini's more refined sensibilities. Together they're a perfect pair, the gentleperson and the rogue, which is pretty much everyone's #relationshipgoals.

VIRGO

CAPRICORN
Your Capricorn soul mate can help you break out of your ordered routines and shake your life up a little. Capricorns are spontaneous but also very caring, so don't worry about your partner pushing you too far out of your comfort zone. Also, seeing as both Virgo and Capricorn are highly intellectual signs, you'll never be bored with your Capricorn love!

LIBRA

AQUARIUS

Libra and Aquarius are both outgoing signs, with the Aquarius being slightly more "out there" than their Libra partner. Because neither of you are afraid of talking, the relationship is fueled by honest, open communication and how well you two relate to each other's social needs.

SCORPIO

PISCES

Scorpio and Pisces are both water signs, so expect affection to flow freely in this pairing. Scorpios are the more practical of the two signs, so any tendency to go overboard with emotion will be checked by them, but the Scorpio's deep feelings are always evident and freely expressed.

SAGITTARIUS

LEO

Sagittarians should find their soul mate in a Leo. Your Leo love will be as free-spirited as you, if not more so, and being with a Leo can mean that you will finally be able to have someone to have all the adventures your other-signed friends might not want to go on.

CAPRICORN

VIRGO

Capricorns and Virgos have that same earth sign compatibility. But the Virgo's more upbeat and sunny personality has the added bonus of lifting you up when you need it (as well as knowing innately when you need them to back off).

AQUARIUS

GEMINI

Your meeting with a Gemini will be a whirlwind! As air signs, you will be immediately swept up by each other. Your collective flightiness may make it hard to get things off the ground, but when you make it work with your Gemini soul mate you can become an unstoppable tornado of LOVE.

PISCES

SCORPIO

Pisces and Scorpio complement each other perfectly. The Scorpio's passion combined with the Pisces' caretaking instinct results in a relationship where your partner is always there to highlight your best self (while having the know-how to drag you out of your own head when you're being your worst self).

What Is Your Celebrity Baby Name?

MONTH YOU WERE BORN

January: Indigo

February: Love

March: Pilot

April: Eiffel

May: Kalifornia

June: Rainbow

July: Champion

August: Pistol

September: Birdie

October: Luna

November: Onyx

December: Winter

LAST DIGIT OF YOUR PHONE NUMBER

0: River

1: Wolf

2: Skye

3: Eclipse

4: Gray

5: Dream

6: Mae

7: Rose

8: Aura

9: Wind

PUZZLE ANSWERS

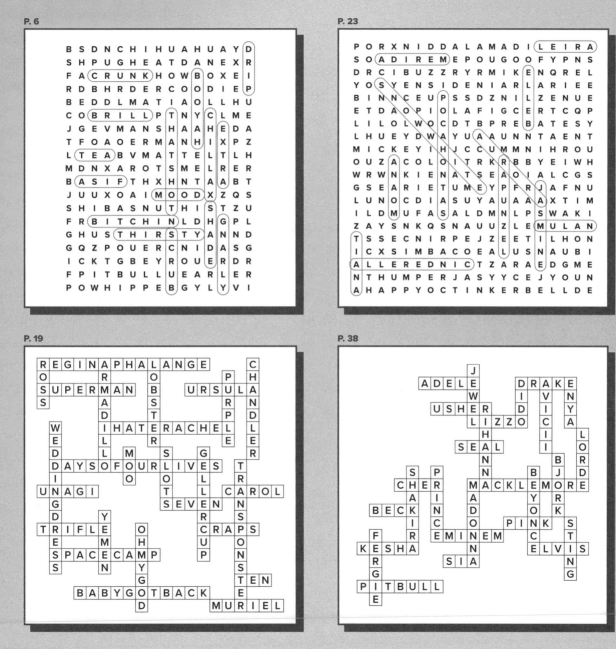

P. 6

```
B S D N C H I H U A H U A Y D
S H P U G H E A T D A N E X R
F A C R U N K H O W B O X E I
R D B H R D E R C O O D I E P
B E D D L M A T I A O L L H U
C O B R I L L P T N Y C L M E
J G E V M A N S H A A H E D A
T F O A O E R M A N H I X P Z
L T E A B V M A T T E L T L H
M D N X A R O T S M E L R E R
B A S I F T H X H N T A A B T
J U U X O A I M O O D X Z Q S
S H I B A S N U T H I S T Z U
F R B I T C H I N L D H G P L
G H U S T H I R S T Y A N N D
G Q Z P O U E R C N I D A S G
I C K T G B E Y R O U E R D R
F P I T B U L L U E A R L E R
P O W H I P P E B G Y L Y V I
```

P. 23

```
P O R X N I D D A L A M A D I L E I R A
S O A D I R E M E P O U G O O F Y P N S
D R C I B U Z Z R Y R M I K E N Q R E L
Y O S Y E N S I D E N I A R L A R I E E
B I N N C E U P S S D Z N I L Z E N U E
E T D A O P I O L A F I G C E R T C Q P
L I L O L W O C D T B P R E B A T E S Y
L H U E Y D W A Y U A A U N N T A E N T
M I C K E Y I H J C C U M M N I H R O U
O U Z A C O L O I T R K R B B Y E I W H
W R W N K I E N A T S E A O I A L C G S
G S E A R I E T U M E Y P F R J A F N U
L U N O C D I A S U Y A U A A A X T I M
I L D M U F A S A L D M N L P S W A K I
Z A Y S N K Q S N A U U Z L E M U L A N
T S S E C N I R P E J Z E E T I L H O N
I C X S I M B A C O E A L U S N A U B I
A L L E R E D N I C T Z A R A E D G M E
N T H U M P E R J A S Y Y C E J Y O U N
A H A P P Y O C T I N K E R B E L L D E
```

P. 19

```
R E G I N A P H A L A N G E       C H
O       R       O           P     H A
S U P E R M A N   B     U R S U L A N
S       A       S       R         N D
        D       T       P         L E
    W   I H A T E R A C H E L E   E R
W E     L   M   S       G   E
D A Y S O F O U R L I V E S     T
I       O       O       L       R
U N A G I       T       L   C A R O L
N       Y       S E V E N   A   N
G       M       R           R   S
D     T R I F L E   O       C R A P S
R       E       H       C U P   O
E     S P A C E C A M P   Y     N
S       N       Y G       E   T E N
    B A B Y G O T B A C K       E
        D               M U R I E L
```

P. 38

```
            J
A D E L E   E       D R A K E
        W           I     N
  U S H E R         D   V I
        L I Z Z O   I   C A
        H           I     L O
      S E A L       I     R D
        N       B         D
    S   P   M A C K L E M O R E
  C H E R   A   Y   R
  B E C K   D   O   P I N K   S
    I   F   O           C     T
    K E S H A   E M I N E M E L V I S
        R       N         N I
        G       S I A     G
P I T B U L L
        E
```

PUZZLE ANSWERS

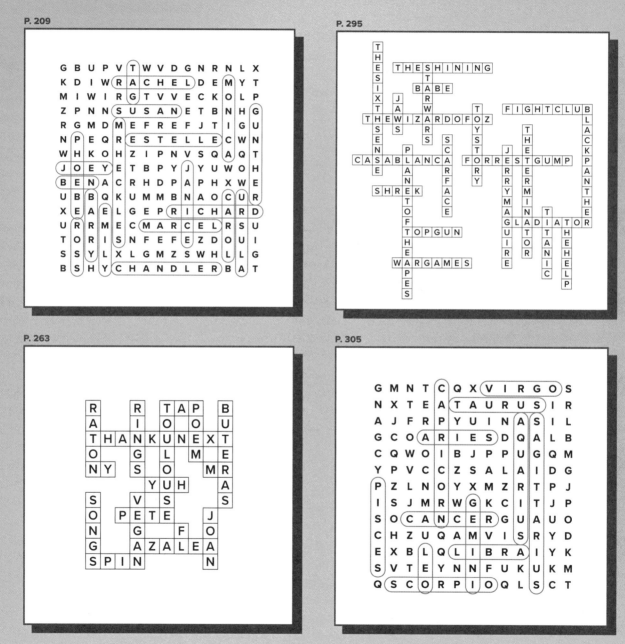

P. 209

```
G B U P V T W V D G N R N L X
K D I W R A C H E L D E M Y T
M I W I R G T V V E C K O L P
Z P N N S U S A N E T B N H G
R G M D M E F R E F J T I G U
N P E Q R E S T E L L E C W N
W H K O H Z I P N V S Q A Q T
J O E Y E T B P Y J Y U W O H
B E N A C R H D P A P H X W E
U B B Q K U M M B N A O C U R
X E A E L G E P R I C H A R D
U R R M E C M A R C E L R S U
T O R I S N F E F E Z D O U I
S S Y L X L G M Z S W H L L G
B S H Y C H A N D L E R B A T
```

P. 295

(crossword answer grid with film titles: THESHINING, THESIXTHSENSE, BABE, JAWS, THEWIZARDOFOZ, FIGHTCLUB, BLACKPANTHER, CASABLANCA, SCARFACE, FORRESTGUMP, THETERMINATOR, PANTOFTHEGRAPES, SHREK, JERRYMAGUIRE, GLADIATOR, TITANIC, TOPGUN, HEHEHELP, WARGAMES)

P. 263

```
R     R   T A P     B
A     I   O   O     U
T H A N K U N E X T  T
O     G   L   M     E
N Y   S   O     M R A
        Y U H     A S
S     V   S       A
O   P E T E   J   O
N     G     F O A N
G   A Z A L E A   N
S P I N           N
```

P. 305

```
G M N T C Q X V I R G O S
N X T E A T A U R U S I R
A J F R P Y U I N A S I L
G C O A R I E S D Q A L B
C Q W O I B J P P U G Q M
Y P V C C Z S A L A I D G
P Z L N O Y X M Z R T P J
I S J M R W G K C I T J P
S O C A N C E R G U A U O
C H Z U Q A M V I S R Y D
E X B L Q L I B R A I Y K
S V T E Y N N F U K U K M
Q S C O R P I O Q L S C T
```